BRONZE
AND THE
BRONZE AGE

BRONZE
AND THE
BRONZE AGE

METALWORK AND
SOCIETY IN BRITAIN
c. 2500 – 800 BC

MARTYN
BARBER

TEMPUS

First published 2003

PUBLISHED IN THE UNITED KINGDOM BY:
Tempus Publishing Ltd
The Mill, Brimscombe Port
Stroud, Gloucestershire GL5 2QG

© Martyn Barber, 2003

The right of Martyn Barber to be identified as the Author
of this work has been asserted by him in accordance with the
Copyrights, Designs and Patents Act 1988.

All rights reserved. No part of this book may be reprinted
or reproduced or utilised in any form or by any electronic,
mechanical or other means, now known or hereafter invented,
including photocopying and recording, or in any information
storage or retrieval system, without the permission in writing
from the Publishers.

British Library Cataloguing in Publication Data.
A catalogue record for this book is available from the British Library.

ISBN 0 7524 2507 2

Typesetting and origination by Tempus Publishing.
Printed in Great Britain by Midway Colour Print, Wiltshire

CONTENTS

Acknowledgements 7

Introduction 9

1 The British Isles and the Bronze Age 17

2 Deposition: anecdote and evidence 43

3 Ancient workings: mining in the Bronze Age 79

4 The work of time: people, processes and places 109

5 Worldly goods 135

6 The Bronze Age: myth and reality 163

Appendix 177

Bibliography 181

Index 189

ACKNOWLEDGEMENTS

Many people have contributed, knowingly and otherwise, to the preparation of this book. Any general introduction such as this inevitably draws heavily on the work of others and I would particularly like to acknowledge, in alphabetical order, John Barrett, Richard Bradley, Joanna Brück, Trevor Cowie, Stuart Needham and Francis Pryor. Their names crop up with what they might regard as alarming frequency, although they have had no opportunity to see what has been done with their thoughts and ideas. They are blameless. Professor Tim Champion may well experience an uneasy sense of déjà vu when reading some parts of the text.

Numerous individuals and organisations helped with the many excellent illustrations and information, including Trevor Cowie and Helen Nicoll at the National Museum of Scotland; Lesley Ferguson and Kristina Johansson at the Royal Commission on the Ancient and Historical Monuments of Scotland; Toby Driver and Medwyn Parry at the Royal Commission on the Ancient and Historical Monuments of Wales; Stuart Needham at the British Museum; Lindsay Jones at the National Monuments Record, Swindon; and Nick Jowett at the Great Orme Mines Trust. Gwilym Hughes allowed me to use the various Lockington images. Michael Lewis provided abundant information and images of finds from Kent in his previous life as Portable Antiquities Officer for that county, and continued to do so after moving to the BM. His replacement at Kent, Andrew Richardson, has been equally helpful. The Portable Antiquities Officers for Merseyside (Nick Herepath) and Suffolk (Helen Geake) also provided images of finds from their respective areas. Euan Mackie kindly allowed me to use one of his photos of Jarlshof; the Flag Fen and Holme-Next-The Sea photographs come courtesy of Francis Pryor; the Tormarton images were provided by Richard Osgood; Bob Bewley let me use one of his photos of the Ewan Rigg cremation pit, and also facilitated use of the Cladh Hallan photo, the ultimate source of which was Mike Parker Pearson. Paul Everson allowed me see his and David Stocker's work on the River Witham in advance. Jon Iveson at Dover Museum provided numerous photographs of the Ripple and Malmains Farm hoards. Last but not least is Dave Perkins, who probably knows more about the Isle of Thanet's past than is sensible, and who provided the photos of the South Dumpton Down metalwork. Of those who provided help that, sadly, remained on the cutting room floor I would particularly like to thank Sally White, Adam Gwilt and Neil Burridge.

Moving to the apologies (aside from those to any of the above for misuse of material), Damian Grady at English Heritage has not yet complained at the amount of time spent staring at bronzes rather than cropmarks; at Tempus, Peter Kemmis Betty and Tim Clarke have proved remarkably patient; and at home, Julie, Jamie and Sian are probably expecting the back room to be tidied up any day now.

INTRODUCTION

It isn't always easy to explain an interest in Bronze Age metalwork to people whose priorities in work, rest and play lie elsewhere. Weaponry and gold can be made to seem acceptable areas of research if couched in the right language, but in contrast a working knowledge of the typological minutiae of tanged chisels is likely to provoke at best sympathy, a state of affairs not helped by the existence of academic papers with titles like 'Inside Socketed Axes' (Ehrenburg 1981a, with apologies). Not surprisingly, then, there will be those who view this book as little more than an extended cry for help.

This book actually owes its existence to a lack of similar introductory texts. Finding out about Bronze Age metalwork is not straightforward, and a glance at websites, newspapers, magazines and television programmes makes it abundantly clear that recent research and ideas are generally failing to have much impact outside a small group of keen and not always bearded researchers. Reading lists for adult education classes tend to comprise a selection of out-of-date (and usually out-of-print) general introductions to prehistory; a selection of recent and not so recent academic papers published in journals rarely encountered outside university libraries; and a sample of excavation reports dealing with sites that actually produced the odd metal find in interesting contexts. Of course, the difficulties of obtaining a reasonable overview of current trends and discoveries applies not just to those learning about archaeology but also to those working in it. It is, after all, hard enough for the specialist to keep pace with new finds and publications, let alone those who merely wish to 'dip in' now and again as and when the urge or the need takes them.

The Bronze Age in general, and the metalwork in particular, has also suffered from something of an image problem. With the odd exception – Flag Fen, the 'Amesbury Archer' and so on – there has been little to capture the interest of a wider audience. Part of the problem stems from the metalwork itself, the detailed study of which was for so long almost the be all and end all of academic research. But, as Alex Gibson (2002, 131) has noted, 'the fascination with intricate metal typologies and debates as to whether such and such an object is really Wilburton do little to fire enthusiasm', reminding us that 'what specialists seem to forget is that an inhabitant of around 3,000 years ago would not give two hoots about what type his axe was, so long as it chopped down that tree or carved that log'. Personally I would argue that there may indeed have been some hooting, but Gibson's main point – that there has been too much abstract debate about artefact typologies and not enough about what he calls 'the reality of the Bronze Age' remains valid.

A brief word about content and scope is necessary. The aim of the book is to offer an overview of recent and current research into, and interpretations of, the roles of metal and metal objects in the British Bronze Age. It is not intended to provide a comprehensive overview of the Bronze Age as a whole – the reader is encouraged to look elsewhere for that (e.g. Parker Pearson 1999; Champion 1999; Brück 2001). As for the metalwork itself, the desire to produce a coherent text within a reasonable amount of time necessitates some sacrifices. The main geographical focus is the British Isles, though that should not be taken to imply any sense of independence or isolation from the adjacent continent or from Ireland during the Bronze Age. The emphasis is placed firmly on copper and bronze; gold is mentioned but receives far less attention than some might think necessary and is deserving of far more detailed discussion than is possible here. It should also be stressed that this is not intended to be a comprehensive guide to the types of objects used in the Bronze Age. Anyone wishing to know, for example, the difference between a 'Stogursey'-type socketed axe and a 'South Eastern' one (and whether the difference should be regarded as significant) is advised to look elsewhere.

The history of Bronze Age metalwork studies receives some fairly lengthy treatment. Some may consider the thoughts of nineteenth-century antiquarians of little relevance to current concerns. In fact, the foundations for metalwork studies were laid down during the later nineteenth and early twentieth centuries, and the work of those 'pioneers' continued to influence the directions of research and the broader understanding of the Bronze Age for many decades afterwards. Indeed, some of that antiquarian baggage remains with us. Current interpretations arose directly or indirectly from, or in reaction to, earlier ideas – there has been no point at which prehistorians have made a completely fresh start and ignored all that went before. Finally, some consideration has been given to ethnographic evidence – ideas derived from the observation and analysis of metal use and metalworking technology in recent and contemporary societies outside Western Europe. The aim is not to seek out direct parallels for what might have happened in Bronze Age Britain, but to show that the 'reality' of the Bronze Age may have been far more complex than previously allowed.

Setting the scene: the Bronze Age in the British Isles

An outline summary of the Bronze Age in Britain written in 2003 is a very different beast to one written, say, 100, 50 or even 20 years ago, such has been the pace of new discoveries and the development of new perspectives on the evidence. In particular, it is now quite common to encounter publications on the period that make little mention of metal, in contrast to previous generations for whom the appearance of metal was a defining moment in the march of progress and of society in general:

the introduction of metal wrought an enormous difference in the lives of men. The Neolithic herdsman, who splintered his stone axe on the skull of a springing wolf, saw the work of months vanish, and was in great danger himself, but when he was the owner of the first of the bronze celts, he walked abroad proudly . . . Trees could be cut down; houses were built more quickly than was possible before, and in a hundred different ways man was given new confidence in his powers and so was able to make progress. The discovery of metal was as important in its own way as the introduction of steam, or the discovery of electricity (Quennell and Quennell 1952, 51-2).

Two key developments may be highlighted here, and they will be referred to on a number of occasions throughout the book. First of all, the identification and excavation of numerous sites over the past three decades in particular have provided a much broader base on which to build historical narratives of the Bronze Age. Secondly, similar developments for the Neolithic and the Iron Age have resulted in shifts in the way the Bronze Age is understood in relation to the preceding and succeeding periods. This is particularly true for the Neolithic, which has undergone considerable reappraisal over the last 15 years. It has, as a result, become increasingly clear that the changeover from Neolithic to Bronze Age is neither so immediate nor so straightforward as once believed. There was no clear break in cultural or economic life, no mass incursion of pots and their makers. Indeed, there is nothing in the archaeological record – no change in artefact styles, in monument types, in modes of subsistence or settlement, in burial rites – that can clearly be attributed to the arrival and establishment in the British Isles of metalworking. That change occurred is undeniable, but the processes that brought it about appear far more elusive and complex than, say, invasion, and were of the long term rather than overnight variety. As for metal itself, instead of marking the onset of wholesale change, the earliest copper, bronze and gold objects were sporadic in occurrence and appear in contexts not wholly dissimilar to the Neolithic objects that they were in time to replace. Effectively, the first metal arrives not at the start of the Early Bronze Age, but during the Late Neolithic. Consequently, some have begun to question (once again) the validity of both the 'Bronze Age' as a concept and the 'Three Age System' as a framework for understanding the prehistoric past.

Instead, attention has now shifted to the social and economic transformations that can be inferred from changes in the ways land was used and occupied from the third to the first millennia BC. The major changes here become apparent during what is traditionally regarded as the Middle Bronze Age – after *c*.1500 BC – rather than at the beginning of the Bronze Age. Over the last two decades the British Neolithic has been subject to quite fundamental changes in interpretation, something of considerable relevance to the Bronze Age once the idea of general continuity of population, economy and culture from one period to the next is accepted. To borrow from the title of Julian Thomas' (1991) book, the Neolithic has been rethought. Once seen as marking a decisive break associated with incoming people, ideas, artefact types and subsistence practices, especially farming, a strong element of continuity from the preceding Mesolithic is now a key theme of discussion. Instead of envisaging a native population of mobile hunter-gatherers effectively replaced by immigrant sedentary farmers, the transition is now seen in more gradual terms, with the indigenous inhabitants adopting and accepting new subsistence practices very much on their own terms. Sedentary agricultural communities, in the sense of farmsteads occupied on a reasonably permanent basis, with associated fields, are no more than an occasional feature of life prior to the Middle Bronze Age.

For an area the size of the British Isles it is difficult to generalise without overlooking a considerable degree of regional variation, but broadly a distinction is commonly drawn between the Neolithic and Early Bronze Age on the one hand, and the Middle Bronze Age onwards on the other. In the earlier phase, the landscape appears as one dominated by funerary and ceremonial monuments and characterised by a fair degree of residential mobility (**1**). In the latter, more 'domesticated' landscapes characterised by settlements and their associated fields become increasingly apparent. In practice of course this is a gross oversimplification, but in general this change appears to reflect a long-term shift from larger to smaller scale communities as the immediate focus for social and economic ties, and a related reduction in the degree of group mobility around the landscape, with a consequently greater emphasis on the long-term occupation of particular places. These are trends that have their roots way back in the Neolithic period. For the Middle Bronze Age onwards, the consequence for the archaeologist is the increasing visibility of the places where people lived and farmed – round house structures, ditches or palisades enclosing farmsteads, networks of fields defined by earthen lynchets, stone walls and clearance cairns – in stark contrast to earlier times when traces of settlement are notoriously ephemeral and elusive.

Over broadly the same period, changes in the nature of burial practices from the Middle Neolithic onwards point to a shift from an undifferentiated community of ancestors (as evidenced by the collections of disarticulated bones from chambered tombs) towards a concern with the genealogical position of particular individuals (as suggested by the interment of those individuals within or beneath round barrows, which are often arranged in clusters or cemetery groups), initially within the broader kinship group and latterly within the immediate co-residential groups. This last change is particularly apparent in the placing of round barrows in closer proximity to settlements by the Middle Bronze Age – the dead were now being buried close to the living places of their immediate surviving family.

Thus the context of the first metal use in Britain is not the farmsteads and fields, nor even necessarily the round barrow cemeteries, archaeological phenomena that have tended to characterise the period in recent times. Instead, to use the long-established Three Age terminology, the first metal belongs in the Stone Age. For

INTRODUCTION

1 *The sarsen trilithons of Stonehenge, a monument whose construction phases span the later Neolithic and earlier Bronze Age, viewed from behind round barrow Amesbury G11 which lies a short distance to the east. The visibility of such features in the modern landscape contrasts considerably with the far lower profile of contemporary and later settlements. The barrow was briefly examined in the early nineteenth century, resulting in the discovery of a cremation deposit and some bone tweezers. Stonehenge's sole bronze finds are an awl from above the ditch near the north-east terminal of the main entrance, and a tubular sheet bead from the upper fill of one of the 'Aubrey' holes. Better known are the numerous carvings, mainly of unhafted axe blades resembling the so-called 'Arreton'-style flanged axeheads of the later stages of the Early Bronze Age. See Cleal* et al. *1995*

the final few hundred years before that first metal, the most visible remains – to the modern archaeologist – are the funerary and ceremonial sites. This is the period when many of the henges and stone circles were being erected in landscapes that were still a patchwork of clearings and forest. Few new long barrows were still being constructed, while the round barrow, whose ancestry itself stretches right back into the fourth millennium BC, was still only an occasional feature of the countryside. The places where people actually lived are represented by far more ephemeral remains than the physically more impressive monuments. What tends to survive are isolated scatters or clusters of pits, postholes and stakeholes, usually only revealed by excavation, and surface spreads of artefacts. Such traces represent places where people stopped for a while, perhaps for a few days, perhaps months, possibly repeatedly over many years, before moving on in a cyclical round of resource exploitation and social obligation. For the most part the Early Bronze Age – in fact almost a millennium of copper and bronze use – remains broadly comparable: monumental burial and ceremonial places, ephemeral living sites, and a population that was still, though to an increasingly lesser degree, on the move.

Studies of stone and flint sources and their products, as well as other classes of artefact, have demonstrated the existence long before metal of extensive networks of contact, trade and exchange both within the British Isles and further afield. It seems likely that rather than disrupting existing networks of alliance and exchange, the first metal probably arrived within those frameworks of social and economic ties. Given the vagaries of the available evidence, it is impossible to be too precise about the date, but somewhere around the middle of the third millennium BC – perhaps as early as 2500 BC – the first objects created from previously unseen materials reached the British Isles. Those earliest tools, weapons and ornaments of copper and gold may have circulated for a while as rumour before first being encountered and held – examined, studied, discussed, valued, coveted – as indeed may tales of the methods used to make them, processes that must have seemed more akin to the techniques used to manufacture pottery vessels or even to prepare food than to the long-established techniques used to work more traditional materials such as stone, bone and wood.

The precise means by which metals arrived are difficult to identify. Attribution of the earliest metalworking to a wave of invaders bringing the technology with them offered a simple and all-encompassing explanation, but it is sadly one that is no longer acceptable for various reasons (see below). The people living on either side of the Channel (and, indeed, the North Sea) were far from being strangers during the Neolithic, but there is almost a sense that metal and metallurgy reached the British Isles despite rather than because of those existing contacts. For example, the famous Alpine 'Ice-man' 'Ötzi' (Spindler 1994) was carrying a copper axehead six or seven hundred years before such items are attested in Britain. Indeed, the particular form of axehead – a flanged axehead – did not occur in Britain for a few centuries more. Yet polished axes of jadeite, many probably derived from sources not too far from where Ötzi lived and died, are known to have been reaching this country by the early centuries of the fourth millennium BC at the latest.

Speculation about these and other problems occur throughout the book as and when appropriate, although it is clearly not possible to deal with every aspect of bronze in the Bronze Age in what is intended to be an introductory synthesis. Indeed, some of the coverage is highly superficial and I will no doubt come to regret some of the omissions. Additionally, some subjects that have received considerable and accessible attention elsewhere in recent years have been dealt with rather briefly. As regards the general approach, I can do no better than borrow from W.B. Wright's (1939) preface to his own *Tools and the Man*: 'An assemblage of dull facts would . . . make a dull book, so the writer has speculated freely when occasion seemed to warrant it. The reader will have little difficulty in detecting when he is being led away on such flights of the imagination, and can tickle his fancy with them or strip them as he so desires.' In the more enlightened twenty-first century, of course, the tickling and stripping is not restricted to male readers.

The next chapter reviews the history of Bronze Age studies in the British Isles, with particular reference to the metalwork, in an attempt to highlight the role of previous generations of archaeologists and antiquarians in shaping the problems faced and interpretations offered by the current generation. Subsequently the focus turns to the matter of deposition. This may seem to be a case of beginning at the end, but in fact the question of how and why metal objects entered the ground is of crucial importance in evaluating the significance of metal in the Bronze Age, as well as in challenging some longstanding assumptions about bronze and bronzeworking. Thereafter attention switches to the beginning of the bronze chain – mining. For Britain in particular this is a subject that has been revolutionised over the past 15 years through extensive fieldwork and radiocarbon dating, offering important insights into processes that previously were simply absent from the archaeological literature. After mining, the metal is followed through the various processing and casting techniques in order to outline the flow of metal from ore to finished object. In both this and the previous mining chapter, ethnographic and historic evidence is added to the archaeological traces in order to offer something resembling a social context for Bronze Age metalworking rather than merely offer description of basic techniques. Finally, the manner in which selected categories of metal object may have been used is examined in order to highlight the variety of social and economic practices and values that they may have represented, and hopefully demonstrating that there is far more to Bronze Age metalwork than meets the typologist's eye. The book ends with an attempt to summarise the broader significance of bronze within the Bronze Age. An appendix summarises the law as regards Bronze Age metalwork finds in England, Wales and Scotland. It may not always be pretty but it is now 'treasure'.

1
THE BRITISH ISLES AND THE BRONZE AGE

All the vital elements of modern material culture are immediately rooted in the Bronze Age . . . Modern science and industry not only go back to the period when bronze was the dominant industrial metal, their beginnings were in a very real sense conditioned and inspired by the mere fact of the general employment of bronze and copper (Gordon Childe 1930, 2-3).

The introduction of bronze was one of the greatest non-events of all time (Andrew Selkirk 1971, 113).

These two brief statements neatly capture the central dilemma faced today when trying to evaluate the significance of the earliest metal objects both to archaeologists and the people who made and used them. Just how important is bronze to our understanding of the Bronze Age? Once the backbone of the period, the core around which its chronology and cultural history were constructed, since the 1970s it has become increasingly difficult to justify retaining that central role for metalwork studies.

No single factor accounts for this change in fortunes. Instead, several developments have combined to relegate bronze to a position of lesser importance. First of all, the impact of the numerous sites excavated from the 1960s onwards has been considerable. Previously, the only type of Bronze Age site excavated in any quantity was the round barrow – the principal funerary monument of the Early and Middle Bronze Age (**2**). Consequently, little was known about the everyday lives of the people who made and used the bronze and who were buried in the barrows. As Colin Burgess acknowledged as late as the mid-1970s, 'Most of our knowledge of the period is derived from burial and ritual sites and unassociated artefacts, which give a biased picture, too concerned with matters spiritual, religious and technological, and not enough with more mundane aspects' (Burgess 1974, 165). As a result, the major artefact types had essentially come to represent the people who used them, cultural history being written from studies of their geographical spread and chronological development. Indeed, Burgess' own

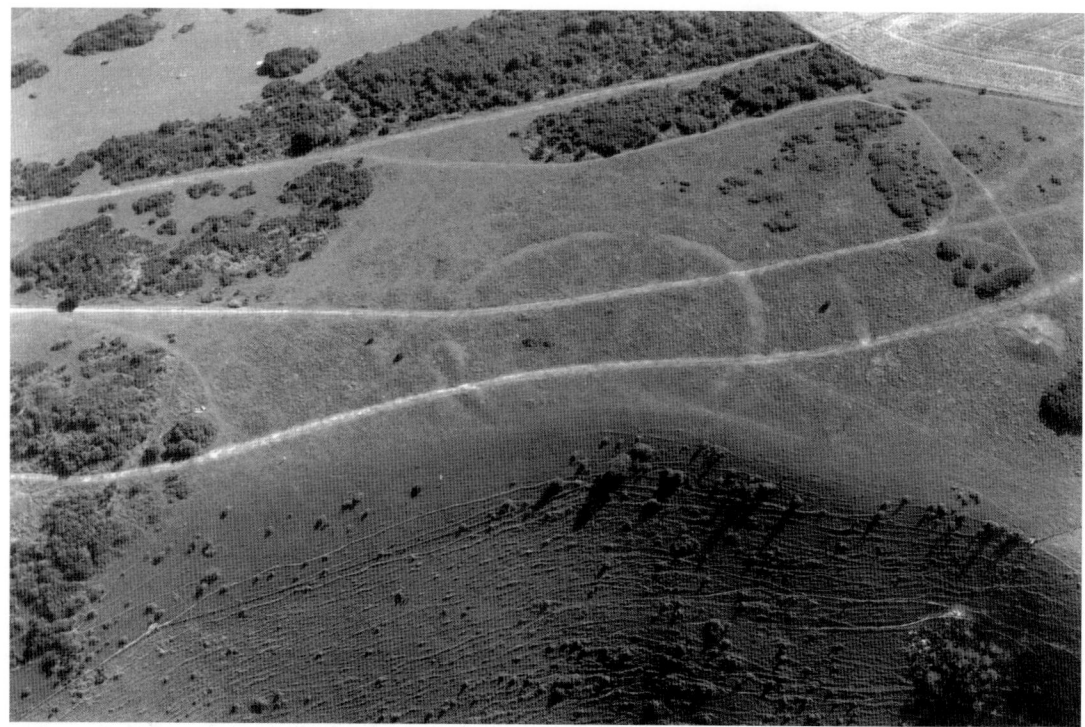

2 Combe Hill, East Sussex. An Early Neolithic causewayed enclosure, first identified as such in 1929 by the wife of Alexander Keiller, and perched on the crest of the scarp of the South Downs. Here viewed from the north, in the Early Bronze Age the enclosure appears to have been a focus for the construction of round barrows. The large bowl barrow to the west was trenched in 1908 by Major F. Maitland, who found three broken flanged bronze axeheads and a fragment of a fourth laid beneath a massive stone just 10in or so beneath the top of the barrow, with no associated burial. RCHME 1995. © Crown copyright. NMR

comprehensive account of the period was still rooted firmly in detailed study of metalwork and pottery, and it is instructive to compare that version of the Bronze Age (Burgess 1974, ironically included within a book entitled *British Prehistory: a new outline*) with the one that, by the end of the 1970s, was emerging from the rapidly accumulating wealth of new settlement data (see for example Barrett and Bradley 1980).

Secondly came the dawning realisation that bronze is, in fact, quite scarce on excavated sites. Few settlements yield more than the odd scrap, and it occurs only with a minority of burials, the attention focused on the 'wealthier' grave assemblages perhaps helping to obscure this fact. This lack of direct association between bronzes and both the living and the dead had long been implicit in metalwork studies, but it was only with the growing quantity and variety of excavated sites from the 1960s onwards that we have been able to appreciate how little we really know about the uses and meanings of bronze in the Bronze Age. Consequently, the grand chronological and cultural scheme for the Bronze Age, constructed largely via the close study of metalwork, effectively became little more than what it had really been all along – a sequential arrangement of the metalwork which had few clear links with the other forms of evidence from the period, and which lacked any reliable form of independent verification.

A third development, only partly a result of the first two, was a decline in the sort of detailed typological analysis that had for so long dominated – indeed typified – the study of Bronze Age metalwork. Burgess and Coombs (1979a, 1) referred to 'the crushing routine of collecting, collating and publishing artefacts' as a key factor in this decline, noting that 'few have emerged in recent years prepared to stick to the grind of gaining familiarity with the material. For many young workers an early sortie into Bronze Age metalwork, resulting in a small regional survey or publication of a hoard, has been followed by an abrupt change of tack' (*ibid.*). Arguably, however, it wasn't the material itself that was the problem but the baggage that came with it – the crushing routine of reading and digesting what had already been written about bronzes. By the 1970s questions were increasingly being asked about the validity of the methods used in studying metalwork, and the conclusions being drawn.

This methodological and interpretative dissatisfaction is alluded to by Burgess and Coombs (*ibid.*) in their attempt to defend the sort of artefact studies that formed the core of their own publication. New theoretical perspectives – retrospectively characterised first as the 'New Archaeology' and later as 'Processual Archaeology' (see e.g. Trigger 1989, chapter 8; Johnson 1999, chapters 2-5) – had begun to emerge from North America during the 1960s and were greeted with a complex mixture of enthusiasm, scepticism and downright hostility in Britain. Though far from being a unified body of ideas and approaches to understanding the past, a key element was an emphasis on the methodological underpinnings of archaeological inference. As will become clear, this was a key weakness of the traditional approach to studying Bronze Age metalwork. For many involved in such metalwork studies, the detailed classification of bronzes was often regarded as an objective process which provided the foundations for broader social and economic interpretations: '. . . it is the artefacts which are the 'stuff', the 'facts' of our discipline, and . . . everything else is inference. There seems to be a widespread belief among today's young (and not so young) prehistorians that methods are an end in themselves, that one can somehow experiment endlessly with methods without having a good grounding in the basic raw materials, the artefacts' (Burgess and Coombs 1979a, 1). The fact that typological classification was itself inference, a subjective method of arranging artefacts according to certain assumptions about what was important in, say, spearhead design and its relationship to technological ability, seems not to have been recognised. Interpretation was being seen as something that arose from the results of classification, when in fact an interpretation of the material was itself central to the classification process.

More recent theoretical perspectives – often characterised as 'Post-Processual Archaeology' despite the variety of views and approaches (see e.g. Johnson 1999 chapters 7-11) – have seen, for Bronze Age metalwork at least, even less inclination to get involved with the typological minutiae, particularly as the ever-growing amount of non-metallic evidence mounts up and offers more varied and interesting avenues of research. However, one interesting development of the last 20 years or so, and one which is rooted in a combination of excavation evidence and the sort of interpretative approaches to the meaning of material culture often seen to characterise Post-Processual Archaeology, is a greater concern with the means by which metalwork entered the ground. As we shall see, for a long time this was a subject that attracted little debate as certain explanations had been widely accepted from an early date.

However, there are difficulties to be faced here. All too often, more recent analyses of metalwork, including those concerned with the symbolism contained within this material and its treatment, are undertaken within classificatory and chronological frameworks whose theoretical foundations have been so heavily criticised, often by the same archaeologists. For example, in his lengthy analysis of hoards and votive deposits in prehistoric Europe, Richard Bradley (1990, 13) noted in regard to Bronze Age bronze hoards that

> All too often studies of such deposits have been concerned with content rather than context. This is a tradition that can be traced at least as far back as the work of Sir John Evans (1881). It has remained important because of the way in which prehistoric chronology has been compiled, by studying groups of associated material. Since so little is known about the circumstance in which this material was deposited, it is perhaps a moot point whether such chronologies can be entirely reliable, but in the present account they are followed for want of anything better.

But to return to the opening quotes. Gordon Childe was writing at a time when the objects themselves held sway among prehistorians – there was after all little else to go on – and were consequently central to the understanding of the Bronze Age, their sheer numbers overwhelming when compared to the number of actual sites known from the period. Although Childe's views on bronze and the Bronze Age are often represented as a watershed in terms of our understanding of the period, they also represented the outcome of a long established approach to interpreting prehistory with particular reference to technology and its products. Selkirk's view, on the other hand, came at a time of increasing recognition that there was much more to the Bronze Age than bronze, and it was proving increasingly difficult to link apparently major technological advances with important developments in other aspects of the archaeological record. The chronological and cultural schemes constructed around the metalwork were largely redundant when it came to interpreting the newly excavated sites. The contrast with earlier generations, who saw the appearance of bronze – indeed of metallurgy itself – and its eventual replacement with iron as events of fundamental significance in the progress of civilisation, is only too clear. Each of these events had been strongly implicated in wholesale economic and social change, ultimately rooted in large-scale population movement. The term 'industrial revolution' had even been applied to various stages of the metal ages, its use underlining the considerable impact envisaged for such great leaps forward in technological capabilities.

The central position accorded by many to metal in later prehistory was typified by the comments of Christopher Hawkes, who argued that

> The issues involved were not only industrial, but intellectual and social no less than commercial and economic . . . Metal was . . . not merely a precious possession: it was capital. Its supply thus became a vital matter in society's economics. Ores were difficult to find, and confined to certain regions, to which access had to be maintained with care. Prospecting, and the establishment and security of trade routes, became consequently essential. And two things followed: first, the growth of organisation within the community had to take on special characters, culminating in adaptation for warfare as the ultimate sanction for protecting coveted wealth; secondly, the territorial growth of civilisation as a whole had to adapt itself to an economic geography not merely concerned with the odd primary consideration of food and water, but with the distribution of mineral resources (Hawkes 1940, 285-6).

Thus the Bronze Age had a distinct character based firmly around the use of and access to metal and metal objects, something that set it apart from the preceding Neolithic ('New Stone Age') and the succeeding Iron Age, the names of the periods themselves seemingly underlining the central role of materials and technology in prehistory (**colour plate 1**).

From Beaker Folk to Hallstatt Warriors

However, the various 'ages' of prehistory are so firmly embedded in the archaeological literature, as well as more generally, that it is easy to ignore the history of their development and to overlook the concerns raised over the years about their usefulness in helping us to understand the past. In particular, it is important to avoid the unqualified assumption that the transition from one age to another must have marked a point of fundamental and fairly rapid change in society. Certainly it used to be believed that the acquisition of metal tools and weapons in particular, and the knowledge needed to make them, would have had rapid and far-reaching consequences in a world used to working various forms of stone. Such views were perhaps inevitable, especially when little of certain Bronze Age date was known except the bronzes and the most conspicuous and frequent of contemporary monuments, the round barrow. Until well into the twentieth century, as with most other periods, research was reliant on what remained visible above the ground and on accidental discoveries. Technology and the dead dominated discussion, with the analysis of metal objects and funerary remains forming the basis of both chronological and cultural frameworks.

Consequently, in explaining the difference between the Neolithic and the Bronze Age, the replacement of a stoneworking technology with metalworking became the central reference point around which other phenomena were arranged. Over time, the significance of this change became further strengthened by its perceived connection with other archaeologically visible developments, most notably a 'new' form of pottery – the Beakers – and the apparently coeval establishment of a funerary rite differing fundamentally from Neolithic practice. Instead of jumbles of bones in chambered long barrows, the emphasis now seemed to be placed on the regular interment of individuals in graves, usually beneath the hemispherical mound of a round barrow. These developments, from an early stage, were assumed to be associated with the arrival of immigrants from the continent. Abercromby's (1902; 1912) studies of Beaker pottery, published at the beginning of the twentieth century, recognised the widespread distribution of Beaker pottery styles in Europe, and established them as the first demonstrably Bronze Age ceramic type in use in the British Isles. The appearance of these distinctive vessels in the British Isles was thus credited to a large-scale incursion of their makers across the Channel, people known to subsequent generations as the 'Beaker Folk'.

The presence of some of the technologically and stylistically earliest metal objects in Beaker graves beneath round barrow mounds allowed these and other (often quite loosely) associated phenomena to be regarded as a distinct horizon of change, something that would take most of the twentieth century and the application of radiocarbon dating to undo. However, at the time further supporting evidence for invasion (or migration) came from a longstanding belief that a physical – and primarily craniological – distinction could be drawn between the occupants of Neolithic long barrows and the dead who resided beneath the later round barrows. The latter seemed to possess more rounded ('brachycephalic') skulls than the people they apparently replaced. Some also argued that the Beaker Folk were generally taller too, proof it appeared that 'two widely-differing races had occupied these islands prior to the invasion of Julius' (Thurnam 1872, 544).

Inevitably, for some the seemingly rapid dominance and spread of a new physical type and their associated, superior, material culture warranted more than mere measurement and description. Thus for Beddoe (1895, 17), 'Whencesoever they came, the men of the British bronze age were richly endowed, physically. They were, as a rule, tall and stalwart; their brains were large; and their features, if somewhat harsh and coarse, must have been manly and even commanding'. More recent analysis of the physical remains, particularly the skulls, suggests that few if any significant distinctions can be drawn between Beaker associated skeletons and those of the Neolithic (Brodie 1994). As for the likelihood of invasion as the underlying reason for cultural change, this was a feature of archaeological thinking from an early stage and lasted well into the twentieth century, eventually prompting Grahame Clark to note that

> So little did British archaeologists of the era from Kipling to Winston Churchill feel the need to underpin the Empire with prehistoric props that they went out of their way to ascribe every good thing about their early past to foreign influences, if not indeed to foreign conquerors. So anxious were some of them to avoid ascribing any innovation to their own forbears that one might say that they were suffering from a form of invasion neurosis. For much of the first half of the twentieth century British archaeologists felt themselves under strong compulsion to ascribe every change, every development to overseas influence of one kind or another (Clark 1966, 172).

The apparent inevitability to many prehistorians of periodic invasion by those armed with some form of superior material culture was underlined by Cyril Fox's (1933, 13) comment that 'The position of these islands . . . is such as to invite invasion from almost any point on five hundred miles of the European coastline from Brittany to the Elbe-mouth and beyond.'

Ironically, of course, Clarke specifically excluded the Beaker Folk from his attack on the invasion neurosis, highlighting the widespread nature of the pottery and its associated artefacts and, in particular, the 'appearance of a new physical type with notably broader heads' (Clark 1966, 180). Subsequently, and particularly with the benefit of radiocarbon dating, a greater range of well-excavated sites, and new interpretative perspectives, much of the rather simplistic narrative centred around the alleged invaders has been disentangled, its constituent parts separated out and no longer regarded as forming a single unified and wholly imported process of change. Following the decline of the culture-historical approach to structuring the past (see below), and continuing criticism of the 'invasion hypothesis', the days of the Beaker Folk were clearly numbered. Their presence on the pages of prehistory always owed much more to the limitations of the available evidence and to the assumptions and beliefs of early prehistorians than the bones, bronzes and Beakers could really bear. Nonetheless their survival throughout much of the twentieth century underlined the extent to which the Bronze Age was regarded as wholly different to the Neolithic, as well as an inherent conservatism in archaeological interpretation and the peculiar appeal of simple but all-embracing explanatory models. This is not to deny that the long-distance movement of people happened in prehistory. As we shall see later, recent discoveries have once again stimulated discussion about the origins of Beaker pottery and the earliest metallurgy in the British Isles. However, such large-scale migration or invasion represents an unsatisfactory and unnecessary explanation for such developments. It is clear that objects and people must have crossed considerable distances before, during and after the Bronze Age, but there is nothing to support the sort of large-scale movements of people once envisaged.

The other end of the Bronze Age has had a broadly similar history. The introduction of iron and seemingly allied novelties were long associated with new and often warlike arrivals from across the Channel. Again, the continuity of cultural and economic life across the bronze-iron divide has become increasingly clear, and any connection between the appearance of iron and changes in other aspects of the archaeological record is also more apparent than real. The changeover to iron had been heralded as marking a major transformation in society, one that would have considerable repercussions on everyday life. Like bronze too, the adoption of a new material and technology was seen as a product of continental influence and immigration, this time largely the fault of 'Hallstatt' invaders (or occasionally 'Celts'), who crossed over to Britain with their weapons, tools and blacksmiths in tow. By the mid-1970s, with continuity in all but the metal of choice for tools and weapons increasingly accepted, the sparseness of the available evidence for invasion was all too clear. Thus, in a remarkable paragraph from his overview of the Bronze Age, Colin Burgess (1974, 212) sought to explain the occurrence in Britain of a particular sword type, with no associated material of continental origin or influence, in the following terms: 'So the likelihood is that Britain and Ireland were penetrated in the seventh century by Hallstatt adventurers, traders and smiths, usually untrammelled by women and the cultural paraphernalia that would have made a broader-based immigration more noticeable.' Soon, of course, even the untrammelled adventurers faded from view.

Though our knowledge remains far from perfect, the ever-increasing number of excavated sites is failing to demonstrate any significant developments that could be blamed on, or attributed to, a switch from stone to bronze, or from bronze to iron. The implication is, as Selkirk (1971) suggested, that such transitions were of far less significance than once believed. Changes in domestic architecture, settlement structure, land division, agricultural practices, funerary rites and so on are all rooted in much longer term processes traceable back over several centuries or longer. However, that metal was important is undeniable, not just from its mere existence but also from the manner in which it was obtained, made, circulated, used and disposed of. Instead of looking for broad horizons of change cutting across a range of artefacts and site types, funerary practices and the like, more subtle and complex interrelationships between metalworking and other aspects of social and economic life are increasingly being sought and identified. These suggest that the impact and significance of metal and metalworking likewise needs to be viewed over a much more long-term perspective. The nature of this impact and those interrelationships will be explored in subsequent chapters. What follows here is a rapid and selective summary of the history of Bronze Age studies in the British Isles, with particular emphasis on the interpretation of bronze, in order to provide a context for much of the later discussion.

A brief history of the British Bronze Age

Until quite recently, as had been mentioned already, the study of metalwork offered the basis for an interpretative and chronological framework that both prescribed and depended upon a significant role for bronze in the Bronze Age. The Three Age System, as it became known, of stone, bronze and iron was created by the Dane Christian Thomsen in the early nineteenth century and was built on subsequently by countless others. It rested upon three basic foundations: raw material, technology and progress. In other words, the material and form of the main cutting tools and weapons, and their perceived development and increasing efficiency over time, lay at its core. Form and assumed function were used to determine types, while changes in form represented increasing technological ability over time, as well as enhanced practical utility of the objects themselves (**3**).

Going beyond this, the associations between different types – their occurrence together in, say, hoards or graves – enabled the linkage of individual type-sequences into broader frameworks encompassing much of the material available. Unassociated items – the stray finds that actually dominate the archaeological record – could then be assigned their position in the grand scheme of things on the basis of a straightforward comparison of material, function and form. Realisation of the potential inherent in recognising stylistic and material change over time thus allowed the creation of relative sequences which could then be linked to similarly constructed continental schemes and, ultimately, to the calendrical dates of the Mediterranean world and beyond.

But, more than providing some chronological backbone to the distant past, the tools, weapons and ornaments were also seen to characterise a way of life via the uses to which they could be put, and the observed level of technological sophistication and scientific achievement. From a social perspective, metal was also perceived as possessing a particular form of value expressed through concerns with factors such as access to the raw material, to finished objects, and to metalworking technology itself. The ability to possess bronzes, and to control their movement and restrict their use and possession became important elements in understanding how Bronze Age society might have functioned. Moreover, links to neighbouring regions didn't just offer a means of obtaining dates for the British material – they also allowed identification of networks of trade and exchange and, of course, patterns of presumed population movement. Going even beyond this, as we have already seen, Gordon Childe, among others, came to view the technological developments as more than just evidence for economic and industrial progress – he saw them as representing the basis of fundamental social and economic change, with considerable impact on society as a whole (Childe 1930; Barrett 1994a).

But to return to the basic framework within which all this work was undertaken – the Three Age System. Dissatisfaction with it is far from new. There were those who refused to accept it from the start, and its delayed acceptance in Britain doesn't seem to have been purely connected with linguistic difficulties. More

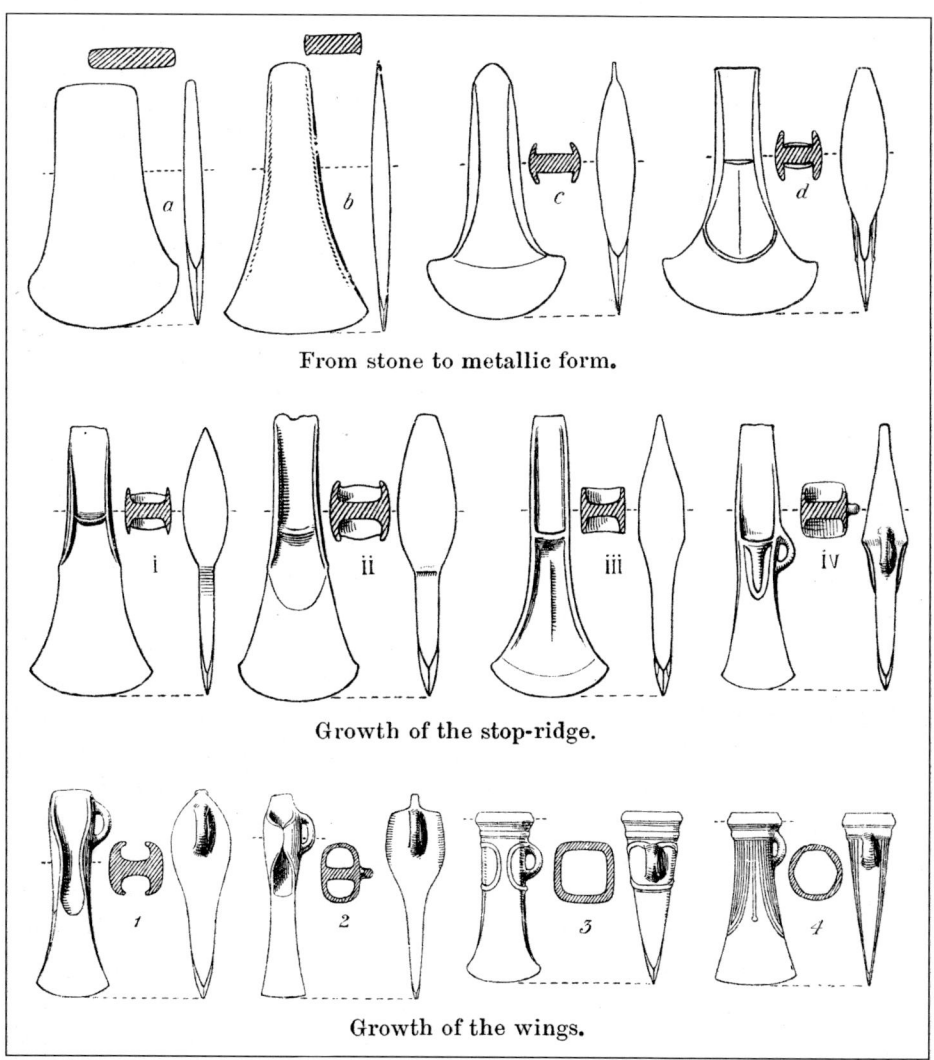

3 'Stages in evolution of the celt', outlining its assumed development from the earliest flat axes, assumed to be metal copies of Neolithic stone axes, down to the latest socketed types. This sort of scheme was commonly used to illustrate not just the development of axeheads, but the potential of typological analysis generally. This particular example comes from the British Museum's (1920) catalogue of Bronze Age antiquities. The scheme remains broadly correct in terms of the relative age of the various forms, but the evolutionary framework can now be seen as far too simplistic, particularly in the relationship between the winged axe forms, more common on the continent, and the wing-decorated socketed axeheads relevant concerns here include those voiced by Peake and Fleure 70 years ago: 'The old division of prehistoric times into the Stone, Bronze and Iron Ages, though it has been of inestimable value during the last century in bringing a measure of order out of chaos, is now revealing signs of failure to meet the needs of today' (Peake and Fleure 1933, iii). Later, Stuart Piggott argued that Thomsen's three ages represented 'a very good model, and still holds valid in many contexts, now co-existing with alternative schemes . . . But we must always remember that we are using the models in question with their limitations and our limitations too. "The Bronze Age" is an intellectual construct to accommodate data viewed within the framework of the technological model of prehistory' (Piggott 1965, 6).

Such longstanding criticisms may come as a surprise to some, given that the scheme and its all too familiar terminology remain with us into the twenty-first century. Its continuing longevity has been aided greatly by its simplicity and familiarity, while the development in recent decades of computerised archaeological databases – sites and monuments records, both regional and national – has seen those familiar divisions of the past used as one of the principal means of characterising the records they hold. Thus an arrangement of the cultural debris of the past that has its origins in the need to display, in a meaningful manner, an early nineteenth-century Danish collection of disparate antiquities continues to exert an influence on modern archaeological practice.

Meanwhile, back in the nineteenth century the Three Age System worked, and it worked beyond Thomsen's immediate concerns with the Danish national collection. Others, both inside and outside Scandinavia, were able to adapt and expand the scheme. Belated but firm acceptance in Britain was marked by the publication in 1865 of Sir John Lubbock's *Pre-Historic Times* . . ., a work which offered a detailed combination of artefact-orientated study with a still novel but increasingly influential presentation of anthropological material. The result was a broader range of phenomena with which to characterise each successive period, although the range of specifically archaeological criteria remained limited for some time to come. At the same time, Lubbock's work confirmed and extended the idea of the principal ages of prehistory as fixed stages through which all human societies would be expected to pass, each marked by specific technological, economic and social advances, and broadly set within an evolutionary framework.

After Lubbock, in Britain and beyond the endeavours of antiquarians and archaeologists continued to focus chiefly on the processes of collection, classification and description – the order from chaos alluded to earlier. Typical, but equally the most notable, of these individuals in Britain was Sir John Evans, who worked his way through coins (Evans 1867), stone implements (Evans 1872) and finally bronzes, his monumental tome on the last with his own personal collection at the core being published in 1881. As well as being an enduring work of reference, the insights and suggestions about the uses and development of bronzes, the nature and purpose of hoarding, and numerous other matters influenced orthodox opinion in Britain for several decades to come. However, towards the end of the volume, when it came to providing a wider picture of life in Britain during the Bronze Age, he was forced to admit that 'on this subject, apart from the light thrown upon it by the tools, weapons and ornaments I have been describing, and by the contents of the graves of the period, we have in this country but little to guide us' (Evans 1881, 486-8), a complaint to be repeated on many occasions over the next century.

The very uses to which objects could be put suggested some of the things that might have been happening throughout the Bronze Age – woodworking, agriculture, fighting, hunting, display, trade and exchange, the accumulation of 'wealth' and so on. Beyond more obvious utilitarian concerns, the finer objects raised the possibility of different levels within society, perhaps determined in part by the possession of wealth and power. But all this was highly speculative, and it was difficult in the late nineteenth century to progress further. Evans' principal material source beyond the barrows and bronzes of Britain was in fact the remarkable and unprecedented discoveries from the so-called 'Lake Villages' of Switzerland and neighbouring regions.

By the close of the nineteenth century, the range of information and the ways of studying it were beginning to show some diversity beyond mere classification and evolutionary sequencing. A sizeable collection of material for study already existed, of course, accumulated by collectors and barrow diggers of varying motives, skill and notoriety (**4**; Marsden 1999). During the latter half of the century, excavators such as William Greenwell, Lt General Pitt Rivers and others did much to put archaeological exploration on a more respectable footing. Pitt Rivers, of course, was also responsible for the first systematic excavation of actual Bronze Age settlements, several examples fortuitously surviving as earthworks (and thus visible to the nineteenth century archaeologist) on his estate at Cranborne Chase in Wiltshire and Dorset. However, such non-funerary sites remained the exception until well into the following century. Nonetheless a broader-based view of prehistoric life was starting to emerge and to complement the work of the bronze typologist.

Such developments allowed each of the Three Ages and their emerging subdivisions to take on even more distinct identities, borne of generalisations derived from artefact and site classification, excavation and, still, anthropology. The differing character of preceding and succeeding periods raised questions about their transitions. Broad patterns of association and the linking of sequences had created, as we have seen for the start and end of the Bronze Age, apparently distinct horizons of change that marked the passing of one period for the next. At the same time, separate traditions of study for individual periods were, by the early decades of the twentieth century, becoming clearly apparent.

Of course, as already implied there was a lot more to the metal ages than metal. A significant step for the British Bronze Age was provided by Abercromby's (1902; 1912) work on pottery. His identification of Beaker ceramics as the first demonstrably Bronze Age pottery type was just the best known of his contributions. His use of distribution maps to plot and interpret the geographical spread of Beakers in

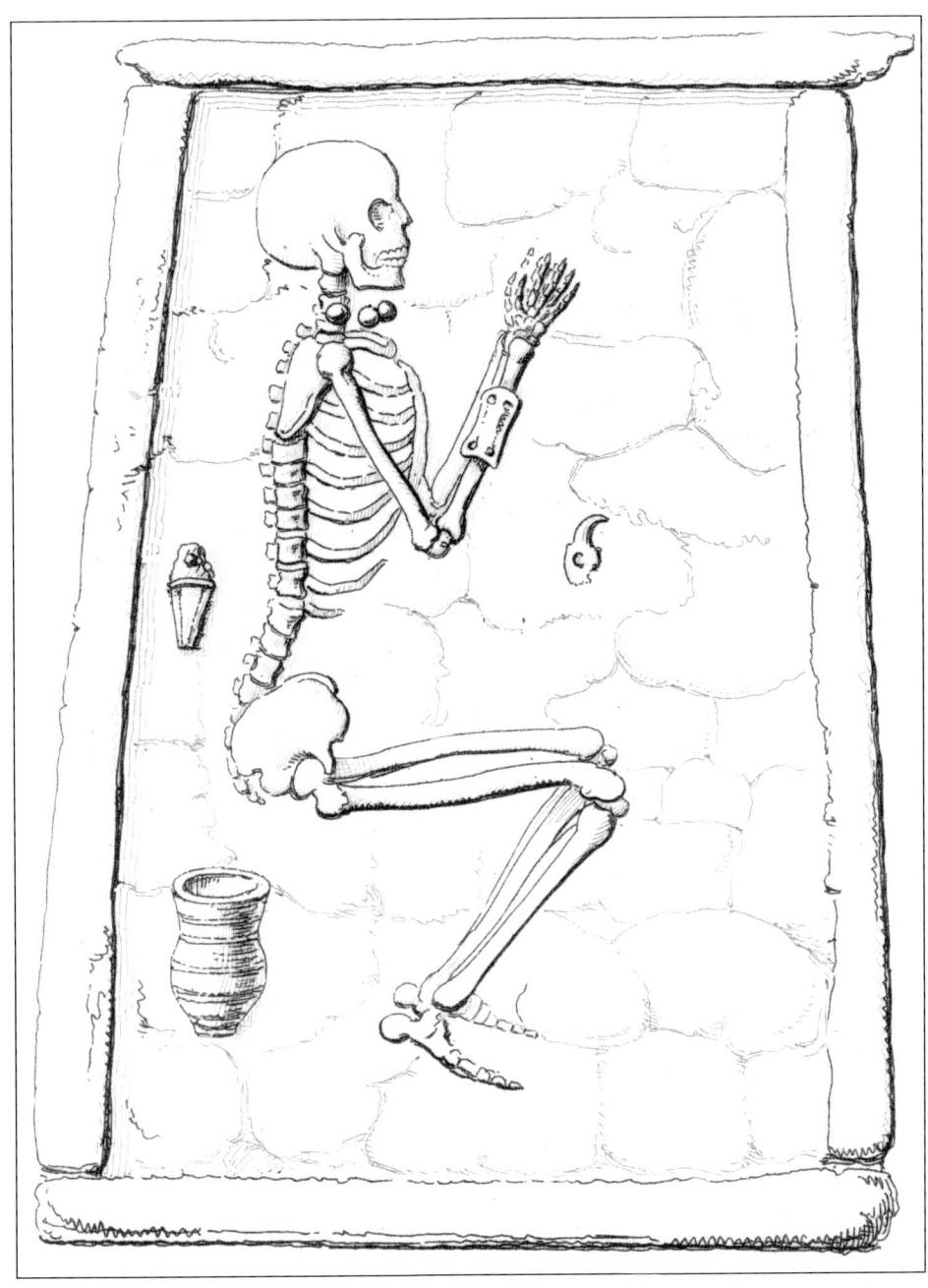

4 *The central interment beneath a round barrow at Driffield, Yorkshire, excavated in 1851 by Lord Londesborough (1852). 'A mass of what seemed to be linen cloth lay under the entire length of the skeleton' — Londesborough suggested that originally the entire body had been wrapped in it. With the crouched male inhumation were a stone wristguard featuring four bronze rivets capped with gold, a Beaker, 3 amber buttons, a copper knife-dagger bearing traces of wooden hilt and sheath, and the head and beak of a hawk*

particular was an important step in archaeological methodology. His detailed examination of comparable continental material, which was ascribed chronological precedence, and his search for a continental source for the origins of change and innovation reflected established practice and typified much of what was to follow.

Chronology and sequence had, aside from bronzes, been notably elusive until Abercromby began to put Bronze Age ceramic studies on a more sound and secure footing, albeit within prevailing analytical traditions. He was able to offer seemingly distinctive cultural groups represented by a significant spread of particular forms of vessel, such work offering a further development between artefacts and people. The Beaker Folk are of course the best known, but a comparable situation was offered for the Deverel-Rimbury ceramics, which were pulled together with some loosely associated metal and monument types and assigned to an incursion of refugees from the continent during the latter stages of the Bronze Age (see also Crawford 1922).

The study of the Bronze Age remained restricted to funerary monuments, metalwork and pottery for a while yet, and the application of calendar dates was often more guesswork than the archaeologists were prepared to admit. The technique was described succinctly and confidently in the British Museum's 1920 catalogue:

> The attempt to assign absolute dates to objects earlier than any historical records is based upon the previous establishment of a *relative* chronology obtained through a classification by sequence of types. It is found that the bronze antiquities of almost any country can be divided into a number of consecutive series in which the development of types of different objects, especially axe-heads and brooches, can be clearly traced. It is further found that the characteristic types of one series are hardly ever associated with those of another, and that the only objects which overlap are those late in the series and early in the next . . . Sometimes, however, the date of a later series can be exactly determined, because the objects which comprise it occur with types also found in Central Europe and Italy, and these in turn come into contact with the old historical civilizations of which the dates are known . . . (British Museum 1920, 22-3).

Thirty years later T.C. Lethbridge reported that he found 'Egyptologists hooting with laughter at the attempts of sages to fix absolute dates for our Bronze Age. It just cannot be done as yet' (Lethbridge 1950, 92), while others such as Gordon Childe had occasionally couched their concerns in more measured prose.

As the Deverel-Rimbury 'Culture' demonstrated, the various classes of evidence could not in fact be pulled together without a fair degree of assumption and generalisation. It was, by the 1930s, widely accepted that metal types, ceramic types, monument and settlement types — sometimes singly but preferably in combination — could represent distinct groups of people, or cultures, whose historical development and fate could be followed in the archaeological record of their particular region. This approach became more formalised within British prehistory via the work of individuals such as Christopher Hawkes, Stuart Piggott and, most notably, Gordon Childe, though its application was seldom as rigorous as the theoretical model suggested. Piggott's 'Wessex Culture', for example, comprised almost exclusively the richer of the known Early Bronze Age burials from southern England (Piggott 1938; Clarke 1966). Inevitably, inspiration was seen to come from abroad.

What constituted a 'culture' for archaeological purposes was first explicitly stated by Gordon Childe, a definition that he was to refine and expand over the years. In his book *The Bronze Age* (1930), he stated that

> During the Bronze Age, as in the preceding period, Europe was divided up among a multiplicity of distinct communities or peoples. These may be distinguished from one another by burial rites, architecture, art and the types of tools, weapons, vessels and ornaments they used. The distinctive metal, bone, stone and pottery types (artefacts), regularly found associated in graves and settlements over a given geographical area, together with the peculiarities of the domestic and funerary structures in which they occur, constitute what is called a culture. In a culture thus defined there is good reason to recognise the material expression of that community of traditions which distinguishes a people in the modern sense (Childe 1930, 41-2).

This approach to ordering and interpreting archaeological material lay behind much of the work on British prehistory undertaken down to the 1960s, whether a particular study was focusing on the totality of archaeological remains in a given geographical area or, as in the case of metalwork, on a single class of artefacts.

An important benchmark in the development of British Bronze Studies – in fact for British Prehistory generally – appeared just a few years after Childe first defined archaeological cultures for an English-speaking audience. T.D. Kendrick and Christopher Hawkes (1932) together offered the first real academic synthesis of British archaeology, incorporating the important developments that had occurred in the years since the First World War. Those developments included not only new discoveries and further artefact studies, but also a burgeoning interest in the survey and excavation of earthworks other than barrows and hillforts, both of which had previously been the principal foci of much excavation effort as far as the Bronze Age and Iron Age (respectively) were concerned. In subsequent years, survey from the air was to reveal entire landscapes of prehistoric remains, previously hidden from the gaze of archaeologists. Understanding of the past was to be transformed as the full extent and complexity of prehistoric activity was revealed, and as 'new' features such as field systems, enclosures and settlements were pulled into the landscapes of particular periods and peoples.

Nonetheless, the artefacts and their sequential arrangement continued to represent the core of archaeological endeavour. They still provided, after all, the primary means of dating sites and monuments – and later, cropmarks – as well as providing the basic building blocks for the chronological and cultural framework of British prehistory. They also comprised the heart of Kendrick and Hawkes' synthesis of the Bronze Age. The extent to which they created rather than reflected orthodox opinion for the period is debatable. British archaeology, professionally speaking, was still a small world and much discussion took place away from the pages of journals and monographs. Aspects of their overview of the Bronze Age can be found in the earlier works of Abercromby (1912), Crawford (1912; 1922), Evans (1881), Fox (1923) and others, but they offered a particularly rigid arrangement of the evidence. They presented a chronological and cultural straitjacket that laid clear foundations for discussion for years to come, with each of the main categories of artefact assigned a clear place in the all-embracing scheme. In fact, despite the wealth of new data to emerge over subsequent decades, their general approach to ordering, describing and explaining the material at hand was not overly dissimilar to that employed in the next major synthesis of the British Bronze Age (Burgess 1974). By 1932, pottery studies had advanced little beyond the pioneering work of Abercromby, but in subsequent years it was the increasing number of non-funerary sites being recognised and excavated that were to offer the greatest potential, if not the most rapid results. Metalwork on the other hand was already beginning to see the sort of organisation that in time would become fossilised into a regional and chronological arrangement of 'industries', defined in the same way as 'cultures' but limited to just the metal.

Kendrick and Hawkes also offered the clearest statement yet of how far the Bronze Age had become separated from both the Neolithic and the Iron Age in the archaeologist's imagination. Begun and ended by invasion from the continent, continuity was neither required nor really looked for beyond a minor concern with the fate of the indigenous populations. Although in years to come the transitions were to become more blurred, the Bronze Age remained a largely self-contained block of time for purposes of study and interpretation.

Mention of Cyril Fox is particularly important here. In outlining what he termed the 'personality of Britain' (Fox 1933), he made extensive use of distribution maps in order to explain the basic geographical spread of certain archaeological phenomena, and by extension the cultural groups they represented. That geographical spread, and any variation within it, was interpreted with reference to geology, topography, climate, flora and fauna. Combined with the culture-historical approach to ordering data, Fox's scheme further emphasised the belief that sizeable blocks of time and space could be characterised by reference to a relatively small suite of archaeological criteria, with regional differences largely explained in terms of the constraints presented by the natural environment. Fox was also largely responsible for fixing firmly in prehistorians' minds the archaeological equivalent of the North-South divide – the Highland and Lowland Zones of the British Isles, separated by a line drawn roughly between the Severn and the Wash, the differing climates, environments and topographies having considerable impact on both culture and the processes of culture change.

After Kendrick and Hawkes (1932), the British Bronze Age as a whole did not receive a detailed treatment to compare with that offered by Stuart Piggott (1954) for the Neolithic until the mid-1970s (Burgess 1974). Of course, Piggott's mid-century framework for the Neolithic was already in trouble by the time he published, and not only because the first radiocarbon dates were beginning to upset some long-held ideas. However, the Bronze Age also saw interpretative and chronological upheaval during the same decade, but this turmoil can seem less obvious in retrospect, perhaps because that major literary benchmark is missing.

Until the 1970s the earlier half of the Bronze Age was still characterised by the Beaker Folk, followed in southern Britain by the chieftains of Piggott's (1938) Wessex Culture. The former, of course, were seen to bring a whole new range of practices and material culture with them, the latter a funerary rite involving the burial with the corpse of wealthy and exotic items, and believed to represent the incursion of an intrusive Breton nobility. Meanwhile, a continuing shortage of house structures and obvious long-term settlements, coupled with the presence of upland enclosures and a greater quantity of animal bones than cereals, offered a vision of a largely pastoral society until well into the second millennium BC, the earliest date to which field systems could then be feasibly pushed. The Deverel-Rimbury 'culture' settlements and their associated features – rectangular earthwork enclosures, palstaves, distinctive pottery vessel forms and so on – had been regarded as intrusive elements of the early first millennium BC since the days of Abercromby and Crawford, but in the 1950s more detailed comparative analyses of the pottery and associated metalwork from southern England and the neighbouring continent (and particularly the Netherlands) highlighted major difficulties (Butler and Smith 1956; I.F. Smith 1961). It transpired that the Late Bronze Age Deverel-Rimbury Culture was not that Late at all, but belonged to the centuries before 1000 BC – the Middle Bronze Age, and with potentially earlier origins. This backdating of a sizeable chunk of material left an apparent gap – a hiatus in the settlement and pottery evidence – at precisely the same time when the greatest quantities of (genuinely Late) metalwork were being consigned to the ground. As Burgess (1969, 30) explained, 'A gap of several centuries is thus opened up between the relevant Bronze Age and Iron Age contexts, with few clues as to what happened to the Deverel-Rimbury complex, and everything associated with it, in between. One is compelled to face again a basic problem of British prehistory; that with rare exceptions, nothing is known about the settlements, burials and pottery of our Late Bronze Age.'

Ironically, of course, this gap was caused by the rigorous application of precisely the same sort of artefact-orientated studies that had misplaced the Deverel-Rimbury material in the first place. Equally ironic was its occurrence – in the late 1950s/early 1960s – just as the indigenous rather than invasion-led roots of the

British Iron Age were beginning to gain acceptance. Of course, the gap was always going to be more apparent than real. Notwithstanding the clear continuity of metalwork evidence from the Middle Bronze Age into the first millennium BC and beyond the end of the Bronze Age, it was radiocarbon dating and pottery studies that ultimately helped close the gap. Little could be done with the bronzes alone as they simply did not occur with sufficient frequency in association with other material. Of particular importance here were developments in research- and, increasingly, rescue-led survey and excavation; there were now far more sites being recognised and excavated.

Initially, and to some surprise, it proved possible to drag some hillforts – hitherto the type site of the Iron Age – back into the Late Bronze Age, along with some other sites. This backdating came either via radiocarbon dating or through the presence of a few bronzes, although in retrospect some of those sites can be seen to offer a more complex sequence of development. This process of infilling is evident to a certain extent in Colin Burgess' lengthy (1974) account of the British Bronze Age, though even here the discussion of settlements was dominated by analyses of pottery styles and their distributions. The few sites firmly dated to the Bronze Age – Mam Tor (**5**; Coombs and Thompson 1979), Grimthorpe (Stead 1968), Ivinghoe Beacon (Cotton and Frere 1968), Dinorben (Savory 1971), Staple Howe (Brewster 1963) and so on – actually received more attention in the subsequent Iron Age chapter (Cunliffe 1974) in the same book, perhaps reflecting confusion about where, culturally rather than chronologically, such places belonged.

The subsequent rapidity with which developments overtook the 'later' Bronze Age (itself largely a creation of the 1970s – see below) is evident in the published proceedings of a conference held at the end of the 1970s (*Settlement and Society . . .*: Barrett and Bradley 1980). Already, based largely on the fieldwork and research undertaken over the previous few years, the editors were able to characterise the distinction between earlier and later phases of the Bronze Age in what are now familiar, if general, terms, and for once they were drawing on a wealth rather than a lack of evidence: 'we can define the *later Bronze Age* as a period of agricultural intensification, contrasting directly with an *earlier Bronze Age* in which the main emphasis in the archaeological record is on ritual, ceremonial and mortuary practices. This change can be recognised in the growing adoption of field systems, land boundaries, durable settlements and defensive sites, and in the progressive disappearance of barrows and ceremonial monuments' (Barrett and Bradley 1980a, 9). This was of course a proposal that both informed and was modified by the editors' own fieldwork on the Neolithic and Bronze Age landscapes of Cranborne Chase (Barrett, Bradley and Green 1991).

Barrett and Bradley (1980a, 10) also made reference to the over-compartmentalisation of the Bronze Age, the artefact- and funerary-inspired sequences of cultural and industrial groupings that still dominated the arrangement of prehistory in the 1970s: 'The truth is that the Bronze Age has been divided up into categories of specialist study, until the relationship between these essentially arbitrary units

5 *The hillfort at Mam Tor, Derbyshire. Excavations between 1965 and 1969 (Coombs and Thompson 1979) demonstrated pre-Iron Age activity at a time when the hiatus in settlement evidence between Middle Bronze Age and Early Iron Age was still puzzling prehistorians. Although Late Bronze Activity on the hilltop appears to have been fairly extensive (Guilbert and Vince 1996), the sole metal find was part of a single socketed axehead. Until the pottery was examined by John Barrett (in Coombs and Thompson 1979; Barrett 1980), confirmation of the approximate date of this phase was heavily reliant on two imprecise radiocarbon dates and the axehead fragment. Note that there is no evidence to associate the hillfort ramparts with the Late Bronze Age phase. © Crown copyright. NMR*

seem to form the really important problems' (*ibid.*). They argued that their aim in arranging and publishing the conference was 'an attempt at integration: its theme – the relationship between the ploughshare and the sword'. In retrospect, they were perhaps more successful in establishing a context for the former than in forging a clear relationship with the latter, but for once attention was squarely focused on the places where people lived and farmed.

The *Settlement and Society* volume presented a great deal of recent work on settlements, and since then of course the number of known sites has increased even more dramatically. A key development here was the introduction in 1990 of Planning Policy Guidance note 16 (PPG 16), which saw archaeological concerns placed firmly within the planning process. To a considerable extent it has also drawn the focus of excavation activity away from the areas of traditional interest to prehistorians, such as the southern chalklands, although inevitably that focus has shifted towards those areas under most pressure from new development. However, this rapid expansion in excavation activity has not resulted in a comparable growth in the numbers of excavated metal objects, further distancing bronze from the mainstream of Bronze Age studies. Essentially, most excavations of Bronze Age sites do not result in the discovery of metal objects. An important corollary to this is that almost all Bronze Age metal objects being found and reported are not discovered by archaeologists (see below).

In contrast, the last few decades have seen pottery studies rise to a position of considerable importance. A major step was John Barrett's (1980) identification of the regional styles and sequences that characterise the Late Bronze Age and earliest Iron Age in southern Britain. These are now known by the admittedly accurate if uninspiring name of 'Post-Deverel Rimbury' (or PDR) pottery. The original framework prepared by Barrett has been increasingly refined and expanded as a result of continued excavations, large and small, undertaken over the past quarter of a century. The initial significance, beyond bridging the ceramic gap opened by the backdating of Deverel-Rimbury material, was to allow the firm identification of sites that belonged to the Late Bronze Age and earliest Iron Age. In the process, the essential continuity from the Middle Bronze Age through to the Iron Age was confirmed.

Moreover it is the pottery, as the most ubiquitous and readily identifiable (if not always aesthetically pleasing) artefact type that continues to be the key indicator of Bronze Age activity on excavated sites. Its relative abundance and its suitability for typological and inter-site studies have seen to that. The gap between Middle Bronze Age and Iron Age has, then, been replaced by another separating metalwork from other aspects of the period. This is particularly apparent in the recent volume *Bronze Age Landscapes* (Brück 2001), the proceedings of a conference that took place in 1999 and which could be considered a successor to *Settlement and Society*. The volume aimed to represent the broad spectrum of Bronze Age studies at the end of the twentieth century, and in doing so confirmed the major shift that had occurred from the artefact-based approaches that had held sway down to the 1970s, to the predominantly site- or landscape-based studies of more recent years.

Nonetheless, the problems with the Bronze Age concern more than just bronze. As the editor of *Bronze Age Landscapes* noted, 'the British Bronze Age has not, with a few notable exceptions, been a focus for theoretical or interpretative debate' (Brück 2001a, v). Instead, 'research on the Bronze Age has not generally been perceived as lying at the forefront of developments in our understanding of prehistoric societies. Synthetic volumes have appeared relatively regularly over the past twenty years for other periods of British prehistory, but again the Bronze Age has lagged behind in this respect. For some years now, one might argue that there has been a sense of fragmentation and a lack of identity for the period' (*ibid.*). A major factor underlying this lack of identity is the continuing retention of the Three Age System and the interpretative baggage that comes with it. Once the role of technology and its products had shifted from centre stage, little remained to give the period any semblance of coherence and, as we have seen, the major social and economic changes appear to occur in the middle centuries of the period rather than at its beginning or end. Moreover, there is little evidence to support a major role for metal in those changes.

However, we have yet to get to grips with the abundance of non-metallic evidence now available, and this too is contributing to the aforementioned sense of fragmentation and lack of identity. Although broad trends can be identified, and a picture of considerable regional diversity is emerging, it remains difficult to characterise the period with any confidence, whether or not one chooses to use tools and weapons of bronze as the criteria for naming and framing it.

In his closing contribution to the *Bronze Age Landscapes* volume, Richard Bradley asked 'Should we go back to the "Bronze Age"? I think not. Over a century after those period divisions were devised, it is time to work out a scheme better suited to the needs of archaeology' (Bradley 2001, 231). The Bronze Age, then, is simply the period when copper and copper alloys were used for the manufacture of the main forms of tools and weapons, and on these terms it remains a fairly arbitrary unit of time (and, of course, space). Consequently, to understand metal there is a need to understand the social contexts in which metal was used, rather than – as had generally been the case in the past – to use the metal itself to define the period in which it was used.

The context of bronze

Since Kendrick and Hawkes' (1932) presentation of a framework for Bronze Age metalwork, studies of bronze objects followed a series of inter-related paths, building on work that had begun during the later nineteenth century. Several important studies appeared in the years between Evans' (1881) offering and 1932. Among the most notable was Oscar Montelius' (1908) attempt to classify and arrange the metalwork of the British Isles, a scheme that had first been presented to a British audience eight years earlier. Montelius, of course, is best known for his work on the classification of prehistoric artefacts, principally of the Bronze Age, from Northern Europe and especially Scandinavia, where the chronological schemes he created via typological analysis still form the basis of current chronological frameworks. His British offering appears to have been politely received and quickly passed over; the following year, when Greenwell and Brewis (1909) published their detailed analysis of British Bronze Age spearheads, they neglected to mention the Montelius scheme, despite the audience (public and published) being the same – the Society of Antiquaries of London.

Greenwell and Brewis' paper represented one of the first attempts at the detailed study of a single class of Bronze Age metalwork from the British Isles. As their full title made clear, they were interested in the 'origin, evolution and classification' of spearheads, a trio of goals that lay at the core of metalwork studies for some time afterwards. Such studies aimed to chart the sequential development of a particular class of object via study of form and technology. Analysis of known associations – graves and hoards – allowed links to be made with other indigenous and continental material, the latter of course offering a route to calendar dates.

At the same time, geographical distribution was rapidly becoming an important feature of metalwork studies, the significance of the spatial spread of particular types being a key building block in the emerging cultural-historical school of prehistory. It was the need to study and understand such geographical patterns that lay behind the decision of the British Association to compile a card catalogue of Bronze Age implements from the British Isles, a card catalogue still maintained today at the British Museum, though for entirely different reasons. Over the years, it is the major classes of object – the most numerous and those considered the most significant culturally – that have inevitably attracted the most attention. As well as spearheads, these include swords (Colquhoun and Burgess 1988), rapiers (Burgess and Gerloff 1981), daggers (Gerloff 1975) and axeheads (Schmidt and Burgess 1981). However, items known in smaller quantities, and those less susceptible to detailed typological analysis, have occasionally attracted in-depth treatment. These include, for example, socketed gouges (Eogan 1966), halberds (Ó Ríordáin 1937), arm-rings (Rowlands 1971), decorated 'plaques' (Coombs 1991) and anvils (Ehrenburg 1981a), though for the most part discussion of lower profile material tends to be confined to specialist reports on particular items from excavated sites.

Hoards likewise have continued to receive considerable attention, both individually and collectively, reflecting continuing adherence to the view that such collections of associated material offer something more than the sum of their parts. Their value in providing evidence of association and for links with the continent has played no small part in this, though considerably less thought was given to the reasons for their existence (see below). Developing the sort of approach typified by Kendrick and Hawkes (1932), a notable stimulus to their study came via the publication of key hoards (and grave groups) in the *Inventaria Archaeologia* series during the 1950s and early 1960s, which saw the standardised presentation and analysis of some of the most significant finds from the British

Isles in a card format. Several other studies emerged around the same time from some of those involved in this scheme, among the most notable being Margaret Smith's (1959) publication of the so-called 'Ornament Horizon' hoards and associated material, primarily from Somerset.

In 1960, a little known but highly influential scheme for the British Bronze Age was presented by Christopher Hawkes. Like his earlier (1931) arrangement of the Iron Age, which ironically was under considerable attack from critics by 1960, this scheme offered a complex arrangement of divisions and subdivisions – perhaps 'pigeon-holes' is in retrospect a better term – for the material culture, funerary and settlement practices of the British Bronze Age. This scheme was never published, perhaps because of the increasing scepticism greeting such treatment of the past for other periods. However, it was widely circulated among prehistorians, and its influence is particularly apparent in the work of Colin Burgess.

Although the current scheme for British Bronze Age metalwork (see below) can be traced back to Kendrick and Hawkes (1932), if not earlier, it was the work of Burgess in particular during the 1960s and 1970s that saw it become fixed in the minds of many. Extensive studies of museums and private collections and a detailed knowledge of the literature led to a series of publications that culminated first in a presentation of the Middle and Late Bronze Age metalwork (Burgess 1968) and then in a more detailed treatment of the Bronze Age as a whole (Burgess 1974; see also Burgess 1980), in addition to lengthy studies of particular classes of object – axeheads (Schmidt and Burgess 1981), dirks and rapiers (Burgess and Gerloff 1981), and swords (Colquhoun and Burgess 1988). However, key criticisms of this work today include a lack of concern for context, as well as the overall scheme being constructed in far too rigid a manner. Moreover, the basis for typological study – the criteria considered important in reconstructing the sequential development of particular artefact types – was often far from clear and not always consistent.

Closely entwined with schemes offered for the continental material (e.g. Briard 1965), which was gradually becoming better known among British prehistorians, what emerged was a series of successive groupings of metalwork. These groupings were held to have both chronological and spatial integrity, and were generally considered to represent the productive output of particular regions for a particular period of time. This scheme was constantly modified and adjusted throughout the 1970s and 1980s (and beyond – see Needham 1990; 1996; Needham *et al.* 1997) as new finds or better dating evidence became available. In true cultural-historical fashion, the clear distinctions between each of these so-called 'industrial phases' led inevitably to the focusing of attention on their transitions, with a complex mix of invasion, migration, trade, exchange and local 'innovation' (usually inspired from outside) accounting for the periodic change in the form of the major classes of object and the technology used to create them.

Recent years have seen a long overdue shift away from tendencies to read too much into these 'industrial phases', particularly as the complexities surrounding deposition are recognised. This is a significant development, as a persistent problem encountered in the literature is an uncertainty over exactly what these phases represent. Deriving from the typological study of metalwork, heavily reliant on hoard and grave associations, and with some acknowledgement of geographical distributions, they have often been presumed (as noted above) to have both chronological and spatial integrity. At the same time, they have been presumed by many to represent the typical output of a local or regional 'industry' for a particular period of time. In fact, the distinctions between successive regional or chronological 'industries' are seldom clear cut. Moreover, as we shall see in the next chapter, what they are more likely to represent is changing trends in depositional practices over time and space. Consequently, the links with any presumed 'industrial tradition', or the belief that the metalwork we study today is in any way representative of the forms, styles and types that circulated in the past, are no more than assumptions.

To deal more specifically with the issue of dating – it may seem remarkable, but the number of radiocarbon dates directly associated with items of Bronze Age metalwork is very small, and a substantial proportion of those that do exist were specifically obtained during the 1990s in order to try and construct a long overdue independent chronology for metalwork (Needham *et al.* 1997). Independent, that is, of the sort of dating by analogy with continental material that had dominated since the late nineteenth century. It can seem surprising that nearly half a century passed between the first application of radiocarbon dating to archaeological material and the first systematic attempt to check that the chronology used for British Bronze Age metalwork was correct, but to a certain extent the delay can be attributed to the fact that many prehistorians saw metalwork itself as the dating medium, so ingrained were the sequences of 'industrial' pigeon holes. Indeed, it still happens – an item of Bronze Age metalwork turning up on an excavated site continues to be regarded by some as potentially valuable dating evidence, whereas the metalwork specialist would now view the discovery as an opportunity to assess the likely date of the metalwork.

Metalworking chronology is a topic with a history best described as tortuous, and it is not intended here to provide anything more than an outline summary. For an up-to-date picture of the current state of play, the reader is referred to Stuart Needham's (1996) periodisation of the British Bronze Age, and the results of the recent British Museum-led programme of radiocarbon dating bronzes (Needham *et al.* 1997). For the individual stages, their gestation is long and complex, and not at all easy to follow in the literature, while the names and dates assigned to then have at times appeared to change according to the whims of particular individuals. Most have been named after particular finds – usually hoards – and consequently some are well known to even the most casual follower of developments.

For many years the Bronze Age had been divided into three parts of unequal length – Early, Middle and Late – these subdivisions being largely but not exclusively based around changes in the metalwork repertoire. The Early Bronze Age was represented by flat and flanged axeheads, daggers and so forth; the Middle

6 *An Early Bronze Age 'hoard' from Migdale, Sutherland, Scotland which, because of its unusually diverse contents, has often seen service as a 'type find' for the 'industrial tradition' or 'phase' to which it is seen to belong. It was discovered prior to 1901 while blasting the top of a granite knoll on the moor at the west end of Loch Migdale (Clarke et al 1985, 302-3). Although the precise circumstances of discovery are unknown, Cowie (1988, 19) noted that a 'contemporary sketch indicated that . . . the striking nature of the rock faces may have been factors [in the choice of location for deposition]; here, however, a further factor may have been the presence of a small ceremonial enclosure, or 'mini-henge' in the vicinity of the site'. Wood extant within one of the tubular sheet beads has produced a calibrated radiocarbon date of 2290-1870 BC.*
© National Museums of Scotland

Bronze Age by the advent of palstaves in particular; and the Late Bronze Age by the appearance of socketed axeheads and swords. This tripartite division has always been less easy to apply more generally, though it remains like the Three Age System itself a part of the territory. Broadly speaking, the Early Bronze Age covers the centuries between about 2300 and 1500 BC; the Middle Bronze Age *c.*1600 to around 1000 BC; and the Late Bronze Age from around 1100 BC to *c.*800 BC. The overlaps are intentional, highlighting the absence of the sort of rapid and widespread change once envisaged.

From the late 1970s there developed a tendency to speak (or write) in terms of an 'earlier' and a 'later' Bronze Age, reflecting the growing recognition that the Early Bronze Age was largely a landscape of funerary and ceremonial monuments, while the Middle and Late Bronze Age saw the advent and development of more settled agricultural landscapes with less overt emphasis on ceremonial structures. This two-fold division clearly has its advantages, but appears to be declining in use.

Stuart Needham (1996; Rohl and Needham 1998) has highlighted the likelihood of an early copper-using phase, dating to around 2500-2100 BC, something that had previously fallen in and out of favour with British prehistorians over the years, in contrast to the situation on the continent where a *Chalcolithic* phase has long been an established feature. However, the cultural context of this primary phase of metal use was underlined by Needham's reference to a 'metal-using Neolithic' to describe the first few centuries of copper and bronze in Britain. The remainder of the Early Bronze Age metal stages have often been simply numbered, though names of key finds such as Migdale (**6**) or Arreton have also been attached to some of them. The use of type-finds has been more closely associated with the Middle and Late Bronze Age, with the sequence established by the 1970s of Acton Park – Taunton – Penard – Wilburton – Ewart Park – Llyn Fawr plus their regional equivalents and variations being familiar to many, though what each actually represents is probably less well known. Essentially, each is represented by a repertoire of bronze types, usually centred around axehead types plus items that occur in association with them. The Middle/Late transition is generally taken as the switch from Penard to Wilburton, though in reality there is no clear link with changes in other forms of evidence. The Llyn Fawr phase, though represented by bronzes, is perhaps more properly regarded as Iron Age. Indeed, the type-find itself famously included iron as well as bronze objects. The available radiocarbon dating evidence suggests that much of the Ewart Park material was deposited before 800 BC.

Given the havoc caused to established Beaker pottery typologies by the rigorous assessment of extant and new radiocarbon dates (Kinnes *et al.* 1991), it arguably came as a relief to discover that for bronze metalwork, the typologists had got it broadly right – the general sequence, that is. However, as should become clear there is rather more potential within bronzes than sequential arrangement. No amount of radiocarbon dating can explain by itself why the stuff was put into the ground in such quantities in the first place, or why there should be so much stylistic variety among technologically comparable types.

2
DEPOSITION: ANECDOTE AND EVIDENCE

As should be more than clear by now, numerous studies have appeared over the years dedicated to establishing some order over the incredible variety of surviving bronze artefacts. Remarkably though, the reasons for the survival of those objects down to the present day have seldom been considered worthy of more serious debate until quite recently – remarkable because, as Bradley (1990) among others has emphasized, bronze is a recyclable material, and the available evidence suggests that recycling was a common practice throughout much of the British Isles (e.g. Rohl and Needham 1998). Why then did so many bronzes enter the ground (or bog or water) never to be recovered or recycled?

A major reason behind the apparent neglect of this issue is the simple fact that contextual information – the sort of detail that could otherwise shed some light on the manner and purpose of deposition – is in almost every instance lacking. It is unfortunately the case that nearly every single piece of Bronze Age metalwork known to us today was neither found by an archaeologist nor recovered in a controlled manner. Nearly all were, until recently, accidental discoveries made in the course of agricultural or building work, road or railway construction, quarrying or dredging. To borrow a phrase much beloved of the media, most have been stumbled upon rather than found as a result of systematic fieldwork. More recently, the growing popularity of metal-detecting (**7**) has added a more purposeful element to the quest for metal objects (of all periods), sometimes with quite spectacular results. The advent of the Portable Antiquities Scheme and recent changes to the law concerning treasure trove (in England and Wales: see Appendix) offer real opportunities for more frequent and detailed archaeological examination of findspots, and hence a greater insight into depositional circumstances, but it will be some time before the real impact of such developments can be properly evaluated.

The importance of excavating the environs of newly-reported finds will become apparent later in the chapter when reviewing the current accumulation of archaeological and anecdotal information surrounding metalwork deposition, and is particularly pertinent given the relative rarity of metal finds from settlement sites – indeed, from any type of site. Although pottery and stone artefacts are often

43

7 *A collection of Middle Bronze Age palstaves found at Ripple, Kent. Four and a half palstaves were found during metal-detector searches in 1994 and 1995. The remaining half had been found independently and some time previously, arriving at Dover Museum only after the rest of the hoard had been found. Excavation of the findspot by Keith Parfitt suggests that three of the palstaves at least had been inserted into the upper fill of a ditch of uncertain function and extent, but of Early to Middle Bronze Age date. The other two were found 75m and 150m away respectively (J. Iveson, K. Parfitt pers. comms).* © Dover Museum

plentiful, and bone common given the appropriate soil conditions, bronze remains an exceptional rather than an expected occurrence.

This shortage of contextual information should represent a major weakness in any attempt to understand the roles and significance of metalwork. If we cannot explain its deposition, how can we make use of it for typological or chronological studies, let alone any broader cultural analyses, with any confidence? In fact, such weaknesses have been effectively concealed by the early establishment and widespread acceptance of quite specific explanations for deposition and non-recovery. These have seen metal finds and by extension metalworking in the Bronze Age characterised in what might be termed 'common sense' social and economic terms. Effectively the economic logic and principles of the modern western world are applied in simplified form to the prehistoric world. Bronze has therefore been viewed as a commodity whose value lay chiefly within its potential to make all manner of objects for undertaking the basic tasks of everyday life, as well as objects for display, prestige, warfare and exchange.

The shortcomings of these established explanations have become increasingly evident with the slow but significant increase in the number of finds recorded *in situ*, as well as the more detailed analysis of the extant corpus of known finds. Today we have, I believe, clear and unambiguous evidence that deposition in the Bronze Age could be non-random, selective and purposeful, with no intention to recover. Furthermore, it appears to have been motivated by factors other than security or economics. However, despite this evidence and the concurrent development of more varied and sophisticated means of interpreting material culture, those traditional interpretations of metalwork deposition have proved remarkably resilient.

Those traditional explanations emerged during the later nineteenth century and offer an extremely limited and limiting range of choices focusing mainly on temporary storage or concealment of personal possessions, plus an element of accidental loss. They revolve mainly around the burial of what became known as 'hoards' (**8**) – accumulations of two or more metal objects concealed, or at least found, together. The term 'hoard' itself carries clear implications for the interpretation of this material. Sir John Evans was not the first to present these explanations of metalwork burial, but his massive 1881 presentation of ancient bronzes represents an important stage in British Bronze Age studies, featuring as it did the first systematic attempt to classify the British hoards according to the perceived reasons underlying their accumulation and burial.

The basic choices offered by Evans remain familiar today, and continue to recur in accounts of fresh discoveries: the founder's hoard, the merchant's hoard and the personal hoard. His explanation of these was concise and straightforward:

> As M. Gabriel de Mortillet and others have pointed out, these hoards are of more than one character. In certain cases, they seem to have been the treasured property of some individual who would appear to have buried his valuable tools or weapons during troubled times, and never to have been able to disinter them. In other cases, the hoards were probably the property of a trader, as they consist of objects ready for use and in considerable numbers, and in others again, they appear to have been the stock-in-trade of some bronze-founder of ancient times, as they comprise worn out and broken tools and weapons, lumps of rough metal, and even the moulds in which the accumulation of bronze was destined to be recast (Evans 1881, 457).

In discussing and tabulating the known British hoards, Evans was concerned to indicate into which category (Personal, Merchant's or Founder's) each should be placed, although he accepted that the dividing lines were not necessarily straightforward. Indeed, he noted that some apparently Personal hoards such as those comprised solely of ornaments might even be sepulchral in origin. As well as dividing the hoards according to categories of ownership, he was also able to suggest two further categories: '. . . the one, in which socketed celts, gouges, or other tools were absent; the other, in which they were present in greater or lesser abundance' (Evans 1881, 459). Evans noted that this two-fold distinction had some chrono-

8 *A Middle Bronze Age hoard found in 1995 by metal detectorists at Malmains Farm, Timanstone, Kent. Excavation of the findspot by Keith Parfitt suggests that the objects had been placed within a small pit [J. Iveson, K. Parfitt pers. comms]. Hoards of this date in the south-east are typically dominated by palstaves. Indeed, often they comprise only palstaves.* © Dover Museum logical significance, with the Founders' hoards generally belonging to a later phase of the Bronze Age than the bulk of the Merchants' and Personal hoards, though why this should be so was not pursued. Indeed, though this shift in depositional behaviour has subsequently been confirmed by further studies of metalwork sequence and chronology, it is one that has seldom been fully appreciated.

Little if any disagreement is to be found with Evans' discussion of the British hoards until quite late in the twentieth century. Indeed many of the ideas contained within his book, whether or not they originated with him, seem to have quickly and quietly attained some sort of orthodoxy (though see Montelius 1908 and Abercromby 1912). Terminology and chronology may have altered but the underlying interpretations remained broadly unchanged. Around a hundred years after Evans' book was published, Colin Burgess and David Coombs offered essentially the same choices. Introducing a volume primarily intended as a vehicle for the publication of a handful of the numerous hoards awaiting such detailed treatment, and in which discussion of the small matter of deposition was unfortunately rather limited in scope and quantity, they suggested that: 'Most would agree that hoards resulted from four sets of circumstances: 1. concealment in the ground for security reasons in an age without safes or secure alternatives; 2. deposits not recovered for one reason or another from their everyday place of storage, in a house or workshop for example; 3. votive offering; 4. accidental loss, whether shipwreck or a bag of metal goods slipping undetected from a belt or pack-horse' (Burgess and Coombs 1979a, iv).

The mention of shipwrecks is a nod to the then-recent finds from Langdon Bay, Dover (**colour plate** 2) and Salcombe, Devon. More noteworthy is the inclusion of a votive category, as is the failure to discuss it (or indeed any of the other choices). They were, it seems, self-evident. Furthermore, they argued that 'many of the owners of the hoards in our museums presumably failed to reclaim them due to death, captivity or exile' (*ibid.*, v), an explanation reminiscent of one offered nearly 40 years previously by Christopher Hawkes, who saw in the image of the itinerant smith operating in barbarian Europe a likely reason for our museum collections: 'Travellers in little civilized lands are always liable to meet accidents, occasionally sudden death, so it is not surprising that throughout Europe and the British Isles the contents of the bronze-smith's workbags are found today in many places where they have lain since they were lost in bogs, or from capsized boats, or were buried in an emergency and never reclaimed' (Hawkes 1943, 78). Burgess and Coombs did, however, note that while three of their explanations should apply equally to all stages of the Bronze Age, the nature (and presumably frequency) of votive deposits should vary with changes in spiritual belief. 'This should mean that there was a fairly even deposition of hoards from period to period, within individual periods, and in all regions. Patently this did not happen' (Burgess and Coombs 1979a, iv). The possible reasons for these peaks and troughs in the frequency of deposition were again sought in the hazardous nature of prehistoric life: '. . . many of those hoards which have survived do not reflect the short-term, everyday unvarying uncertainties of Bronze Age life, but must point to intermittent, much more serious disturbances' (*ibid.*).

That so little attention was paid to votive deposition can seem surprising today. It has become a familiar and recurring theme in the discussion of metalwork over the past twenty years or so, with the discoveries at Flag Fen (Pryor 2001) providing a notable focus for debate. This lack of apparent interest until recently is even more remarkable given the longstanding acceptance of the possibility of votive deposition among continental scholars (see summaries in Bradley 1990; Taylor 1993). While rarely accepted in the British Isles, the possibility didn't go unremarked. Indeed Evans himself mentioned the suggestion that some religious motivation might have lain behind the burial or disposal of metal objects, noting that some foreign scholars had 'suggested that some of these hoards may be of a votive character and have been deposited in the ground as precious offerings to the gods. I am not, however, aware of any of our British hoards being of such a character that they can safely be regarded as votive' (Evans 1881, 457-8). This was a question he returned to the following year when discussing the then newly-found Wilburton hoard, the collection of bronzes having been found resting on clay beneath peat during drainage work in Wilburton Rush Fen.

The Wilburton hoard presented clear problems for Evans and his scheme for classifying hoards:

> Whether the Wilburton hoard is to be regarded as personal, or as that of a merchant or bronze-founder, is a difficult question. There is an entire absence of moulds, jets from castings, and portions of cakes of metal, and the only fragments of fused metal which are present are such as might have originated in the burning of the peat in which the hoard was buried. On the other hand, the broken condition of the swords, which from the bending of the metal appears to have been brought about before their burial in the peat, affords an argument against the hoard being merely that of a merchant intended for sale or barter, or of the whole being weapons in personal use. The varied character of the spearheads, both in size and form, is against their being the weapons belonging to some detachment of a native army, and on the whole I am rather in favour of regarding the hoard as the property of some early merchant of bronze, whose stock was in part old metal destined for the crucible, and in part tools and weapons possibly intended to be bartered away for a greater weight of metal in the form of broken or worn-out instruments. If, as seems probable, the site where the hoard was discovered was in the Bronze Age of Britain a waste of waters, we must assume that the deposit of these instruments in the peaty bottom of the mere was unintentional, and was probably caused by the upsetting of a canoe. There is one other possibility, viz., that they may have been thrown into the water as precious offerings to the gods, as has been suggested by Mr

> Worsaee; but where votive offerings of such a kind were made it seems to have been the practice, as with the gold coins offered to the divinity of the Seine, to deface and injure the offerings, so that they could not again be restored to their pristine worldly uses. In the present hoard, though, the swords and some other articles seem to have been broken in ancient times, many of the spear-heads, and several other objects, are absolutely uninjured. The spot where they were deposited must also before the drainage of the fens have in all probability inaccessible, except by a boat or a canoe (Evans 1884, 113-14).

Thus Evans wasn't opposed to the idea of votive deposition itself. He simply couldn't see any justification for its application to any of the British material, though the discussion of the Wilburton hoard suggests that it wasn't a possibility he favoured greatly.

Such reluctance to allow for 'irrational' motives in prehistoric Britain outside explicitly funerary or ceremonial contexts proved remarkably long lived. Recent shifts in outlook owe much to Francis Pryor's discoveries at Flag Fen (Pryor 2001), although a broader trend in the study of material culture deposition in the Neolithic (see for example Richards and Thomas 1984) were arguably of greater significance. The constraints on interpretations presented by the ideas of Evans and others, particularly with regard to hoard deposition, effectively removed the need to consider the act of deposition in individual instances save where the circumstances were clearly exceptional. However, even then it could prove difficult to break with tradition, as demonstrated by O'Neil's (1941) struggle with the circumstances of the Late Bronze Age hoard from Bourton-on-the-Water, Gloucestershire (see below).

A little more overt was Cyril Fox who, in his discussion of the archaeology of the Cambridge region, attempted to classify hoards from the area according to Evans' scheme, including the recognition that for the most part Founders' hoards were of a later date. However, he too encountered some difficulty in placing all hoards satisfactorily into one of the three principle categories. Some hoards which might normally be assigned to the Personal or Merchants classes he felt might be otherwise interpreted: '. . . several, such as those of flanged axes from Grunty Fen and Mildenhall, and the shields found together in Coveney Fen, may be votive offerings; and in both [Personal and Merchants'] groups some of the larger hoards may be those of chiefs, following the contemporary Homeric and later Teutonic custom' (Fox 1923, 51). A little later, discussing the hoard of Early Bronze Age axes found beneath a stone at Finglenny Hill, Stevenson (1947-8) noted that the circumstances – some of the axeheads had been deliberately broken before concealment – suggested that each axehead was 'a religious of magical offering, of which some . . . were deliberately destroyed' (**9**; Stevenson 1947-8).

Votive deposition played little part in the writings of Gordon Childe either, presumably reflecting his broader beliefs on the social and economic role and

9 *A hoard of Early Bronze Age flat axeheads from the Hill of Finglenny, Aberdeenshire. Parts of eight axeheads are present, and some of them seem to have been deliberately broken in half prior to deposition beneath a stone on the Hill. Several of the axes had been 'tinned', a process which would have given them a more silvery appearance. Cowie (1988, 19-22) noted that the findspot overlooked a henge, and lies close to 'the significant watershed separating the Deveron valley and the western end of the Garioch'.*
© National Museums of Scotland

impact of metallurgy, as well as the role played by associated finds in the establishment of sequences, chronologies, and links with continental material. The existence of bronze hoards was, he felt, 'a result of the extensive trade of the Bronze Age and its peculiar conditions' (Childe 1930, 43). The nature of their contents reflected their origin:

> Hoards are of various kinds: some appear to be just the personal possessions of an individual or a household and may be termed 'domestic hoards'. Such consist of a few tools, weapons and ornaments, comprising as a rule only one specimen of each type and normally showing signs of use. They have probably been buried by their owner in time of danger or while he was travelling and never retrieved so that their survival is an indication of the owner's misfortune. Domestic hoards may be regarded as closed finds guaranteeing the contemporary use of all the articles deposited together. They are valuable for synchronizing types, but otherwise of no special interest (Childe 1930, 43-4).

As for the merchants' hoards, or 'traders' hoards' as Childe characterised them, they 'normally contain several examples of each type of tool, weapon, or ornament. In the Early Bronze Age the traders' hoards consist almost entirely of new or half-finished articles. Some at least seem to have belonged to travelling tinkers, bartering metal products which they were prepared to finish off on the spot to suit the taste of the customer . . . The contents of the foregoing commercial hoards in all probability were in contemporary use' (*ibid.*, 44). As for their deposition,

> The accepted explanation of traders' hoards is that they were buried by the travelling merchant, when he saw himself threatened by some danger, with the intention of reclaiming them when the peril was past. And in point of fact when plotted on a map, they are seen to lie along natural routes and to be thickest just where danger might be expected, for instance on the frontier of two cultural provinces. Hence a multitude of hoards, whether commercial or domestic, is anything but a sign of prosperity. It was rather in times of unrest that valuables had to be entrusted to the preservation of the earth. (*ibid.*, 45)

Clearly there was the potential for confusion, or at least overlap, between the roles of the travelling trader and the bronzesmith, something that Childe recognised and sought to clarify in distinguishing traders' hoards from founders' hoards, which

> seem in some cases to have been left by a class of trader. They are characterized by the presence of old and broken tools, obviously scrap metal collected for remelting, and often too of metallurgical tools, moulds and ingots of raw metal; such are termed 'founders' hoards' to distinguish them from ordinary traders' hoards. The distinction is vital since the objects included in them may be of very different date, being in fact any old pieces of scrap metal. Yet some such hoards probably belong to gangs of travelling tinkers who went around the countryside repairing broken tools and collecting scrap metal at a time when the demand was particularly intense. Others are so large that they must represent the stock of a village smithy buried at a moment of danger or of a station in the international metal trade. (*ibid.*, 45)

Some tinkering with such ideas occurred over subsequent years – Hodges (1957, 51) for example added a new class – the personal tool-kits of specialist craftsmen, and also noted potential confusion between large personal hoards and smaller traders' or merchants' hoards. Typical of the general situation was Campbell and Coles' (1962-3) discussion of the finds from Torran, Argyll. The first finds were made in 1881 when digging for a ferret which had apparently got lost down a rabbit hole. 'Six feet down the rabbit hole ceased, and there, where the rabbits had lain, were found the two [spearheads] and the gouge' (Strachan 1884). In 1962, the original findspot was relocated on 'a very steep slope . . . among tumbled boulders, some very large, which had fallen from the cliff above' (Campbell & Coles 1962-3). Further bronzes were found in the immediate area – some rings, socketed axeheads, a knife – and 'in view of the steepness of the hillside and the obviously recent rock-movements, it seems that the original hoard may have been deposited in some rock-shelter, now collapsed, under the crag, and rolled downhill with the fallen rocks to its eventual findspot' (*ibid.*). And what were the objects doing there? 'The group of objects taken together is best considered as a personal hoard of tools and weapons, perhaps a woodworker's set, although this is not certain. By some definitions, the presence of three similar objects (here, the axes) would suggest a merchant's hoard, but the axes are of such distinct types, that if a merchant's hoard, it must have been in the nature of a travelling salesman carrying a sample of his wares' (*ibid.*). Throughout, the terminology and the explanations offered remind one not so much of the Bronze Age but of much more recent times, with modern notions of trade and commerce effectively being projected backwards into prehistory. Deposition in the ground, whatever the precise circumstances or the awkwardness of the location, was all too frequently viewed as a response to danger, whether real or imagined. Moreover, there was seldom any attempt to justify such interpretations, which appeared to occupy the realms of 'common sense'.

In general though, the reluctance to look closer at the reasons behind the accumulation and deposition of the bronze hoards had repercussions for other aspects of metalwork study. Chronology and sequence, as well as the classification of hoards itself and the accepted explanation for their very existence required belief in the idea, usually implicit rather than explicit, that all objects within a hoard (or other form of association) should be broadly contemporary in terms of date of manufacture and period of use.

The uneasy relationship between traditional explanations of deposition and the available evidence was clearly demonstrated by Stuart Needham in a study of depositional patterns in the Early Bronze Age of Britain and Ireland (Needham 1988). For example, he was able to demonstrate that clear distinctions existed between the types of metal object appropriate for use as grave goods and those that appeared in contemporary hoards. He also noted an uneven geographical distribution in the archaeological record: the mapping of hoard findspots, arranged by chronologically successive 'Metalwork Assemblages', indicated a trend throughout the course of the Early Bronze Age from a highland- and Ireland-dominated distribution towards a lowland concentration. As for the reasons for depositing those hoards, he argued that

> None of the British hoards has any evidence connecting it explicitly to the process of metal-working; explanation of the broken objects in

some hoards is ambiguous, and therefore they cannot necessarily be regarded as the unretrieved stockpiles of merchants . . . Only rarely are the circumstances adequately recorded, but sometimes they give evidence of considerable care taken in the arrangement of objects, thus hinting that deposition was not only deliberate, but intended to be permanent . . . here is something beyond a purely functional requirement in their act of burial (Needham 1988, 232).

These are also ideas that can be applied to the metalwork deposits of the Middle and Late Bronze Age as well, as the examples in the next section will show.

Going underground

One of the most depressing features about museum collections and published gazetteers of metalwork finds is the regularity with which each item is accompanied by, at best, a place-name and a probable date of discovery. Occasionally, however, some detail survives to offer a tantalising glimpse into the process of deposition. The quantity of metalwork recovered from watery contexts – rivers, lakes, bogs – represents an exception of sorts, but the manner in which those items reached their resting place remains open to debate. They are as in need of proper evaluation as any dry land discovery.

The following discussion considers a number of finds from all over the British Isles, though the choice of what to include is clearly determined not by geography but by the surviving documentary record. This selection is arranged initially under two rather broad headings: associated and unassociated finds. The arbitrariness of such a distinction should become clear, and its use here is partly a reflection of the way metalwork has been studied in the past, but it will also help to demonstrate the very real difficulties involved in trying to impose a clear line between the two. Essentially, such a distinction can only work if other factors, such as the place and manner of disposal, are ignored. Ironically, of course, the distinction is now enshrined in legislation (for England and Wales at least) – Bronze Age metalwork only constitutes 'treasure' if two or more items are found in direct association (see Appendix). Finds from settlements and other site-types and 'watery places' are considered under the 'unassociated' heading. Finds from funerary contexts are also considered briefly, while further discussion occurs in later chapters. Throughout what follows there is a considerable degree of overlap, reflecting both the complex nature of prehistoric depositional practices and the perpetual tendency of archaeological material to ignore the criteria we use to organise it.

Associated finds

This section concerns both 'hoards' and other accumulations of material in a single place, other than those from funerary, settlement or wet contexts, which are discussed later. Despite the previously mentioned rarity of useful information, enough discoveries have been reported in sufficient detail for some questions to be asked about established ideas on deposition. That many of these bronzes are far from being new finds merely underlines the extent to which those established ideas essentially overrode the detail of individual cases.

Often, all we know for sure is that certain objects were found together, or at the same location, sometimes both. A worrying proportion of cases lacks even this bare minimum of information. When observations of the circumstances of discovery survive, it has often been noted that the bronzes were closely packed, as though held within a pit or similar feature dug specifically to hold them and little else, or as if the objects had been stored within some kind of organic container when buried. Observations of recent hoard excavations appear to confirm the former at least – that the bronzes were often held within a pit that may have been dug specifically to receive them. Of course, this simple fact does not invalidate ideas about hoarding as a method of storage or safe-keeping. Neither does it offer unequivocal support.

The use of organic containers is less easy to prove than the presence of a pit. Organic material seldom survives in any form, and with earlier finds we cannot be sure that traces would have been spotted anyway. Typical are cases such as the Late Bronze Age hoard from Winship, Cambridgeshire ('evidently buried in a bag of which some indications survived'; *VCH Cambridgeshire* Vol. 1 1938, 278), and the Early Bronze Age hoard from Coombe Dingle near Bristol (three flanged axeheads and a chisel found in 1899 apparently lying on a mat of twigs or reeds; Britton 1963, 286-90). Going back even further of course is the collection of material found wrapped in 'linen' near St Michael's Mount (see p.98). A more recent example – the assemblage from the upper levels of ditch fill at Petter's Sports Field, Runnymede, Surrey (Needham 1990a) – where two 'hoards' broadly similar in content appear to have been buried one on top of the other underlines the possibility of such containers having been used.

The use of ceramic containers is better attested, pottery being a relatively resilient material (see Coombs and Bradshaw 1979 for a gazetteer of such finds). Nor are wooden containers unknown, although clearly appropriate soil conditions are necessary for their survival: for example the Middle Bronze Age hoard from Edington Burtle, Somerset which was contained in a square wooden box (Rowlands 1976, 255); a Late Bronze Age hoard from Winmarleigh, Lancashire found within a large oak box fastened with oak pins (*VCH Lancashire* Vol. 2, 236-7); and the large Late Bronze Age hoard from Stuntney, Cambridgeshire evidently contained within a wooden tub or bucket (Burgess and Gerloff 1981, 82). Alternatively, the tying together of objects is also occasionally noted. In the 1860s, a man was trenching a small round knoll which lies immediately behind the west-most houses in Monadh-mor [Killin, Perthshire] when in turning over the ground with his pick-axe he came upon these bronze articles on the south-west side of the knowe, and within a few yards of the top of it. They were about a foot below the ground all lying together, and had apparently been tied, he thinks, with some kind of fastening, not unlike medium twine, the strands being distinctly visible, but the substance crumbled in to dust the moment it was touched (Stewart 1881-2).

Going beyond mere containment, evidence for the concealment (or just possibly marking) of a deposit is also far from uncommon, though that evidence is heavily reliant on the manner of discovery and recovery of the objects concerned. A well-known Irish case concerns eleven Early Bronze Age axes found at Carhan, Co. Kerry within a hollowed rock. A stone slab had been placed over the hollow (Needham 1988). Three Early Bronze Age flanged axeheads were found at Cragg Wood, Yorkshire in 1866 beneath a stone (Schmidt and Burgess 1981, 80). Another Early Bronze Age collection, this time from Plymstock in Devon, was found in 1868 beneath a flat stone at a depth of 2ft (Pearce 1983). Four flat Early Bronze Age axes recovered during excavation of a bowl barrow at Combe Hill, East Sussex, just outside a Neolithic causewayed enclosure, were also laid beneath a stone (**2**; RCHME 1995). Seven Early Bronze Age flat axeheads were found in 1947 under a stone 'at a Forestry Commission quarry at about 1,000ft OD far up a glen' at the foot of Finglenny Hill, Aberdeenshire (**9**; Stevenson 1947-8).

Along with ceramic containers, large stone slabs represent highly visible and durable associated material, unlikely to escape the attention of the fairly observant onlooker, though the manner of discovery can sometimes obscure or perhaps even destroy clear evidence of their relationship to the bronzes. The means by which metalwork is revealed – ploughing, ditch digging, road building and so on – can mean that much contextual information is lost even before the artefacts are first noticed. When the association is with a pottery or wooden container, for instance, some debris may remain – potsherds, for example – but any evidence for the way in which objects were arranged is likely to be lost forever. This is particularly unfortunate given the few occasions in which recovery of bronzes from largely undisturbed contexts has been observed.

In many such cases, particularly the so-called Founder's Hoards of the Late Bronze Age, there often appears to be no clear order to the manner in which items were deposited. They seem to have been bundled up in an organic container, dropped into a pottery vessel, or likewise dropped into a hole in the ground. However, without a proper record of their recovery, such a disorderly approach to disposal is as much an assumption as is the suggestion that greater care and formality may have been involved. In the case of the aforementioned hoard from Carhan, Co. Kerry, the eleven Early Bronze Age axeheads in the hollowed rock were laid out in a circle, cutting edges outwards, around a heap of what were described as wood ashes and bones of deer. Four Early Bronze Age axeheads were recovered from a round barrow at Wold Farm, Willerby, North Yorkshire during excavations by William Greenwell in 1889 (Needham *et al.* 1985). The axeheads were within the body of the barrow mound, and had been placed on their sides rather than flat on their faces. Another well-known Early Bronze Age example is the Arreton Down hoard, a collection of axeheads, spearheads and daggers discovered *circa* 1735 '. . . ranged in a regular order, the axes laid on the spearheads' (*ibid.*). The hoard from Colleonard, Banffshire was found during trenching in 1857, 'the pot containing the axes . . . found about 1ft below the surface, protected on two sides by two stones of its own height. The axes were closely packed in the vessel, cutting-edges uppermost' (**10**).

A more recent find, and this time of the Middle Bronze Age, is the collection of 90 palstaves from Marnhull, Dorset (Lawson & Farwell 1990) which had been packed into a small pit. 'The first palstaves to be discovered had been closer to the surface than the rest; the second to ninth had been placed flat in a rough crescent at the top of the pit'. At Plumley, Bovey Tracey, in Devon four Middle Bronze Age palstaves were found placed 'end on end' beneath a boulder. Another four were either similarly arranged under an adjacent boulder or were found scattered nearby – accounts vary (Rowlands 1976, 230). At Grunty Fen, Cambridgeshire, in 1844, three Middle Bronze Age palstaves and a gold torc were found. The palstaves were three feet below the surface, and the torc another foot below the palstaves (Rowlands 1976, 226). The Middle Bronze Age hoard sited to the Quantock Hills, Somerset (Rowlands 1976, 257-8) was found in 1794, some six feet below the surface in marshy ground. It comprised two torcs, one on top of the other, and placed within each was a palstave.

Among the best known of these 'arranged' hoards is that found within the later prehistoric enclosure on Hollingbury Hill near Brighton, East Sussex (**11**). In 1825 a labourer digging for flints hacked into a low mound and found 'in a slight excavation in the face of the chalk rock' a palstave, a bronze torc, three coiled finger rings and four so-called 'Sussex loops'. The torc was laid flat, with the four loops arranged around it. The rings had been threaded onto the torc, while the palstave was placed at the centre, within the torc (cf the Quantocks hoard above).

Moving into the Late Bronze Age, it was noted above that there was a tendency for the later hoards, particularly the so-called Founders' Hoards of southern and eastern England, to present rather less evidence of formality in their burial, the occasional wooden or ceramic container notwithstanding. However, some of the most remarkable evidence for careful placement belongs to these latter stages of the Bronze Age. A hoard found at Bourton-on-the-Water, Gloucestershire has already been mentioned in passing (above, p.49). In 1907, eight socketed axeheads were found arranged in four pairs in a circle in a hole which was a little over 2ft in depth. Mr Bowles's (the finder) description, by letter, is as follows:

10 *Discovered during 'trenching operations' in 1857, the hoard from near Colleonard Farm, Banff comprised five complete and two incomplete flat axeheads, all contained within a coarse pottery vessel and arranged with their cutting heads uppermost. The pot was also standing upright, protected by two vertical stone slabs. There is a possibility that the items were buried close to the site of a now-destroyed stone circle (Clarke et al. 1985, 300-1).* © National Museums of Scotland

BRONZE AND THE BRONZE AGE

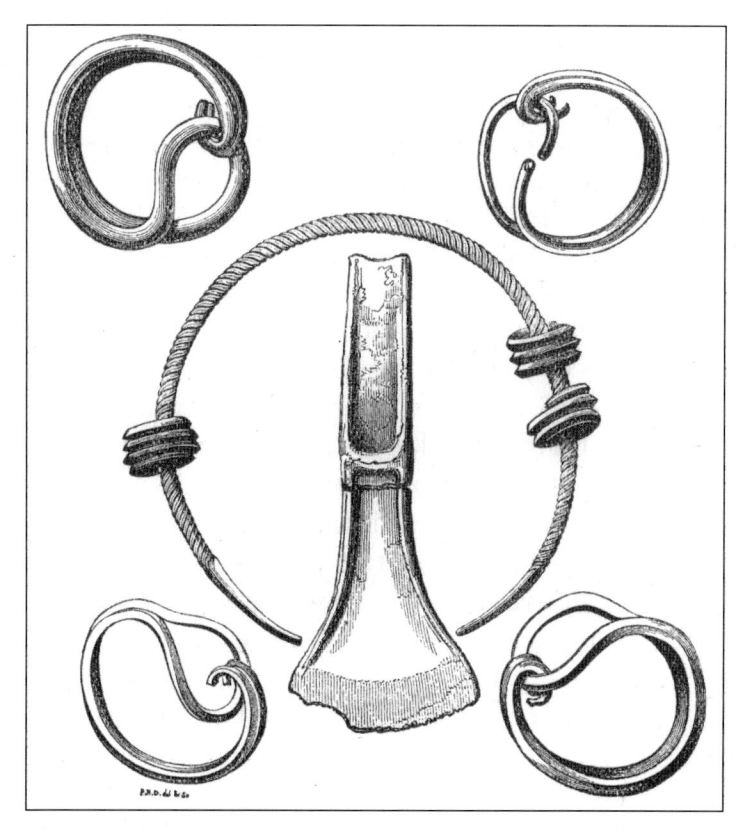

11 *A collection of Middle Bronze Age items found under a low mound within the hillfort on Hollingbury Hill, Brighton, East Sussex, a hillfort which probably has Late Bronze Age origins. The illustration here (reproduced from the* Archaeological Journal *V, 1848, 324-5) is said to represent the objects as they were arranged in the ground when discovered. The collection comprises a palstave, a spiral twisted bronze torc, three coiled finger rings and two 'Sussex loops', an unusual form of bracelet or armlet which, as the name suggests, has rather a limited geographical distribution*

Below 25 or 26 inches of soil I came upon some flat stones arranged one overlapping the other in a large circle, with one large flat one on the top to keep the rest in place. After carefully removing these I found four pairs of axes of different sizes, arranged two and two in a circle in the hole, with hardly any soil on them at all . . . Whether the Bourton hoard can be considered as an example of a votive burial, at present had better remain an open question until further finds help with corroborative evidence, but the careful arrangement of the axes does not suggest the hastily hidden store of a bronze founder. (O'Neil 1941)

At Kilkerran, Ayrshire, a hoard was found at Dalduff Farm in 1846. Most of the bronzes were contained within a pottery vessel, but two sword fragments had been placed over the mouth of the pot (Colquhoun and Burgess 1988, 124). At Barrow in Suffolk, two leaf-shaped swords were found in 1850 or 1851 lying side by side, surrounded by stones and 'blackened earth' (*ibid.*, 32). The eponymous Ewart Park, Northumberland find comprised three swords found in 1811 on a grassy knoll following its first ploughing – all three sword blades had been forced vertically into the ground (*ibid.*, 97). Further north, on the island of Shuna, Argyll, three more Ewart Park swords were found *c*.1875 'in digging a ditch through peaty soil, within a short distance of each other, at some depth below the surface, and all sticking vertically in the peat with the points downwards, as if they had been designedly thrust in and not casually lost' (Anderson 1878-9, 332). Such circumstances are reminiscent of the swords and spearheads found at Whittingham, Northumberland, where two swords and three spearheads were all found

> by some workmen digging drains in a field near Thurston Farm . . . The spot must formerly have been a quagmire, and is supplied with a copious spring of water. The arms were found sticking in the moss with the points downwards, in a circle, about two feet below the surface, perhaps left thus by a party of soldiers who had halted at the spring and been surprised (*Proceedings of the Society of Antiquaries of London* Vol. 5, 1870-3, 429).

No suggestion was offered as to the nature of the surprise. Such circular settings were not confined to swords and spearheads. In 1780, at Beith, Ayrshire, five or six bronze shields were 'discovered in a peat moss several feet below the surface, and were stated to have been arranged on their edges, so as to form a circle' (McCulloch 1862-4). Meanwhile, at Brading Marsh on the Isle of Wight, in 1830 eleven armrings were found arranged in a crescent around a spearhead, all of Middle Bronze Age date (Rowlands 1976, 238). In 1968 at Gosport, Hampshire, 18 Middle Bronze Age palstaves and a single armring were uncovered, the palstaves set vertically in the ground, blades downwards (Rowlands 1976, 239).

Finally, on the subject of arrangement in the ground, come three recent examples, two of them so-called 'founder's hoards'. The first of the latter was discovered in 1993 at Withersfield, Suffolk (Anon 1996). A rare instance of an excavated hoard, its presence was suggested by a small surface scatter of bronzes on the surface of a ploughed field. Excavation revealed a remarkable arrangement: a tightly packed mass of metal, comprising from the top

> a layer of packed bronze-cake fragments . . . at a depth of 30cm, the whole mass being roughly circular, with a diameter of 25 cm . . . the depth of this layer of fragments was 15cm. Below this level, five axes were visible, deliberately packed to the sides of the whole with cake

fragments, all five axes being positioned vertically . . .; a small socketed chisel/gouge had been placed lying flat, together with five broken axe fragments, all lying centrally.

Three of the axeheads surrounding the deposit were blade-upwards, the other two face down. Secondly, and even more recently, an excavation at Hollingbourne, Kent, in March 2003, following an initial metal-detector find, uncovered the *in situ* residue of a Late Bronze Age hoard at the base of a broad, shallow pit. The undisturbed bronzes comprised three socketed axeheads standing upright and framing a deposit of ingot/cake fragments (A Richardson pers. comm.). This hoard was the first to be reported in England following the recent changes to the Treasure Act (see Appendix).

The third example is of Middle Bronze Age date, but like the last is also from Kent. A subrectangular enclosure associated with Deverel-Rimbury pottery at South Dumpton Down on the Isle of Thanet was excavated by the Trust for Thanet Archaeology (**12**, **13**; Dave Perkins, pers. comm.). The enclosing ditch contained a pit, dug once the ditch had already become more or less completely backfilled. Towards the base of the pit were four palstaves, placed together on their sides and arranged in an arc or fan shape. The four palstaves were broadly similar in form and were unused, broadly as cast although tidied up to a certain extent. The blades had never been sharpened; the palstaves had never been used. Covering them was a large slab of tabular flint. A little higher in the pit fill was another palstave, this time lying on its face, and with a bronze bracelet resting on top of it and another fragment nearby. The circumstances suggest two (connected?) acts of deposition late in the history of the enclosure, or perhaps after it had been abandoned.

But the objects alone are only part of the story – the place of burial is equally worthy of consideration. Settlements and burial places are of course considered later on, as are lakes and rivers, but there is good evidence from many different parts of the country for the choice of natural places, sometimes quite difficult of access, for the deposition of metalwork. One possible candidate is the collection of ornaments and razor found at the Braes of Gight, Aberdeenshire in 1866 'by some workmen who were engaged in the construction of a private carriage road . . . A man who was present at the discovery informs me that the ornaments were got during the removal of some huge old fragments of rock which were lying at the bottom of a lofty precipice' (Muirhead 1890-1). On more certain ground, at Skelmore Heads, Cumbria (**14**), just outside a later prehistoric hilltop enclosure, six Late Bronze Age Sompting-type socketed axeheads were found in 1902 in a narrow limestone fissure (RCHME 1996). Interestingly, in the late 1950s a small group of Neolithic stone axeheads were found in a similar context nearby (Powell 1963). At Glentrool, Kirkcudbrightshire, a large collection of Middle Bronze Age bronzes including a flanged axehead, a spearhead, a rapier, razors, a knife, torc fragments and so on were found in 1915 underneath a large

12-13 *The upper and lower deposits found inserted into an enclosure ditch at South Dumpton Down on the Isle of Thanet, Kent.* © The Trust for Thanet Archaeology

14 *Skelmore Heads, Urswick, Cumbria, viewed from the north. Generally presumed to represent an Iron Age hillfort preceded by a palisaded enclosure of probable Late Bronze Age date, the dating evidence from excavations undertaken in the 1950s is slight, and an alternative suggestion of a Neolithic origin has been offered, albeit on even less certain evidence. Circumstantial evidence includes a long barrow a short distance to the north (just visible in the photograph right of centre and above the field boundary crossing left to right), and the discovery in 1959 of four roughed-out stone axeheads placed within a crevice between two stepped limestone boulders circa 20 yards from the enclosure's north-western entrance. Others have been found in the vicinity. In 1902, six Late Bronze Age socketed axeheads, all of 'Sompting' type or similar, were found in a fissure between two limestone blocks during quarrying (RCHME 1996).* © Crown copyright. NMR overhanging boulder, the spearhead projecting above the surface (Coles 1959-60). The Late Bronze Age hoard from Wotton, Surrey was found in 1787 'in a cavity in the rock' (*VCH Surrey* Vol. 1, 241). In 1874, two socketed axeheads were found in a cleft in the rock at Park House Quarry, Birtley, Northumberland (Schmidt and Burgess 1981, 195).

Moving further north into Scotland, Early Bronze Age Migdale-type flat axeheads bearing 'evidence of considerable usage' were found during the nineteenth century at the edge of a bay called 'The Maidens', in the course of clearance of rock faces prior to the construction of a new shipbuilding yard. At the end of April 1883, the workmen 'came upon five bronze celts and a bronze ring lying together, as if concealed in a lateral crevice', the ledge under which they had been placed said to have been 'at the time of their deposition, open to the shore' (Monro 1882-3). In 1906 a pair of Middle Bronze Age palstaves were found at Craig-a-Bhodaich, Sutherland, lying side by side on a small shelf in a rock shelter, close to the confluence of the Crask and the Farr:

> The place has all the appearance of having been a rock-shelter or lean-to, for the rock, which is about 12 feet in height, overhangs a little ... The palstaves lay side by side on a small shelf near the base of the rock, as if placed there by the hands of the ancient craftsmen, the soil afterwards covering the tiny ledge over, and so protecting them. They lay so closely together as to preclude the possibility of their having handles attached to them when deposited there, and the marks of casting on either side of them are so very pronounced that it looks as if they had been little used. (Mackay 1908-9)

Amongst the more spectacular locations for hoards is Roseberry Topping (**15**), on the northern edge of the North York Moors, a landmark feature rising some 200m from the floor of the Tees Valley which 'cannot fail to have early impressed itself upon the imaginations of the inhabitants' (Turton 1913). In 1826 a Late Bronze Age hoard was found in a crevice some way up the south side of the hill, the hoard including socketed axeheads, socketed gouge, a chisel, a hammer, a sickle and other items including a two-piece mould for casting socketed axeheads (Ord 1846; Sherlock 1995). Meanwhile, at Dail na Caraidh, Inverness-shire, near to Fort William on the West Highland coast, several Early Bronze Age items were found between 1980 and 1984, initially by metal detector and subsequently by excavation. Mostly axeheads (or fragments of axeheads), they appear to represent at least two and possibly more distinct episodes of deposition focused upon a prominent natural feature — a long mound in a spectacular position — 'at the confluence of the rivers ... and set against the backdrop of Ben Nevis' (Barrett and Gourlay 1999).

15 *Roseberry Topping, 'a place of pilgrimage for generations of poets and sightseers' (Sherlock 1995, 119), and the scene in 1826 of the discovery of a small collection of Late Bronze Age objects by a labourer in a crevice around halfway up the southern side of the hill. The collection included socketed axeheads (complete and fragmentary), a two-piece socketed axehead mould, socketed gouges, a socketed chisel, a socketed hammer, a socketed sickle, a 'bugle-shaped object' (probably a belt, strap or harness fitting), ingot or 'cake' metal said to weigh 5-6lb, a piece of plate metal with crescent-shaped openings, a whetstone and a piece of jet.*
© Crown copyright. NMR

Unassociated finds

Despite their reputation as little more than dots on maps, or as little more than typological or chronological markers, single and/or unassociated objects of metalwork have been discovered in circumstances similar to those outlined above for hoards. Moreover, the sometimes sizeable quantities of such 'unassociated' material from rivers, lakes and bogs have played a major role in establishing the idea of votive deposition in the Bronze Age, the sheer quantity of such material overcoming alternative explanations such as disposal of unwanted items (though see below) or pure (and extraordinarily frequent) carelessness.

Pottery or organic containers for single items are rare, though not wholly unknown – a highly decorated Early Bronze Age flanged axehead from Brockagh, Co. Kildare, Ireland was found contained within a leather pouch (Brindley 1994, 19). Similarly, special arrangements or the careful positioning of items is clearly more difficult to spot when dealing with individual bronzes. Inevitably, the most information derives from those encountered during archaeological excavation, or from watery contexts.

At Long Rigg Field, Urswick, Cumbria in 1829, some labourers 'engaged in stone getting' lifted a large flat slab of limestone and discovered beneath it 'as if it had been concealed there, a spear. The shaft had been about four feet long, but although quite distinguishable it had crumbled away to powder' (Schmidt and Burgess 1981, 259). Similarly at Tosson, Northumberland in 1868, a Ewart Park-type sword was found lying under a rock (Colquhoun and Burgess 1988, 92). At Highclere, Hampshire, a sword was found 'beneath the roots of a large oak tree . . . lying flat with its tip to the south' (Lawson 1985). In contrast, in 1875 at Cerrig-y-Drudion a rapier was discovered in a peatbog, wooden hilt still attached, standing point upwards (Burgess and Gerloff 1981, 32). A similarly upright position was reported for the remarkable Oxborough dirk (see p.150).

One of the more unusual of unassociated finds, and one which perhaps more than many others underlines the difficulties of finding a plausible, rational explanation, concerns a palstave found at Wood Walton, Cambridgeshire in the winter of 1941-2. The finder, Mr C. Fuller of Abbey Farm, Wood Walton discovered the palstave stuck in the trunk of a bog oak at Castle Hill Farm. The find was confirmed on behalf of the members of the Cambridgeshire and Huntingdonshire Archaeological Society by a Major Gordon Fowler, who was able to inspect both palstave and oak. Reporting the find, J.R. Garrod reported quite matter-of-factly that

> It would seem probable that this axe was embedded in the tree when it was alive or not long dead and certainly before it was covered by the peat, giving a date in the middle bronze age for the catastrophe which caused the trees to die and fall, being subsequently covered by the peat. This peat having shrunk, the dead trees form an obstruction to agricultural operation and have to be removed (Garrod 1952).

Thus the axe dates the tree, but what on earth was it doing there in the first place? Why leave a perfectly serviceable axehead embedded in a tree? And why had no haft survived?

Among excavated non-settlement finds, the socketed axehead/chisel from Barford is worth highlighting (Oswald 1967). The site itself was a triple-ditched ceremonial and/or funerary monument of Late Neolithic/Early Bronze Age date. In the early first millennium, a number of pits were dug into the monument, some partially cutting into the ditches. One of these pits contained a complex sequence of fills – it seems that after the pit had been dug and backfilled, it was dug into once more for the purpose of inserting the aforementioned bronze tool, accompanied by what the excavator described as a small fossil sponge, both items then being covered by a single large potsherd prior to final backfilling.

An interesting comparison can be made between situations like that at Barford and the previously mentioned South Dumpton Down find, and discoveries on excavated settlements such as the well-known South Lodge Middle Bronze Age enclosure on Cranborne Chase, just in Wiltshire, excavated in the 1890s by Lt General Pitt Rivers and again nearly a century later by Richard Bradley and John Barrett (Barrett *et al.* 1991). The site comprises a rectangular enclosure defined by ditch with inner bank, and set within a lynchetted field system. Barrett *et al.* argued on the basis of their own work and re-analysis of the earlier excavations that the enclosure phase had occurred late in the site's history.

More recently, David McOmish (pers. comm.) has argued that the enclosure earthworks actually represented almost the final act in the settlement's history, the enclosing earthworks being constructed at or soon after the site had been abandoned. This suggestion finds support from both excavation and survey evidence, and has clear implications for the interpretation of any artefacts present in the ditch fill. Particularly noteworthy are the fact that the enclosure ditch and bank on the north side cut through a sizeable spread of burnt flint that had accumulated during the life of the settlement, and the observation that the lynchet running across the enclosure's main western entrance still survives as an earthwork, even though 'heavy traffic through that entrance would surely have caused more erosion' (Barrett *et al.* 1991, 183). The enclosing ditch, once cut, had been backfilled rapidly – perhaps almost immediately, the excavators noting that 'the excavated profile [of the ditch] is steeper than we would expect from a chalk-cut ditch which had silted naturally' (*ibid.*, 153).

The bottom three feet or so of the ditch fill was composed entirely of chalk rubble and above this was what Pitt Rivers referred to a the 'mixed silting'. A bronze razor and a bronze awl were found at the base of the ditch, beneath the chalk rubble (**16**). The razor was in the north-eastern corner of the enclosure, the awl in the opposite south-western corner. Another razor plus some bronze wire and a bracelet were found close together but not in direct association at the northern end of the eastern ditch, all at the base of the mixed silting. Finally, a bronze side-looped spearhead came from high in the ditch fill on the southern

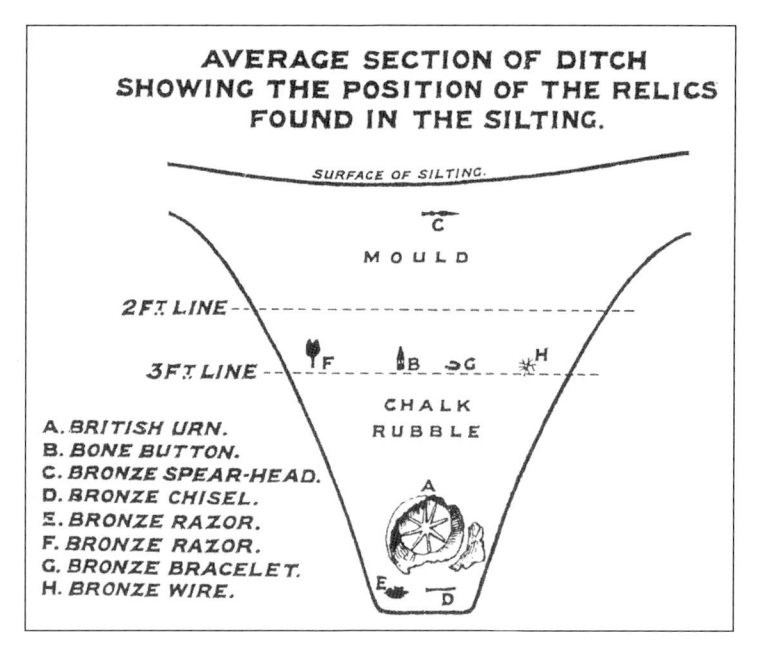

```
           AVERAGE SECTION OF DITCH
        SHOWING THE POSITION OF THE RELICS
              FOUND IN THE SILTING.
```

16 Pitt Rivers 'Average' section for the South Lodge enclosure ditch, showing the relative depths of the key finds. Note the three apparently clear horizons of depositional activity: at the base of the ditch; on top of the rapid primary backfill; and towards the top of the upper fill

side, near the south-eastern corner and close to a possible break in the line of the enclosure bank. The timing of the enclosure's construction, the nature of the ditch fill, and other artefactual evidence from the ditch all argue against the metalwork representing settlement debris incorporated accidentally in the ditch, as of course does the presence of an internal bank. Such circumstances are far from unusual on sites on Cranborne Chase, and similar stories can be told about sites across southern England and beyond. The example of South Lodge also serves as a reminder that the reasons for constructing earthworks around a settlement are equally problematical, and by no means restricted to the most obvious explanations such as defence, or stock management (see for example Bowden and McOmish 1987; 1989).

An equally complex set of circumstances appears to lie behind the metalwork found within Sculptor's Cave at Covesea on the Moray coast of Scotland. The cave faces north across the Moray firth towards the Caithness hills and, as the excavator Miss Sylvia Benton noted, 'The sun never touches it, and a north wind made sieving at the entrance an unpleasant proceeding' (Benton 1930-31, 178). Interpretation of the finds from the cave is problematic, the standards of excavation being somewhat short even of 1920s standards: 'A dump is always a nuisance, but inside a cave it produces intolerable confusion of mind. Everything was put on a barrow and taken out into the daylight. Here we soon learnt that the topsoil was full of small bronzes which were quite invisible inside. Once on a barrow the earth might as well be put through a sieve' (*ibid.*, 177).

The bronzes included six pieces of so-called 'ring money' – small penannular rings comprising gold over a bronze core – plus two bronze rings and four penannular bracelets. Not untypically for the time, Miss Benton's thoughts were occupied not by why the bronzes were there, but who had brought them. She regarded the cave as a dwelling, its inhabitants being immigrants from Switzerland, primarily based on a visual comparison with some objects she had once seen in Zurich Museum. More recent excavations by Ian Shepherd have offered an alternative explanation for the cave's contents. As Cowie (1988, 38-40) noted, 'The presence of several jawbones of children aged between six and nine trodden into the clay floors, combines with other evidence for decapitation or the removal of skulls to suggest that the cave was a focus for ritual activities. These may have involved the display of the heads of children in the entrance area of the cave'.

The relationship between metalwork deposition and the abandonment of sites is even clearer in some examples from Cornwall, though here the emphasis is on individual houses rather than entire settlements. Nowakowski (2001) has demonstrated that the reasons for abandonment can be many and varied, but considered the evidence for planned abandonment being associated with events marking the end of the lifecycle of a house, a settlement, a community etc. These involved more than just metalwork – some house sites were clearly levelled and backfilled, incorporating sometimes sizeable quantities of artefactual material, including pottery, but one of the most remarkable concerned a house site at Penhale Moor, in which a bronze side-looped spearhead was found 'piercing the upper earthen floor of structure 1013 at a 70° angle, and had the appearance of having been speared into the floor as though it was used to "kill the house". It is likely that it was in a broken condition when it was discarded in this fashion . . .' (*ibid.*, 145).

The evidence so far has focused chiefly on finds from dry land. This is intentional, as it is arguable that far too little emphasis has been placed on understanding such deposits until quite recently. Instead, much discussion has centred on finds recovered from rather wetter locations (see discussions in Bradley 1990; Taylor 1993). The presence of quantities of Bronze Age metalwork in rivers, lakes, bogs and other such 'watery' places is a long and widely recognised phenomenon of the archaeological record, and has been seen as particularly characteristic of the Later Bronze Age. For example, among other developments Bradley (1990, 97) characterised this period as one which saw a 'clear identification between finds of weaponry and watery locations', a statement which is undoubtedly correct but which also conceals a considerable degree of variability in depositional practices and motives.

The discoveries at Flag Fen (Pryor 2001) where large quantities of bronze, along with items of other metals and materials, were deliberately cast or dropped into the waters played a key part in concentrating attention on the idea of deliberate, votive deposition in such places, as well as facilitating broader acceptance of ritual deposits more generally. Flag Fen has been discussed often and published in full (Pryor 2001) so it is not intended to offer more than a brief outline here. The principal feature of the site (for our purposes, that is) was a droveway that approached the fen-edge from the west and was linked to a complex of stock enclosures and settlement features. At the fen-edge, where it met land that was at least seasonally flooded, its course was continued west by five parallel rows of timber posts. These posts continued west for some 1,200m to the higher ground of Northey. Then, 200m before it reached Northey, the post alignments crossed a sizeable timber platform, the purpose of which is not entirely clear though it was certainly connected with the alignments. Dendrochronology suggests that the major construction phase for the timber alignments and platform probably belonged in the first half of the thirteenth century BC, with evidence for further episodes of work at intervals down to the late tenth century BC. In other words, they were maintained for perhaps 400 years. Associated with these structures was a remarkable collection of artefacts that accounted for hundreds of individual acts of deposition over an even longer period – from the early thirteenth century BC down to the Late Iron Age (c.300 BC) and perhaps beyond, much of the post-Bronze Age material probably being deposited long after the alignments and platform had been abandoned.

The metalwork was not limited to weaponry, though these were clearly important. Also present were pins, rings, awls, razors and other small tools and ornaments, plus items of tin and lead. There were also wooden items (**17**), complete pots, quernstones, and the buried remains of several dogs, among other things. Many of the artefacts appeared to have been intentionally broken before being placed in the waters. Some of the bronzes are unlikely to have been used – some of the swords were poor quality castings, for example, while some of the non-metal objects such as the quernstones featured little or no evidence for the sort of wear one might expect had they seen service: 'There is a strong argument for concluding that these objects were destined for Flag Fen almost from the start' (Pryor 2001, 427).

The widespread publicity accorded the Flag Fen discoveries provided a clear focus for ideas of deposition in water having been deposition with ritual intent, something already suspected for some of the major rivers in the British Isles, and something already widely accepted on the continent (see Bradley 1990). However, at the same time this emphasis on votive acts associated with water led to potentially misleading distinctions being drawn at times between 'wet' and 'dry' contexts, the former being viewed as more likely to have a ritual motive, and the latter falling prey to more traditional explanations of deposition, individual circumstances notwithstanding. As many of the examples quoted above demonstrated, the potential of dryland finds for questioning traditional explanations of metalwork deposition is, with the exception of a few places like Flag Fen, far greater than for wetland finds.

17 *Complete haft for a Late Bronze Age socketed axehead from Flag Fen. The 'hook' has been split out of an oak tree trunk and the handle is a side branch, with bark still in place. Marks left by the axe's mouth are still just visible and the 'hook' has been notched from both sides above the axehead, presumably to secure the line attached to the axe's loop. Note that despite the excellent conditions for preservation at Flag Fen, the majority of the metal was deposited in an unhafted state.* © Francis Pryor

Funerary contexts

'Grave goods' were an essential component in early attempts to create sequences and consequent understanding of the Bronze Age. The presence of artefacts, sometimes in close association, in closed contexts confirmed the stone-bronze-iron sequence in the broadest terms and also assisted in finer subdividing of the period. They also allowed antiquarians and archaeologists to consider the possibility that artefacts, including bronzes, could have a use and a meaning beyond the purely functional or utilitarian. However, it was some time before such ideas received proper consideration rather than straightforward, unquestioned acceptance.

Generally, such items have been viewed in fairly straightforward terms, with the life and death of the individual being linked with the grave contents either by regarding them as possessions of the deceased, or as gifts deposited by mourners, in either case with the frequent assumption that they did in some way reflect the social status of the deceased. While not denying the plausibility of these suggestions as genuine reflections of funerary ritual, the growing corpus of archaeological data and the development of different theoretical and interpretative perspectives highlights the inadequacies of regarding such ideas as the only possible explanations for the presence of artefacts in graves.

Barrett (1991; 1994) has highlighted the long-standing practice of drawing social inference from funerary practices. To a considerable extent this reflects the enduring dominance of funerary remains and rituals in the archaeology of the earlier Bronze Age in particular. An understanding of the significance of artefacts from graves requires an assessment of the funerary practice as a whole – not just the act of burial itself – as well as an appreciation of the roles of the living. As Barrett (1994, 50) has argued, funerary rites are as much about relations between the living as they are about the status of the dead.

For the Earlier Bronze Age, as we have seen, Stuart Needham has highlighted the processes of selection evident in the types of copper and bronze objects that were appropriate for deposition in graves. For the most part they differed from the types of objects present in contemporary hoards. Where types more usual in hoards do accompany the remains of the dead, they tend to differ in important respects – size for instance – from equivalent objects in non-funerary contexts. The handful of Early Bronze Age axeheads known from graves are generally much smaller than their counterparts in hoards (Needham 1988, 245), for example.

There are of course other issues to be aware of. Not all metal deposits from a funerary site or monument need be contemporary with a burial or with the main phase of use of the funerary site (**18-19**; **colour plate 3**). The examples already noted from Combe Hill, Wold Farm, and Barford are worth recalling. In some cases, metalwork deposits appear to have been broadly contemporary with the funerary phase but did not accompany burials. Also, not all artefacts in graves arrived as grave goods. Some items of weaponry appear to have arrived inside a body, with examples being known from the Neolithic onwards. Among the best known examples are the spearheads embedded in human remains found at Queensford Mill, Dorchester-on-Thames and Tormarton, Gloucestershire (see chapter 6). In addition, the presence of pins or awls with cremations might be viewed as a fastening of some kind of organic container, or with inhumations as a fastening for clothing. Barrett (1994) has suggested that the presence of razors and other blades in graves might relate to the dressing of the corpse, the objects utilised for this purpose having to be deposited because of their association with the corpse.

At the same time, it is important to note that among Bronze Age burials, most are either accompanied by a pot or by nothing (with the obvious caveat about non-survival of organics). Among the minority of graves that do feature something in addition, metal objects are relatively scarce. Corpora of barrows and of items commonly occurring in graves (Beakers, Collared Urns etc.) highlight the infrequent occurrence of copper and bronze objects in such contexts. Needham (1988, 245) has stressed the sparing use of metal in graves, and questioned the manner in which 'the few metal-rich grave goods . . . are misleadingly allowed to dominate' our understanding of funerary rites.

Of equal importance is the fact that formal human burial of human remains was not a widespread and continuous practice throughout the Bronze Age in all parts of Britain. Indeed, formal burial is something that cannot be regarded as a

18 *The Lockington 'hoard', one gold armlet and pottery vessel just visible, in the process of being excavated.*
© Gwilym Hughes/BUFAU

common event until well into the third millennium BC, and only becomes truly widespread, though not universal, after the first appearance of metal in the British Isles. But the flat graves, cemeteries, round barrows and related structures of the later Neolithic and early Bronze Age do not account for the total population, although the proportion of the population accorded an archaeologically visible burial seems to have increased by the Middle Bronze Age. The manner of burial and the nature of funerary ritual also vary and change considerably over both time and space, while funerary rites could clearly be lengthy, multi-phase processes possibly involving many individuals in their observance. Furthermore, by the end of the second millennium BC, formal burial practices (in the modern sense of insertion of a body, whether complete or cremated, into a grave) fade almost completely from view (Whimster 1980; Burgess 1976). Recent work (e.g. Brück 1995) has highlighted a continuing use and presence of more fragmentary human remains throughout the later Bronze Age and into the Iron Age, sometimes in a manner which recalls earlier, Neolithic practices as attested at causewayed enclosures, henges, and in more isolated pit scatters. Such occurrences also further highlight the problems inherent in trying to draw clear distinctions between domestic and ritual activities, particularly where the undertaking of both seems to utilise the same place.

19 *The site of 'Barrow 6' at Lockington, excavated in advance of the Derby Southern Bypass in 1994. The site had several phases, but the key ones here are the most visible, the substantial ring ditch, which surrounded a round barrow mound, and the earlier and narrower palisade slot, visible in the foreground, which represented an earlier pre-barrow enclosure. The 'hoard' was buried within a shallow pit close to an entrance on the enclosure's northern side. It thus appears to be associated with use of the enclosure rather than the barrow. Certainly the radiocarbon dates obtained suggest that the 'hoard' may have preceded the funerary activity sealed beneath the barrow by perhaps three or four centuries or more. (The excavation has been fully published in Hughes 2000).* © Gwilym Hughes/BUFAU

Rubbish or ritual?

As has already been hinted on several occasions, the evidence presented above for selective, formal and deliberate deposition of metalwork inevitably leads in the direction of a ritual or votive interpretation. These are concepts with a rather chequered history in archaeology, although the past twenty years or so have seen the recognition and understanding of ritual practices in the archaeological record placed on a rather more sound footing than had once been the case (e.g. Garwood et al. 1991; Barrett 1994, ch. 3; Brück 1999). However, these developments have not necessarily filtered far beyond the academic world. Previously the term 'ritual' saw service as a means of categorising phenomena that seemed otherwise inexplicable – whether illogical, uneconomic, or of uncertain function, and its continued use remains caricatured as such by some. Also, ritual behaviour has often been associated with religious practices or performances, the aims of both being depicted on occasions in quite simplistic terms, for example as a means by which particular groups or individuals might attain or maintain control over people and things. At the same time, the performance of rituals has been seen as something ultimately quite distinct from the realities of everyday life and consequently requiring little further attention or elucidation once identified.

A general belief that a clear distinction could be drawn between the sacred and the profane in prehistory has been a persistent, if implicit, feature of the archaeological literature, as is the assumption that this distinction can be observed in the archaeological record. Such beliefs have received much comment and criticism in recent years (e.g. Barrett 1991; 1994, 77-84; Brück 1999). There is a growing acceptance of the ongoing, if largely subconscious interaction between the mundane – the everyday social practices and subsistence activities of individual groups – and the broader cosmological concerns that help to shape social and economic relationships and activities, and this is something that is also evident in later chapters on mining, metalworking and, indeed the use of objects themselves. Effectively, what we might characterise as religious beliefs and ritual practices were an integral, if sometimes hidden, element of everyday life. However, putting such awareness into practice is another matter entirely.

For British prehistory, there have been noteworthy studies of the orientation and internal workings of round houses and settlements (e.g. Hingley 1990; Parker Pearson and Richards 1994; Oswald 1997), while discussion of the use and symbolic potential of material culture, including its deposition, has been a marked feature of Neolithic and Early Bronze Age studies for some time now. By and large, metal has not featured in such discussions. Part of the problem appears to be a perception that it is an inherently utilitarian material used to create objects that served a primarily practical purpose. At the same time, the landscape of the Middle Bronze Age and later periods is perceived to be more 'domestic' in nature, as the monuments characteristic of earlier millennia cease to be constructed or actively used (see Barrett et al. 1991, 143-444, 223-6). This decline in the archaeological visibility of ceremony and ritual is underlined by the apparent disappearance of funerary practices over the same period. By the later Bronze Age, of course, the focus of ritual is less physically tangible. The archaeological record is instead dominated by the monuments of everyday life – settlements, enclosures, field systems and so on – accompanied by an increasingly broad range of artefacts. The latter are generally used to build a picture of the sort of activities occurring at these sites, and can provide invaluable dating evidence. The disappearance of material and monumental evidence of an overtly non-utilitarian nature has led to the Later Bronze Age being viewed primarily within a framework that highlights the economic, the technological and the subsistence-related aspects of life and only occasionally acknowledges the spiritual side (see also Brück 1999). However, formal, stylistic and contextual analyses of these artefacts, metalwork included, highlight the continuance of ritual and ceremonial practices.

More than just metal

Of key importance in coming to terms with both metalwork deposition and the relative significance of bronze is the evidence for the treatment of other kinds of material. In the Late Bronze Age, for example, Needham (1992, 60) has noted how 'the settlements themselves can contain, amidst the general domestic debris, occasional deposits of material goods, or the remains of food, animals or humans, in contexts which suggest their deliberate placing to non-utilitarian ends'. At Runnymede Bridge, the site with which Needham was principally concerned, these deposits included a lamb and a ewe buried on either side of a round house. Also found was a pit containing a lengthy sequence of horse-related depositions.

Similar deposits of animal remains have been encountered at many other sites. At Ram's Hill in Berkshire, these included the remains of dog, sheep and pigs in the entrance post holes of a palisade trench, remains regarded as 'foundation deposits or event-making deposits' (Bradley and Ellison 1975; Needham and Ambers 1994). At Dean Bottom, Wiltshire (Gingell 1992, 27) the burial of a neonatal calf was found concealed beneath some sarsen blocks. At South Lodge, Wiltshire (Barrett *et al.* 1991, 157 & 161), in the interior of the building designated Structure 1, a single pit had been cut through the clay fill of the terrace on which the house had stood and into the underlying chalk. The upper fill contained a cluster of flint nodules. At the bottom of the pit, lying against its northern edge, was the left half of the carcass of a small cow. It is clear that only the left half had been buried. At Blackpatch in West Sussex, the skeleton of a lamb or kid had been buried between two of the post holes of the round house within the Middle Bronze Age enclosure (Ratcliffe-Densham 1953). Meanwhile, at Itford Hill, West Sussex, in 'Hut N' 'at the foot of the scoop on the north side of the platform was a large portion of the skeleton of an ox. It lay directly on the chalk floor and was covered with clean undisturbed chalky silt. It must have been coeval with the occupation or abandonment of the site' (Burstow and Holleyman 1957). No limb bones were present, and one presumes that a legless ox was unlikely to have resided or been placed in the house while it was still occupied by humans.

Moving away from animal remains, artefacts such as quernstones and pots, among other items, were also treated and deposited in ways that suggest more than mere rubbish disposal. At South Lodge again (Barrett *et al.* 1991, 183) a mound of pottery with a quernstone placed on top was found within 'Structure 2'. At Petter's Sports Field, Egham, Surrey (Needham 1990a) a substantial dump of pottery lay in a ditch terminal immediately above the well-known deposit of Late Bronze Age metal. The deposition of this pottery appears to have been part of the process of levelling – i.e. completing the backfilling – of this ditch, the sherds possibly coming from a midden deposit elsewhere (Needham 1992). At Loft's Farm, Essex, excavation revealed evidence for the dumping of a substantial amount of 'domestic' debris, including quantities of ceramic finewares and bowls, objects associated with the presentation and consumption of food. This material had been placed in the top of the ditch enclosing the settlement. Atypical of the ceramics recovered from elsewhere on the site, this deposit was seen as part of the process of abandonment, perhaps representing the debris of feasting (Brown 1988). Other notable deposits include Black Patch in East Sussex, where threshed grain had been deposited in pits within round houses, some associated with metalwork (Drewett 1982). Similar discoveries occurred at Itford Hill, where finds also included a chalk phallus inserted into one of the porch post holes of a roundhouse (Burstow and Holleyman 1957). Deposition at its most extreme is documented in the Middle Bronze Age at Grime's Graves, Norfolk (Longworth *et al.* 1988; 1991) and most spectacularly at Late Bronze Age sites such as Potterne (Lawson 2000) and East Chisenbury (Brown *et al.* 1994), both in Wiltshire, and Runnymede Bridge, the last being described by its excavator as 'so awash with depositional activity that it is difficult to explain solely in terms of rubbish disposal' (Needham 1992).

However, there are some who continue to question the application of 'ritual' explanations to phenomena such as metalwork deposition in the Bronze Age. For example, Colin Pendleton (1999; 2001) has recently argued from a study of the metalwork from Norfolk, Suffolk and Cambridgeshire, that 'There is no evidence to support ritual deposition of metalwork in northern East Anglia during the later Bronze Age. Although I have not undertaken the necessary work for other areas, I would tentatively suggest that the same is likely to be the case in the rest of Britain' (Pendleton 2001, 177). This is not the place to embark on a detailed rebuttal of Pendleton's case, but a few general points are worth highlighting. First of all, Pendleton fails to consider what is meant by ritual. Instead, he merely notes the beliefs of some archaeologists that deposition in rivers and bogs was probably votive in intent, and seeks to determine whether or not the objects concerned were really deposited in wet conditions. Secondly, and following on from the first, is a subsequent failure to explain just why so much recyclable metal was discarded or abandoned. Furthermore, to suggest that some items were actually thrown into

DEPOSITION: ANECDOTE AND EVIDENCE

rivers after being ploughed up during the Roman period 'to prevent accidents occurring with children' (Pendleton 1999, 71) is surely far less satisfactory.

One point made by Pendleton has been made by others – that items of later date, including swords, are also found in rivers without the apparent need to resort to anything other than a purely rational explanation for their presence. Pendleton (2001) noted in passing the quantity of material from the River Witham in Lincolnshire, while 'an examination of Saxon Christian period swords from Suffolk (when one would presume ritual was not a factor in their disposal) shows 40 per cent occur in rivers . . . It has been estimated (Ewart Oakeshot, pers. comm..) that between 75 per cent and 80 per cent of medieval swords from England with a known provenance come from rivers' (*ibid.*, 173). Clearly these are statistics that need further investigation. Just why are so many Saxon and later swords found in rivers? Is it enough to assume that just because they belong to the time after the establishment of Christianity in the British Isles that some ritual explanation cannot possibly apply?

Recently, David Stocker and Paul Everson (2003) have looked again at the material from the River Witham as part of a study focusing on the Witham valley monasteries and the medieval causeways which led to them across the fens. They were able to show that in many cases, deposition of artefacts in the river had begun by the Bronze Age and continued through the Iron Age, Roman and early medieval periods and beyond, with the latest datable items probably belonging to the fourteenth century. Throughout this long period of time, intermittent depositional activity appears to have concentrated in the vicinity of those causeways suggesting that their origin lay not in the medieval period but much earlier. The medieval finds included swords, daggers/knives, axeheads and spearheads. 'Some of the swords carry incantations inscribed into their blades, which emphasise the superstitious (and presumably ritualistic) character of their depositions' (*ibid.*, 280). Stocker and Everson argue that the occupants of the monasteries were far from being unaware of what was happening:

> The great majority of offerings of the Christian era are of swords, and this also demonstrates a continuity of ritual with earlier periods, where weaponry had also been predominant. By the date these medieval swords were deposited in the river, however, the causeways were under the control of a chain of monastic houses. Clearly, the practice had been christianised in some way. The prehistoric ritual had been given a meaning that sat acceptably within the ideology of the new religion: a 'conversion' had taken place (*ibid.*, 281).

Moreover, they note that

> it may be no coincidence that the first recorded instances of aristocrats hanging military equipment around their tombs come from the four-

> teenth century also . . . , just when the practice of depositing such equipment in the river apparently ceased . . . Did this new behaviour replace earlier customs of reverent disposal of the trappings of lordship, such as depositing them in a local river? Despite the Church's reluctance to accommodate weaponry in ecclesiastical buildings, one can see that it might sponsor such a move; by finally bringing the deposition within the church itself, it eventually assimilated completely this evidently pre-Christian practice (*ibid.*, 282).

There is, of course, an interesting parallel here with the funerary associations of weaponry during the Bronze Age (see p.169).

Overall then, there is good reason to suggest that the intention behind much metalwork deposition was more complex than had once been presumed, something that is further emphasized by the better known quantities of material known from rivers such as the Thames, Trent and Witham as well from other waterlogged locations. All this supports the idea that bronze was valued during the Bronze Age for far more than its utilitarian potential – as a raw material for making tools, weapons and ornaments. Of course, bronze was not alone. As has been noted, other types of artefact made from other raw materials – stone, bone and so on – could equally be disposed of in a formal or purposeful manner, and in similar contexts. At the same time, however, there are differences between the treatment of bronze and these other materials. The phenomenon of 'hoarding', for example, and the clear choices being exercised in the selection of material for deposition according to different depositional contexts, and the regional and chronological variation evident in depositional practices are all hard to parallel among other artefact categories. Some of the possible reasons for this treatment of bronze will be explored at the end of the book. However, the properties that made metal a desirable medium for ritual or votive expression did not arise out of nowhere at the moment of deposition. To explore more fully the meaning of bronze, it is necessary to look at the entire lifecycle, beginning with its original removal from the ground.

3
ANCIENT WORKINGS: MINING IN THE BRONZE AGE

> I presume to think, indeed, that without full attention to the mining history of Britain . . . the opinion which may be formed of the ancient British people would be altogether conjectural, derogatory, and erroneous (Phillips 1859, 21).

The discovery of firm evidence from the British Isles for the mining of copper ore during the Bronze Age is a very recent development. For other important metals such as tin and gold, such firm evidence is still awaited. Although many thousands of gold, copper and copper alloy objects have been recovered and their possible significance pored over, the origins of the metal used to make them was, until the 1980s, largely a matter of informed speculation. In retrospect, the silence of key summaries of the period (e.g. Kendrick and Hawkes 1932; Burgess 1974; Megaw and Simpson 1979) on the matter can seem particularly remarkable given the effort expended from the later nineteenth century on the discovery and exploitation of Neolithic stone sources (see for example Clough and Cummins 1978; Bradley and Edmonds 1993; Barber *et al.* 1999) or the amount of ink spilled over the years in trying to explain the origins of metallurgy and the flow of metal around western Europe.

In many cases, the apparent absence of physical evidence for actual mining was obscured by the assumption that at least some of the known ore deposits in Britain must have been exploited in prehistory. For example, Peake and Fleure (1931, 22) noted that 'Cornwall had both copper and tin, while Alderley Edge and many other places produced copper; Britain would, therefore, not be forced to look to Ireland for supplies of copper', an opinion that contrasted with the contemporary views of Cyril Fox (1933, 36-7) who suggested, with reference to the Irish ore sources, that 'The precious and accessible riches which she possessed greatly extended her influence over Britain, for though copper and gold occur in the Highland Zone of Britain, Anglesey and Carmarthenshire for example, there is no evidence as yet that they were here worked until Roman times'.

This view was echoed by Gordon Childe, among others, who envisaged the arrival in Ireland of miners and metalworkers from the Iberian peninsula, stimulating the growth of an industry that, in the Early Bronze Age at least, dominated the supply of metal to the British Isles: 'The Beaker lords in Great Britain and subsequently Continental communities purchased the products of the Irish metalworkers. To supply their needs more often regular trade was maintained' (Childe 1949, 117). As recently as 1986, Ian Longworth of the British Museum, in discussing the advances in our knowledge of British prehistory since 1945, offered only the following comment: 'The availability of copper deposits, primarily in south-west Ireland but also in western Scotland, North Wales, Devon and Cornwall, provided a ready supply of raw material' (Longworth et al. 1986, 43). Others meanwhile questioned the very occurrence of mining in the British Isles, Briggs (1988) for example querying whether the technological capability had existed at all to exploit anything but the most superficial surface exposures.

William O'Brien (1996, 12), in his excellent account of Bronze Age copper mining in Britain and Ireland, offered some additional reasons for the apparent neglect of ore sources by prehistorians. He suggested that the study of mines had generally been 'dominated by geologists, mining historians and industrial archaeologists' whose primary interest in more recent mining and a reliance on documentary sources might make them slow to recognise the early date of some mine workings. At the same time, however, prehistorians have until recently proved remarkably reluctant to investigate potential sites, perhaps put off by a limited knowledge of mining techniques, geology and metallurgy. Certainly the specialist literature (e.g. Craddock 1995) can appear intimidating to the newcomer or casual reader, though mining historians, geologists and archaeometallurgists might feel the same way about some recent archaeological publications.

Before metal: sources of stone

The history of investigation within the British Isles of Neolithic stone sources provides many useful points of comparison and contrast with the search for and study of metal sources. In Britain, the study of flint mines is almost as old as the idea of the Neolithic itself (see Barber et al. 1999 for a more detailed history and bibliography of flint mine investigations). Grime's Graves in Norfolk and Cissbury in West Sussex were both being excavated just a few years after Sir John Lubbock (1865) first presented his twofold subdivision of the Stone Age into earlier (Palaeolithic) and later (Neolithic) phases. By 1870, William Greenwell's work at Grime's Graves had established the reality of deep underground mining prior to the use of metals. Within a few years Colonel Lane Fox and others finally confirmed that Cissbury too was another Neolithic flint mine, and both sites were rapidly elevated to a position of key importance in understanding the period (see for example Dawkins 1894). Despite the apparent ubiquity of flint across large parts of southern and eastern Britain, here it seemed was proof that the best quality flint was deliberately sought out and mined from depths of up to 40ft. So keen were the miners to obtain raw material of the desired quality for making their axes, knives and arrowheads that sometimes they were prepared to cut through two or more seams of flint before settling on the seam they considered most suited to their needs.

In the early twentieth century the flint mines, more of which were gradually identified across the chalk of southern England, were joined by sources exploited for other types of rock – the so-called 'stone axe factories'. These of course tend to be located in the appropriate geological zones – the upland areas of northern and Western Britain. Unlike the flint mines, these did not involve underground working. Instead, rock was quarried from surface outcrops. Among the first to be recognised was the site at Graig Lwyd on the north coast of Wales, just a few miles west of Llandudno (Warren 1919), a discovery that helped to reinforce the notion that the raw material for axe production in particular was obtained from quite specific locations, with more widespread secondary sources such as glacial erratics or, for flint, the river gravels or clay-with-flints deposits, being of much lesser significance.

By the 1930s, for the types of stone other than flint, major advances were underway in trying to link the sources of stone to the places where axes were being found – in other words, to try and understand the movement of stone implements around the British Isles and beyond during the Neolithic. Scientific analyses of individual implements were undertaken to try and match them to the 'factory' or outcrop from which the raw material had originally been quarried. Eventually a number of definite and possible sources were identified, allowing attempts to chart the flow of axes in particular from their presumed point of origin, studies which resulted in a number of remarkable, if sometimes flawed, conclusions. Since the 1960s, some efforts have also been made to try and match flint implements to possible sources, mainly the mines of course, but with very limited success.

Recent decades have seen a shift in focus away from an emphasis on individual sources, as questions have increasingly been asked about the methodologies being used and the assumptions underlying much of the work (see e.g. Berridge 1994). For example, it is now clear that the geological distinctions drawn between geographically different stone sources are not as clear-cut as once believed. Furthermore, it is now acknowledged that the more widely distributed secondary sources – glacial erratics, for example, and for flint the river gravels and clay-with-flints – were widely exploited throughout the Neolithic and after. However, far from downgrading the likely role of flint mines and 'axe factories' during the Neolithic, such changes serve to reinforce perceptions of them as important places, though with a major shift of emphasis. If suitable stone was so widely distributed and accessible, why were places like Grimes Graves in Norfolk and Great Langdale in the Lake District returned to repeatedly, over a period of centuries, in order to extract stone in a manner that was both extremely laborious and highly dangerous?

Copper mining in the British Bronze Age

Despite initial appearances to the contrary, the archaeological investigation of Bronze Age copper mines in the British Isles has a history almost as long as that of flint mines. What it most clearly lacks is the sort of continuity of effort that meant few summers passed in the twentieth century without some kind of excavation or survey occurring at a Neolithic stone source – those interested in lithics grew increasingly concerned with the sources of their raw material; those interested in metal seemed content to rely on assumptions. Instead, the initial phase of interest and observation, following on from a lengthy if intermittent period of antiquarian recording and speculation, was not maintained and it was not until the 1970s that the quest resumed for evidence of Bronze Age copper mining in the British Isles.

To date, around 10 sites in Wales and England – none so far in Scotland – have yielded good archaeological evidence of mining or prospection of Bronze Age date, while a number of others have provided circumstantial evidence of varying quality (see the excellent summaries in Timberlake 1992 and O'Brien 1996 for more details). Most have attracted attention because more recent copper mining, particularly during the nineteenth century, had encountered – and often destroyed – earlier workings frequently described by observers as 'ancient' or 'primitive' in nature. Further evidence was provided by the recorded distribution of grooved stone hammers or mauls. Since at least the mid-nineteenth century these have been accepted as usually, though not exclusively, associated with the mining or working of copper ore and as being of early, perhaps pre-Roman, date. John Evans (1872, 208-12) for example discussed them at length in a work otherwise devoted largely to the Stone Age, justifying their inclusion in his book on the grounds that 'though belonging to a period when metal was in use, [they] are in all probability of a high degree of antiquity'. As for their purpose: 'It is uncertain whether or not they were merely used for crushing and pounding metallic ores, or also in mining operations; but they seem to occur exclusively in the neighbourhood of old copper mines'. Their discovery actually within some of the mines provided further indication of the latter's antiquity – among the examples Evans cited were hammers from Great Orme and Parys Mountain (see below). In fact, many of the sites now proven to have been worked during the Bronze Age have been known since the nineteenth century – and in some cases earlier – as sources of these distinctive hammers and as sites of the once-mysterious 'early workings'.

Given the extent of known copper ore sources in the British Isles, it is probable that more mines await discovery. The recorded distribution of the stone hammers is also far more extensive than the known distribution of Bronze Age mines, though it is important to remember that they need not have been used solely as mining tools. Moreover, some ore sources will have been beyond the means of prehistoric miners even to find, let alone exploit. A further possibility – that some cultural factors may have prevented exploitation – will be considered later.

20 An aerial view of Great Orme's Head from the south. © Crown copyright. RCAHMW

Among the known sites, most attention has been focused on Great Orme's Head (**20**), a prominent limestone headland which climbs to a height of more than 200m above the Irish Sea. Located on the North Welsh coast beside Llandudno, the site is exceptional in a number of respects. It is the only known prehistoric British copper mine where sufficient ore and good drainage, combined with a relatively soft ore-bearing rock, allowed underground exploitation via the cutting of shafts and galleries (**21**).

The extent of the workings is quite remarkable. Claimed to represent the largest prehistoric mine ever found, Great Orme's vital statistics are certainly impressive (O'Brien 1996; Roberts 2002). Underground passages explored to date total over 6km in length, with workings extending over an area of 24,000m^2. Evidence of mining has been recovered from depths of up to 70m below the surface. Over 100,000 tons of mining waste have been removed so far, and estimates suggest that perhaps 10km of underground passages await exploration. Some 33,000 bone tools (**22-3**) and fragments and 2,400 stone hammers have been recovered. Estimates of the amount of copper ore likely to have been removed are more problematic. Lewis (1990) suggested that over 200 tons of copper metal may have been extracted, an estimate that Timberlake (2001) has described as 'plausible' given the sheer scale of the workings, but 'optimistic' when compared to the quantity of metal artefacts known from the British Bronze Age. Estimating the extent of workable ore among the rock removed from the mine is clearly open to a number of assumptions, while

21 (Left) *Inside the underground workings at Great Orme, the relatively spacious gallery contrasting somewhat with* **36**

22 (Below) *Two of the many bone tools recovered from Great Orme, the limestone being soft enough to work with such materials. The bone is coloured green from the copper*

23 (Opposite) *Toolmarks within one of the underground galleries at Great Orme, their clarity in the photograph suggesting a freshness that belies their true antiquity*

21-3 © Great Orme Mines Ltd

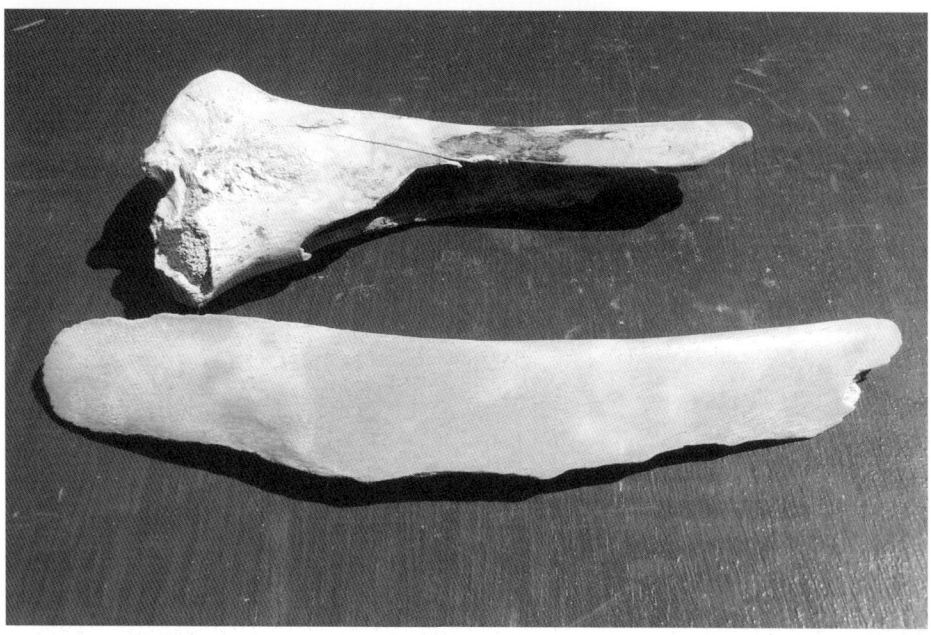

the question of how representative the surviving artefacts are of the amount of metal circulating during the Bronze Age is an equally complicated one.

As with Neolithic flint mines, it is important not to be misled by the extent of the surviving traces into thinking that intensive, industrial-scale activity (in the modern sense) was occurring. The available radiocarbon dates suggest that mining at Great Orme occurred over at least a millennium – indeed it is the only British mine to provide evidence of such longevity of exploitation. Set against that sort of timescale, the suggested annual output appears tiny and has clear implications for the social and economic organisation and context of mining (see below).

Another confirmed North Welsh site is at Parys Mountain, which rises to nearly 150m above sea level on the north-eastern coast of Anglesey, *c.*30km west of Great Orme. As with the latter, eighteenth- and nineteenth-century mining was intensive – in fact Parys Mountain was the site of one of Europe's largest copper mines – which inevitably will have destroyed many traces of earlier activity (**colour plate 4**). However, evidence of Bronze Age mining has been located close to the summit, with excavations in 1988 recovering stone hammers from an old spoil tip, plus radiocarbon dates placing the mining in the Early Bronze Age. Unfortunately, the actual mine workings from which this spoil came have not been identified. More recently, though, evidence has come to light suggesting that underground workings of Early Bronze Age date may survive (Timberlake 2003, 1).

A notable cluster of sites in mid-Wales has been identified and investigated. The largest occurs at Copa Hill, Cwmystwyth, in the valley of the river Ystwyth around 25km inland from Aberystwyth (**colour plate 5**). Investigations spanning a decade and led by Simon Timberlake (2001) suggest that this is the largest of the known mid-Wales sites. The Bronze Age workings occur close to the top of the hill overlooking the valley, at a height of around 420m above sea level. It has been argued (O'Brien 1996) that this was probably the only point at which the copper mineralisation was visible during the Bronze Age. Excavations have revealed the existence of a substantial cutting into the hillside measuring up to 50m in length, 15m wide at the surface, and up to 15m deep. In places, the ore veins appear to have been followed via galleries cut into the face of the pit using fire-setting techniques and stone hammers.

Fire-setting is a technique common to most early copper mines, a notable exception being Great Orme where the soft nature of the limestone meant that for the most part it wasn't necessary there. The technique simply involves piling wood against the rock face and setting light to it. The heat, sometimes aided by dousing the rock face with water, causes the rock to weaken or shatter. The rock and the ore it contains can then be removed by prising open cracks using bone or antler tools, and by pounding the surface with stone hammers, which can either be hand-held or hafted, the latter evidenced by the characteristic groove around the middle of so many of the hammers. Fire-setting, though simple, can be extremely effective, as has been demonstrated by numerous recent experiments (e.g. Crew 1990; Lewis 1990; Timberlake 1990), though clearly the nature of the rock encountered can have an impact on its efficiency.

The excavations at Cwmystwyth have also demonstrated the potential for prehistoric mines to preserve organic remains, providing a wealth of detail from the mine workings and of the lives of the miners. Flooding is almost inevitable once mineworkings reach sufficient depth, and at Copa Hill, waterlogging has led to the survival of numerous fragments of organic material, including 'broken antler picks and hammers, bits of withy (hazel) basketry, rope, handles for hammer stones, fragments of worked wooden stemples and the remains of brushwood brought up to the site for use in the mine' (Timberlake 2001), as well as evidence for the techniques developed by the miners themselves to deal with the flooding. The most remarkable of the latter was a 4m length of wooden guttering, hollowed out from a tree trunk and still in position. In addition, the survival of such items allows the evidence for mining to be radiocarbon dated with far more precision than is usually possible from charcoal derived from spoil.

Further evidence for ore exploitation in mid-Wales includes a marked cluster of sites north and north-west of Copa Hill, all a short distance from the 750m-high peak of Plynlimon. Definite sites include Nantyreira and Nantyrickets, both close to the source of the River Severn (see Timberlake 2001). To date, no sites in other areas of Wales have seen real proof of Bronze Age activity, despite the presence of both ore and of eighteenth- and nineteenth-century mining. There are odd finds of stone hammers, but none firmly associated with the Bronze Age.

Moving across the border into England, Bronze Age copper mining has to date been confirmed only at Alderley Edge, a high and prominent scarp in Cheshire, although it seems likely that the nearby Mottram St Andrew site was also worked at an early date. Alderley Edge emphasises the difficulties in recognising Bronze Age mineworkings. Although first identified around 130 years ago, it was radiocarbon dating that produced evidence of Bronze Age activity when, in 1992, an oak shovel found in 1878 produced a date of 1888-1677 BC (Garner *et al.* 1994), placing at least some of the workings firmly in the Early Bronze Age. Stone hammers have been reported from copper workings at Ecton, Staffordshire, in the Peak District, but otherwise the evidence from England (and indeed Scotland) is sparse, the distribution of stone hammer finds offering the only indication of any mining occurring in, for example, Scotland, Cumbria or the Isle of Man.

Aside from excavation evidence, the first major application of lead isotope analysis to Bronze Age copper and bronze artefacts from the British Isles (Rohl and Needham 1998) has thrown up some intriguing results with regard to the probable exploitation of insular ore sources. The technique can aid the provenancing of the copper in artefacts to particular ore bodies, thereby indicating which sources were likely to have been contributing to the metal supply at any given phase of the Bronze Age, though neither the technique nor the interpretation of its results are without problems. Rohl and Needham sought to minimise these by considering the results in conjunction with the results of more traditional chemical composition analyses, a careful consideration of the archaeological data – the provenance, context and associations of the sampled objects – and the extensive sampling of ore bodies (in England and Wales) themselves.

Overall the research programme, which sampled some 460 objects, confirmed the impression of periodic change in the character, and therefore the possible range of sources, of the copper in circulation during the Bronze Age, already suspected from more traditional analytical techniques. The results confirmed the likely importance of an Irish source for much of the earliest copper used within the British Isles – 'a link with the Ross Island mine, Co. Kerry, seems highly probable. Here it is the early date of circulation and hence the limited number of sources under exploitation and the lack of opportunities for mixing, which has favoured the matching process, aided of course by the timely confirmation of Copper Age activity at the site' (*ibid.*, 182). Irish metal continues to occur among later phases, while other regions within and beyond the British Isles may also have contributed – a lack of sampling of continental ores creates problems here, but sources in the Pyrenees and the middle Rhine, for example, have been suggested for some of the sampled artefacts, and indeed continental sources seem more likely than British or Irish ones for some of the earliest copper items known from the British Isles, including the copper knives that accompanied the so-called 'Amesbury Archer' into the grave.

Copper from the Great Orme mines has been suggested as contributing towards bronzes from the Arreton, Acton Park and Taunton assemblages in particular, a period spanning the eighteenth to the thirteenth centuries and which ties in tolerably well with the available radiocarbon dates, without matching the full extent of the latter (see below). Rohl and Needham actually 'identified three separate metal types as potentially coming from this source . . . If indeed all are from the one source, it shows that the character of the ores actually smelted changed. In part this could be due to a change with depth; the upper copper deposits are primarily malachites and azurites, whereas the primary ore below is chalcopyrite and was presumably exploited later' (*ibid.*, 181). The other Welsh sources made a more limited showing, again broadly in line with the radiocarbon dates but equally suggesting that more sampling of both ores and artefacts, particularly from the more immediate locality of these sources, might be worthwhile. This was particularly emphasized by the case of Parys Mountain. The sampled deposits from the area produced quite distinctive lead isotope signatures but only one sampled object – a pin – could be matched to the site (*ibid.*, 181).

Interestingly, in the light of the archaeological evidence, the south-west of England showed little indication of being a major copper provider during the British Bronze Age. The most likely candidates belonged to the initial copper-using phase, though in far less quantity than the probable south-western Irish source, for example, and to some of the later Early Bronze Age assemblages, notably Brithdir (*c.*2200-2000 BC), but certainly not beyond the Willerby stage (*c.*1900-1700) (*ibid.*, 182). According to Rohl and Needham (*ibid.*, 182) 'a resumption of exploitation in the Iron Age, beginning with Llyn Fawr metalwork, is possible'.

The question of chronology has already been touched upon. The available evidence for the duration of copper mining in the British Isles, at least as far as radiocarbon dating is concerned, falls some way short of spanning the entire Bronze Age. Timberlake (2001, 190) has argued that the available evidence points to 'copper mining and prospection [being] widely undertaken during a 400-year period between 1900-1500 BC . . . within certain areas of England and Wales', with only Great Orme currently providing evidence for the continuation of mining into the first millennium BC. The lead isotope analyses of Rohl and Needham (1998) point to some British sources being in use during the earliest, copper-using, phase as well as of course during the Middle and Late Bronze Age, but the precise sources of this material remain a matter for speculation, as does the relative contribution during each phase of Irish, British and Continental sources.

The history of investigation

Of course, as has already been indicated, evidence for ancient mining had been recorded at a number of locations from at least the eighteenth century onwards, almost always in the course of recent extraction, a process that was certainly responsible for the destruction of much valuable evidence. For example, at Great Orme, mid-nineteenth-century workings uncovered extensive traces of earlier mining as well as finds of antler, bronze, animal bones and the inevitable stone hammers. These ancient workings were soon blasted away in the continuing quest

ANCIENT WORKINGS: MINING IN THE BRONZE AGE

for copper (James 1990, 1; Dutton and Fasham 1994, 250). The main discoveries at Great Orme occurred in 1831 and in October 1849. The latter was described in some detail by William Stanley (1850):

> . . . the miners broke into another ancient working of considerable extent. The roof and sides were encrusted with beautiful stalactites, to which the mineral had given beautiful hues of blue and green. The workmen, unfortunately, broke the whole in pieces, and destroyed the effect, which was described as very brilliant when torch-light was first introduced. On the ground were found a number of stone mauls, of various sizes, described as weighing from about 2lb to 40lb, and rudely fashioned, having been all, as their appearance suggested, used for breaking, pounding, or detaching the ore from the rock . . . (**24**).

24 *Within one of the largest chambers in Great Orme, the scene reminiscent of Stanley's (1850) account but without the dynamite.* © Great Orme Mines Ltd

Other finds included large quantities of animal bones, identified as ox, deer, goats and 'a small breed of swine'. The preferred interpretation was that the bones represented food refuse rather than broken tools. Some bronze was also found. Stanley explained that 'The miners at Llandudno observed, however, that their predecessors of former times had been unable to work the hardest parts of the rock, in which the richest ore is found, for they have recently obtained many tons of ore of the best quality from these ancient workings . . . There was some appearance of the effects of fire or smoke upon the sides and roof of the cavern, when first discovered.' In the light of the latter, Stanley noted suggestions that 'ancient' mining had sometimes involved the use of fire and water to help break down the rock containing the ore.

However, recognising the date of these early workings was a problem. Yates (1858) for example seemed happy to treat the early mining at Great Orme as Roman. Nonetheless some early observers were able to make, in retrospect, some remarkably pertinent comments. Briggs (1976) for example quoted an extract from Sir Christopher Sykes' manuscript *Journal of a Tour in Wales, 1776*. Sykes, a Yorkshireman, briefly described his visit to the copper workings at Parys Mountain, Anglesey, stating that

> It is a curious fact that this mine has been worked, not only before the use of gunpowder was known, but also before Iron was used in this Kingdom. I saw several places from whence Ore had been taken within the rock of the Mountain they followed the inclination of the rock and no mark of any tools is to be seen. They are very smooth but discoloured and the opinion of an intelligent workman here was that fire had been applied to soften it. I cannot say I saw anything to induce me to think so, but all around there was laid parts of oval cobbles split from the ends as they would be if used as hammers and most of them battered at both ends . . . Possibly this mine may have been opened when the Phoenicians traded to Cornwall for Tin, they can not be of a later date.

Sykes lamented the fact that these early workings were unlikely to escape destruction by the mining occurring around them, though as we have seen, sufficient surface traces survived to allow more recent investigation and confirmation of an Early Bronze Age date.

Sykes had no means available of dating the workings. His speculative suggestion that they pre-dated the use of iron is not the same thing as dating them to the Bronze Age, a concept then still to be invented. It was simply assumed that if iron tools had been available, they would have been used and there was no evidence that they had been. There was at the time little guidance beyond church teachings and the writings of some Greek and Roman historians and geographers when it came to understanding the more distant, undocumented past, hence the reference to the Phoenicians (and see also Phillips 1859 for a remarkably clear demonstration of the reliance on classical authority for fleshing out the more distant past). Similarly, the discoveries at Great Orme during the mid-nineteenth century were variously attributed to 'Old Welsh' or 'Celtic' miners (Lewis 1990), such labels merely reflecting uncertainty over the age of the workings rather than any real knowledge of their origins.

A notable advance in understanding came in 1874, with two visits to the mining complex at Alderley Edge, Cheshire by William Boyd Dawkins, the second in the company of Colonel Lane Fox, better known today in his later guise of General Pitt Rivers. During both visits they collected stone hammers (**25-6**), a type of implement already firmly associated with 'early' mining. As Dawkins noted, 'They have been found equally in the ancient copper mines of Anglesea [sic], of Spain and Portugal, and of Lake Superior . . . They undoubtedly represent one of the ruder and probably earlier stages in the art of mining' (Dawkins 1875). At Alderley Edge, many of the hammers recovered by Dawkins and Lane Fox had been found in an area where rock had been 'hollowed out irregularly and evidently artificially, and to a depth in some cases of from 8 to 11 feet from the surface. And from an examination of the ground it was perfectly obvious that the ancient users of these tools had worked the metalliferous portions from above, without attempting to make galleries. The tools lay buried in the *débris* which had been thrown into the old surface workings after which they had been discontinued . . .' (*ibid.*). Dawkins further speculated that the workings represented attempts to obtain copper, rather than the cobalt, lead, iron and manganese that also occurred in the immediate vicinity. As for their date, the Three Age System was already well-established among the leading antiquarians and archaeologists of the day, providing a real framework for understanding the pre-Roman past. Thus Dawkins concluded that 'these implements imply a ruder phase of the art of mining than has hitherto been known in the neighbourhood of Manchester, a phase which may point back to the Bronze Age, when the necessary copper was eagerly sought throughout the whole of Europe' (*ibid.*).

There is, however, a clear note of uncertainty in Dawkins' attempt to date the workings, and while his speculations did not go unnoticed, they do not appear to have attracted much more than local interest, something that may seem surprising given the involvement of Lane Fox who, at the time, was about to restart his investigations at the Cissbury Neolithic flint mines. Some follow-up work was undertaken by Dr Sainter, the value of which was largely overlooked until the wooden shovel he found was radiocarbon dated over a century later. A quarter of a century after Dawkins, Charles Roeder (1901) provided a brief taste of the local debate:

> The discovery at the time created widespread interest, and attracted Mr R.D. Darbishire, the late Mr John Plant, the North Staffordshire Naturalists, and all our local societies. The speculations it led to were divergent, some of them highly amusing — particularly those of Plant, who tried to pour ridicule on their real nature, and declared [the stone hammers] in all earnest to be stones for the attachment of tents, or for the rope-weights to hold the thatch on the roofs of the huts of the miners, and not perhaps gone long out of existence.

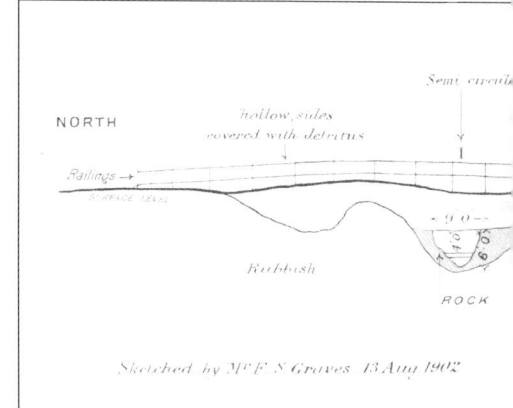

25-6 (Left and below) *Some of the thousands of stone hammers and mauls, and other stone tools, recovered during the past two decades of investigation at Great Orme.* © Great Orme Mines Ltd

27 (Above) *Grave's 1902 sketch section of the 'ancient superficial pits' at Alderley Edge, noting amongst other things the discovery of some stone hammers. Neither Roeder nor Graves (nor indeed anyone for some time) seemed willing to offer a definite date for such features until the close of the twentieth century.* From Roeder and Graves 1905

ANCIENT WORKINGS: MINING IN THE BRONZE AGE

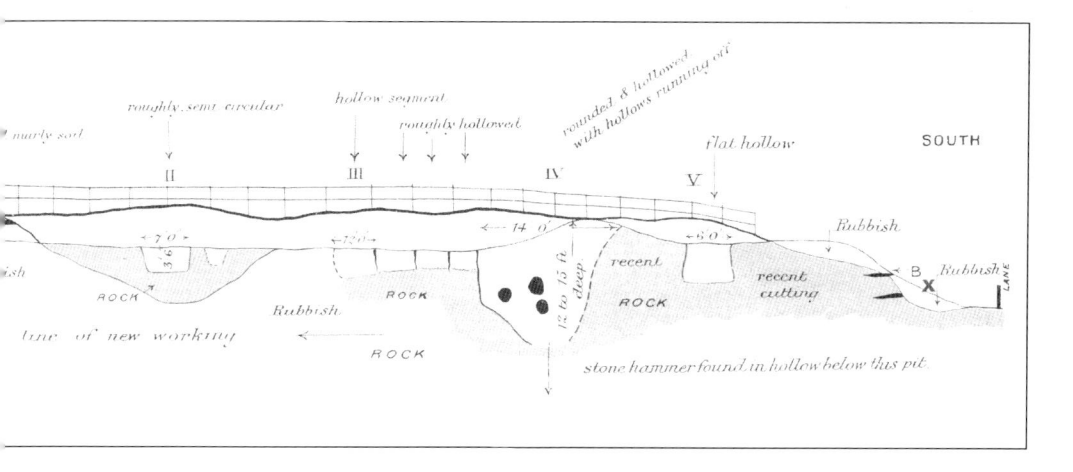

Roeder's interest in the Alderley Edge mines had been sparked by the 'fresh and interesting discoveries that have been made by Mr F.S. Graves, of Alderley Edge, who has given great attention to the matter, and undertaken a very systematic search of the whole Edge, which puts the whole subject on a new basis'. What Roeder and Graves presented between them (Roeder 1901; Roeder and Graves 1905) was a descriptive account of the archaeology of Alderley Edge, detailing all surviving monuments and recorded finds, in an attempt to provide a cultural setting for the early mining. However, although they noted Dawkins' suggestion of a Bronze Age date for some of the early workings, at no point did they explicitly state their agreement with this, preferring instead to describe the earliest mining as simply 'prehistoric' or 'ancient' (**27**). Nonetheless, they were able to recognise the sheer extent of these 'ancient' mines in the area, mapping numerous workings in addition to those noted by Dawkins, the location of which according to Roeder (1901) had, remarkably, already been 'forgotten' before Graves began his explorations *c*.1894. Their location was 'reidentified by the former captain of the mine, Mr John Lawton, now an old man'.

In addition, Roeder and Graves were able to understand and describe the 'ancient' methods of ore extraction:

> What the miners did was to work directly from the surface to the first ore-bearing bed; so they sunk, at close points, a number of small hollows along the line, and then knocking out the sides of these hollows or pits they made a clear face; parallel to these they formed similar new sets of pits, and so on and on until the whole ground floor of the ore-bed was laid open and cleared from the incumbent dead rock. In like manner the second and third beds were successively attacked, reaching the same by forming terraces . . . We also find that, to facilitate the cumbrous work of removing the rock, they deeply under-cut the face first, and by the aid of fire loosened the rigid strata . . . (Roeder 1901).

This new work stimulated a little further local interest. For instance, on Saturday 27 August 1904, up to 50 members of the Lancashire and Cheshire Antiquarian Society visited the workings at Mottram St Andrew under the guidance of Graves, who rather fortuitously discovered fragments of some stone hammers during the tour. The anonymous writer of a brief sketch of the tour noted that 'At Mottram St Andrew the tools are of the most primitive kind. There they seem to have used the first stone that fell their way; instead of the carefully and laboriously contrived central and transverse grooves, we have the sides only deeply and roughly knocked out for attaching the withy and thongs. The men who worked here were either less particular or of an inferior status as compared with the miners of the Edge . . .' (in *Transactions of the Lancashire and Cheshire Antiquarian Society* vol. XXII, 1904, p.202).

After the writings of Roeder and Graves, the possibility of Bronze Age copper mining in the British Isles largely vanished from the archaeological literature until the 1970s. Thus Varley and Jackson (1940, 51), writing about prehistory in Cheshire, merely mentioned that 'It has been suggested that the ancient copper workings at Alderley Edge go back to the Bronze Age, on the strength of the discovery there of grooved stone hammers which, admittedly, have been found elsewhere in Bronze Age contexts. Alderley Edge was certainly a centre of Bronze Age population, and, to put the matter no higher, there is a case for investigation'. Of speculation, there was plenty as was noted earlier, but never did it lead to any fieldwork, at least as far as the Bronze Age was concerned. Scott (1951) mused briefly on the possible exploitation of Scottish ore sources, while Clark (1952, 186-92) discussed Bronze Age copper mining across Europe, noting the possibility of Bronze Age mining at Great Orme and at Alderley Edge but was able to offer little real evidence, noting for instance that the stone hammers 'cannot be narrowly dated, since they continued in use in parts of the Roman world down to the first century AD' (*ibid*, 188).

However, the mines now known to be Bronze Age did not completely escape archaeological attention. Prior to the most recent renewal of interest, the most important episode occurred during the 1930s. In 1935, the British Association for the Advancement of Science established a committee to investigate the evidence for the earliest mining in Wales. Membership of the committee naturally included leading archaeological figureheads of the day, including Gordon Childe and Cyril Fox, but its key member in terms of the committee's achievements was its secretary, Oliver Davies, then best known as an expert on mining in the Classical world and author of *Roman Mines in Europe* (Davies 1935). That book had included a lengthy chapter on the British Isles, in which evidence for early mining, primarily in England and Wales, was considered. He was aware, for example, of Bronze Age finds from Cornish tin-streams (see below) and was clearly familiar with the eighteenth- and nineteenth-century finds and observations relating to both the Welsh mines and to Alderley Edge, though rather than see the stone hammers as evidence of prehistoric mining, he instead suggested that 'these tools afford proof of the use of stone as late as Roman days' (Davies 1935, 156). For

Great Orme, he felt that 'these mines were probably opened before the Roman conquest' (*ibid.*, 157), while Alderley Edge 'is partly prehistoric' (*ibid.*, 160).

Davies now undertook a fresh appraisal of the extant evidence from Wales, focusing particularly on the reported finds of stone hammers, before selecting a handful of sites for closer investigation. Beginning in 1937, Davies paid visits to Parys Mountain, Nantyreira, Nantyricket, Cwmystwyth and Great Orme, conducting small-scale excavations on old spoil tips at all but Nantyricket. No datable artefacts were recovered from these trenches and the advent of radiocarbon dating was still some years off, so Davies was forced to rely on his own experience to interpret his findings. He opted for a Roman or 'Old Celtic' date for the workings he examined, being partly influenced by pottery of second-century AD date recovered from a possible settlement site at the foot of Great Orme, a site that also produced some stone hammers similar to those from the mines, as well as the discovery of stamped Roman copper ingots elsewhere in North Wales. Clearly his background as an acknowledged expert on mining in the Roman period may have influenced his thinking, but it also allowed him to acknowledge both the limitations of the dating evidence and the likelihood that the stone hammers were not Roman tools. Instead, he tentatively accounted for their presence by suggesting that the stone hammers were in fact evidence for the local population being forced to work the mines for their Roman masters.

It would be easy to dismiss Davies merely as someone who reached the wrong conclusions on the basis of quite sparse evidence. However, this would ignore also the quality of the conceptual tools available to him, and would completely overlook the value of his work to more recent investigators. Indeed, Timberlake (1992) has argued that Davies' 'pioneering work laid the foundation for the modern discipline of mining archaeology in this country'. He identified many of the major sites known today; he recognised the reality of early (pre-medieval) mining, and was able to link the use of stone hammers and fire-setting within those early mines. The difficulties he faced in trying to correctly date these sites are underlined by more recent successes, which in the general absence of associated material culture – contemporary pottery, for example – have been largely reliant on radiocarbon dating, a technique unavailable to Davies, to establish their true antiquity.

The next real breakthrough came in 1960s and occurred not in the British Isles but in the Republic of Ireland, at the time another country blessed with ore but equally reliant on assumptions about their exploitation rather than actual evidence. Nonetheless, Ireland had often been regarded as the source for much of the early copper used in the British Isles. John Jackson, then Keeper of Natural History at the National Museum of Ireland, became interested in the mines at Mount Gabriel, located on the Mizen peninsula on the south-western Irish coast. In 1966, along with Joseph Raftery, an archaeologist from the National Museum, he cut a trench through one of the surface spoil heaps. Charcoal from the trench was submitted for radiocarbon dating, producing an uncalibrated date of 1500 ± 120 bc, a date whose historical value in the study of ancient mining far outweighs its value today in

28 Andy Lewis seen collecting charcoal for radiocarbon dating. This technique has been essential in dating mining activity to the Bronze Age, as there is nothing distinctly Bronze Age about any of the sites. As with the Neolithic flint mines in particular, there remain problems to be overcome. So far only Great Orme has produced dates spanning most of the Bronze Age. The other excavated sites in the British Isles have yet to provide evidence of activity beyond the Early Bronze Age. © Great Orme Mines Ltd

understanding the site – it was the first scientific evidence for Bronze Age mining from Britain or Ireland. Although the dating evidence was subsequently questioned by some (e.g. Briggs 1988), a major programme of research undertaken by William O'Brien of University College, Galway and focused on Mount Gabriel has, since 1982, more than adequately confirmed Jackson's date (see e.g. O'Brien 1994).

In the British Isles, the next major step came with the work undertaken by Duncan James in underground workings at Great Orme during the late 1970s (James 1988). James' work uncovered a network of mined galleries associated with stone hammers and bone tools. Charcoal stratified among the mine deposits produced a radiocarbon date of 2940±80 bp (HAR-485), which calibrates to 1410-920 BC. Again, the value of this date has been superseded by subsequent working at Great Orme, particularly by the Gwynedd Archaeological Trust and by the Great Orme Exploration Society (**28**), but its importance lies in proving that some at least of the early mineworkings at Great Orme were as old as the Bronze Age. Since the 1970s, considerable attention has been focused on the surviving evidence for Bronze Age mining, in particular under the auspices of the Early Mines Research Group, led by Simon Timberlake, which has since the mid-1980s been responsible for much of the work undertaken at the Welsh mines (other than Great Orme) in particular.

A Briton of the Interior

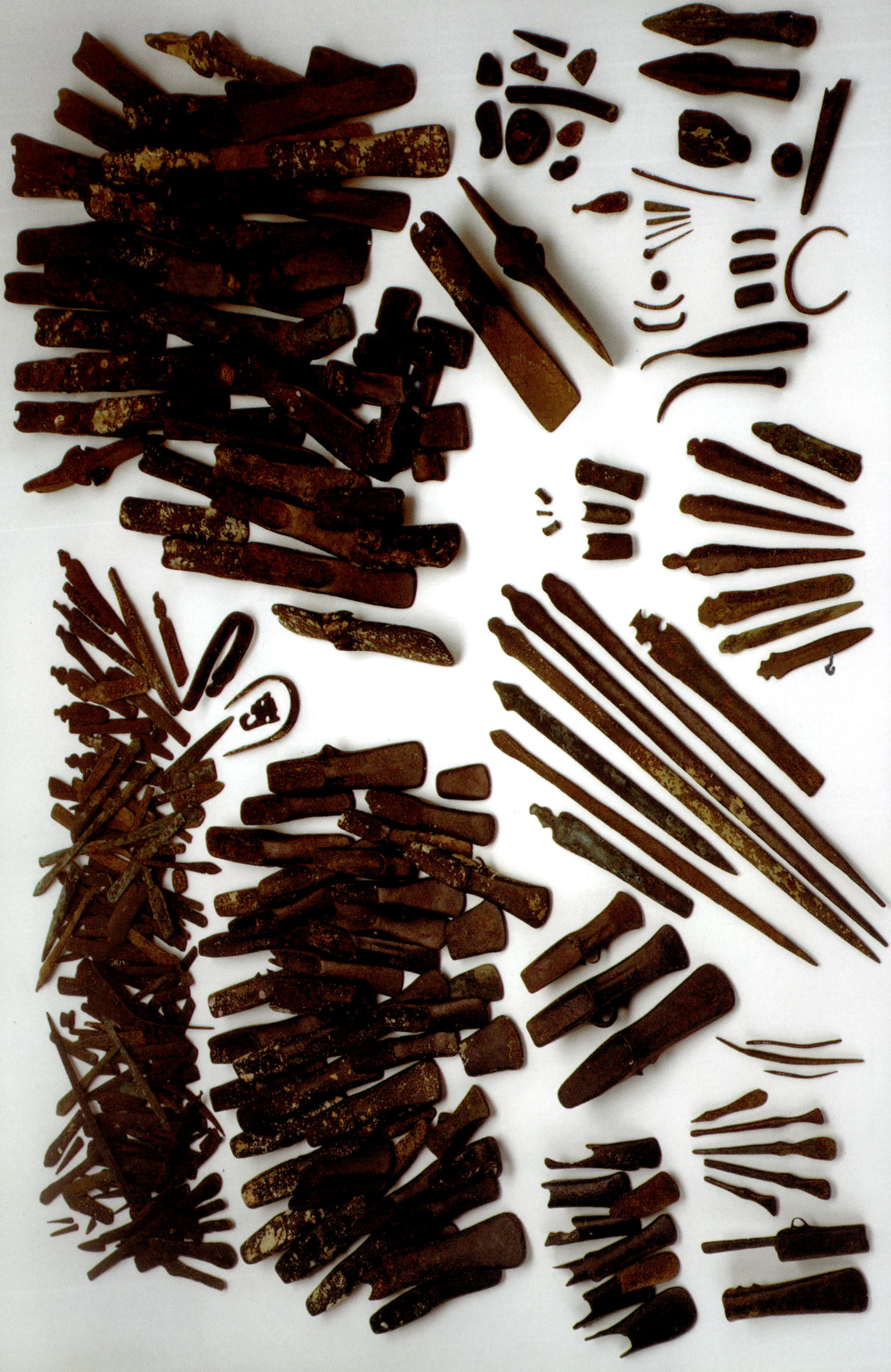

1 (Previous page) *Samuel Rush Meyrick's 'Briton of the Interior' appeared in 1821, just after Christian Thomsen first formulated what became the Three Age System. The notion of a Bronze Age was something of which Meyrick knew nothing, yet he and his artist colleague have managed to deck out their Briton entirely with Bronze Age metalwork. As far as Meyrick was concerned, the Bible told us that the descendants of Cain had discovered the art of metallurgy, while more earthly authority suggested that this art had been lost by the Celts as they migrated across Europe. It was reintroduced to them in Britain by Phoenician traders. In his 'Pre-Historic Times…' of 1865, Sir John Lubbock still credited the Phoenicians with the first exploitation and trading of British metal. In return, as many a website still informs us, they gave the Britons clotted cream, the pasty and the Margate shell grotto.*
From Meyrick and Smith 1921

2 (Opposite) *A large collection of material recovered from the seabed at Langdon Bay, Dover, Kent during the mid- to late-1970s, and presumed to derive from a shipwreck, though unfortunately no trace of any vessel has been located. The collection raises important questions about the circulation of metal. Most of the contents are more typically continental, with few parallels from the British Isles, suggesting that if forms more common across the Channel were reaching here, they were being melted down and recast according to local preferences in form and style. The situation is further complicated by the fact that the collection dates broadly to a period (Penard phase, c.1275-1140 BC: Needham 1998) when comparatively little metalwork was being deposited in south-eastern England. Lead isotope analysis appears to confirm the continental origin of the Langdon bay assemblage (Rohl and Needham 1998, 99-100).*
© The British Museum

3 (Above) *The excavated pit at Lockington contained two gold armlets, a copper dagger, and two pottery vessels. When found, the two pots were inverted, one inside the other. Both were incomplete when found, and were almost certainly incomplete when buried. Typologically they proved hard to identify but are considered probably to be Beakers. They partially covered one of the armlets. The other armlet and the dagger lay beside them. There was no evidence for any funerary deposit with them. The dagger blade was distorted when found, a series of gentle undulations clearly visible along its length. Organic material adhering to it represents the remains of the sheath. The damage, which was deliberate and occurred before burial, must have occurred while the dagger was within its sheath, as Stuart Needham (in Hughes 2000) pointed out, otherwise it would have been rather difficult to get it back in. The dagger itself is unique in Britain but resembles Breton material in a number of respects. Both armlets are made of hammered sheet gold, skilfully decorated. One featured traces of cassiterite beneath its rim, suggesting that the gold had been turned around some tin wire. There is nothing about their form to suggest anything other than manufacture in the British Isles.*
© BUFAU; photographer Graham Norrie

4 (Above) *An aerial view of part of the predominantly nineteenth-century AD workings at Parys Mountain, Anglesey, highlighting the difficulties of pinpointing the traces of earlier activity, the dating of which often relies on radiocarbon dating rather than any distinctly Bronze Age working techniques or material culture*

5 (Left) *An aerial view of the workings at Copa Hill, Cwmystwyth. The definite Early Bronze Age workings are to be found in the deep scar close to the hilltop on the right of the photograph, just above centre. Much of the remainder is later in date. See Timberlake 2003 for a detailed account*

6 (Opposite) *Meyrick and Smith's (1821) 'Romanised Briton and a Feryllt', the latter 'deemed to have been the first teachers of all curious arts and sciences, and more particularly are thought to have been skilled in everything that required the operation of fire'. Note the scatter of distinctly (to our eyes) Bronze Age metalwork, while the 'Feryllt' himself works on a coin in front of a customer smugly satisfied with his iron sword*

4-5 © Crown copyright. RCAHMW

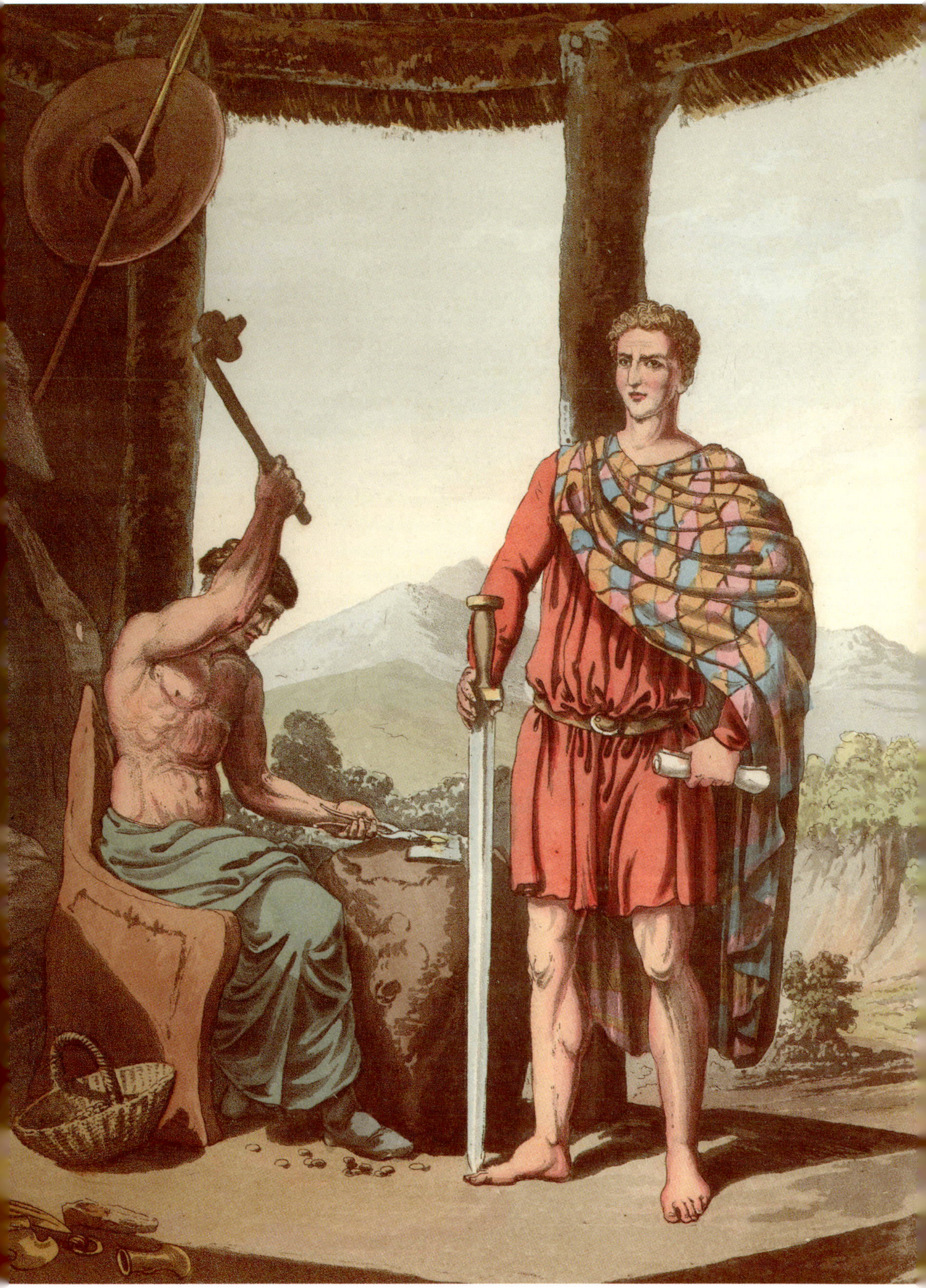

7 *Two bronze bar-armlets and a tripartite Food Vessel from Kinneff, Kincardineshire, Scotland, whose discovery has been subject to much confusion. The earliest detailed account appears to be that in the 'New Statistical Account of Scotland . . .', published c.1845, volume 11 of which deals with Kincardine. According to the Rev. A. Steward, minister of the parish, 'These relics of antiquity were found on the 15 December 1831, by my workmen, while trenching a field on the top of a cliff overhanging the German Ocean, and near the site of the old Castle of Kinneff. The piece of metal resembling the point of a spear, or part of a sword, was discovered about twelve inches below the surface of the ground, lying across the mouth of the urn, but separated from it by a layer of earth about two inches thick. Round the mouth of the urn there was an outer edge or rim about two inches in depth, and of the same material as the urn itself; but it crumbled to dust on being handled. The urn was quite full of earth compactly pressed together. And on the surface of this earth, were found the inner rings set upon their sides, and which were broke into their present state by the workmen attempting to pull them out of the earth. At the bottom of the urn, were found the latter rings entire, and also two button-shaped ornaments, the one made of a substance resembling bone, the other of a substance like coal. The latter was quite entire when discovered, but has since fallen to pieces'. The spearhead may be a millennium older than the urn and its contents, and there appears to be no mention of any human remains, despite later sources referring to a headless skeleton. Cowie (1988, 15) has again emphasised the degree of skill involved in the creation of these armlets and others like them during the early centuries of bronze use. These are smooth, near circular rods of metal that have been bent around so tightly that the ends fit right up against each other, the join barely visible in the photographs.*
© National Museums of Scotland

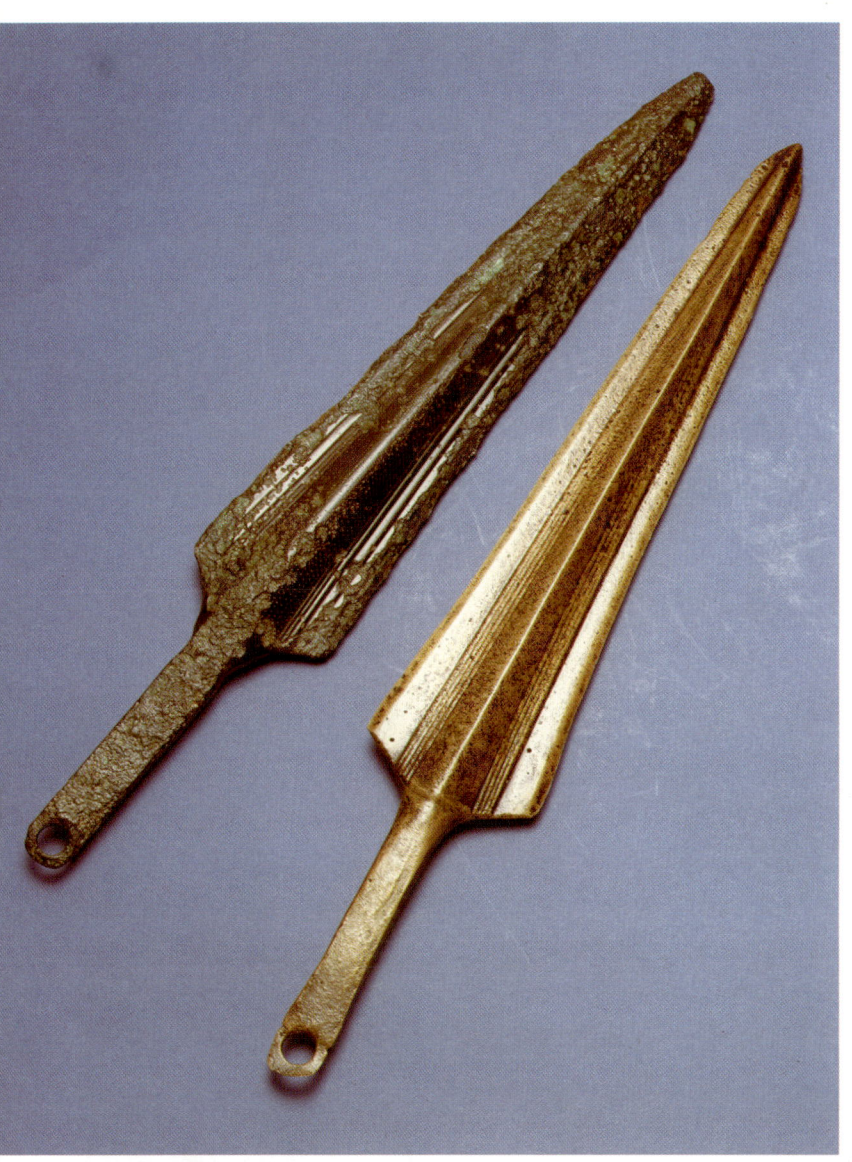

8 (Left) *A pair of tanged bronze spearheads from the later stages of the Early Bronze Age, from Crawford Priory, Fife, Scotland (left) and Whitehaugh, Moss, Ayrshire, Scotland (right). The former is 264mm long, the latter 272mm. Both appear to have been isolated finds, with no associated material recorded. The Crawford Priory spearhead was found c.1874, only the general provenance known for certain. The Whitehaugh example was found by a labourer some time prior to 1884, apparently projecting from the side of a drain about 6ft deep*

9 (Below) *A bronze razor, from a grave at Magdalen Bridge, Midlothian, Scotland. The broken blade is c.74mm long, and was found in a pottery vessel containing cremated human remains in January 1882. Several other pots containing cremations were also found. In one the bone fragments were stained green from contact with another bronze object of which only a fragment survived (Clarke et al. 1985, 294-5)*

8-9 © National Museums of Scotland

10 *Decorated Early Bronze Age axeheads from (left to right) Cornhill-on-Tweed, Berwickshire; possibly Banffshire; and near Eildon, Roxburghshire. The largest, that from near Eildon, measures 179mm in length. Note that in all three cases, the punched decoration continues well beyond the area that would have been exposed once hafted.* © National Museums of Scotland

11 *The Oxborough 'dirk' is a quite spectacular member of a small but clearly related group of similar items known, after two key continental finds, as the 'Plougrescant-Ommerschans' type (see Fontijn 2001 for a recent discussion of the group as a whole). Despite a geographical distribution spreading from Brittany to the Low Countries, as well as the British Isles, their formal similarity is remarkable: 'In addition to their common style, the group seems to have in common a specialized function, denoted by the unwieldy scale, lack of hafting and quasi-sharpened cutting edges . . .' (Needham 1990c, 245). In addition, analysis of metal composition across selected items has raised the possibility of some sort of common origin, given the level of heterogeneity observed (ibid., 242-4).* © The British Museum

The tin problem

> Searching for field evidence of prehistoric mining nowadays seems to me rather like looking in the proverbial haystack for needles which formerly existed but which may no longer do so (Penhallurick 1997, 23).

Tin presents something of a problem when it comes to understanding the exploitation and circulation of metals in Bronze Age Britain and, indeed, in Europe. Tin deposits across the continent as a whole are far less common than copper, and one of the largest tin fields in Europe occurs in Cornwall and West Devon, yet physical evidence for its exploitation is remarkably limited. For the south-west, of course, this is not just a problem for tin – the region is also notable for the marked absence of evidence for prehistoric exploitation of its copper sources. As Sharpe (1992, 35) noted, 'not one securely-dated prehistoric mining site has yet been found in the south-west, despite considerable efforts to locate them. This is not to suggest that they did not exist, nor that they will not be found in the future, nor more importantly, is it to say that there is no evidence whatsoever that prehistoric exploitation of ore deposits did not take place.'

As far as physical traces of mining are concerned, workings at Wheal Coates near St Agnes on the Cornish coast highlight some of the problems to be encountered. A tin and copper mine of primarily nineteenth-century AD date, some of the workings visible on the surface today suggested activity of an earlier date and led to some recent exploration in the hope of finding some evidence to indicate when these workings occurred. However, the results were inconclusive (Budd and Gale 1994) – the shallow surface workings seemed pre-industrial, but beyond this, little could be said. A few cobblestones were found, but with little to indicate use as hammerstones. One appeared to have been modified for hafting but this and other stone tools found 'may have been used at virtually any date up until relatively recent times' (Budd and Gale 1994, 19), underlining the value of recovering *in situ* organic material for radiocarbon dating in order to identify the likely age of an activity that seldom leaves behind any clearly diagnostic artefactual evidence.

The scanty evidence for the exploitation of the south-western tin deposits largely comprises observations by antiquarian and miners in a similar vein to those made about 'ancient' copper workings prior to the twentieth century. All refer to discoveries made during the course of more recent mining. The last such recorded discovery appears to have been a stone axehead found in tin workings at St Erth in the south-west corner of Cornwall *c.*1930, the trailing off of finds a result of shifts in the emphases of modern extraction and the gradual decline of the tin industry itself. Despite renewed archaeological interest in recent years, largely stimulated by the discoveries of prehistoric copper mines, further evidence has proved disappointingly elusive.

The available data has been collated and published by Shell (1979) and Penhallurick (1986; 1997). As a whole it presents a strong, if circumstantial, case for the widespread exploitation of tin deposits in the Bronze Age, but when compared with what is now known about copper mining, it underlines the sense of disappointment that no prehistoric tin extraction site has yet been discovered and subjected to modern techniques of investigation. Almost all of the known Bronze Age finds were discovered during the course of medieval and modern working, usually tin streaming, something that supports the assertion of Penhallurick and others that the major source of tin during the Bronze Age was also streamworks rather than the mining of tin lodes. Despite its name, streaming is essentially a form of opencast mining exploiting alluvial deposits of tin. These deposits have been eroded from weathered lodes and tend to occur at the base of alluvial sediments which themselves can attain depths of between six and thirty feet on the higher moorland and may be even deeper in the lower valleys (Penhallurick 1997), although the extent of post-Bronze Age alluvial deposition is clearly an unknown factor here at present.

The earliest probable references to the discovery of Bronze Age artefacts from tin workings refer to sixteenth-century discoveries. Around 1540 John Leland mentioned a then-recent discovery of 'Spere Heddes, Axes for Warre, and Swerdes of Coper' wrapped in linen in 'Tynne Works' near St Michael's Mount (Chandler 1998, 67), while in his 1602 *Survey of Cornwall*, Richard Carew when writing of tin workings noted that 'There are also taken up in such works certain little tools' heads of brass which some term thunder-axes, but they make small show of any profitable use'. Carew wrote that the Cornish tin miners believed the streamworks they encountered to be 'very ancient and first wrought by Jews with pickaxes of holm, box and hartshorn', such items being 'found daily amongst the rubble' in contrast to the less frequent metal objects (Halliday 1953, 89), though it is the metal objects which have tended to attract attention. This is somewhat ironic, as it is the wooden and antler implements which probably represented the mining tools.

Of the Bronze Age finds reported from tin workings, almost all belong to the Middle or Late Bronze Age. The sole metal find datable to the Early Bronze Age is a flat bronze axehead found in 1790 at a reported depth of 26ft below the surface in a streamwork in the Carnon valley. The only other potentially Early Bronze Age finds, neither of them metal, are the stone axehead from St Erth mentioned above and a jet 'slider' – perhaps a belt or strap fitting – of a type broadly attributed to the Late Neolithic or Early Bronze Age. Later items include a Middle Bronze Age pin 33cm in length, decorated and featuring an amber setting in its head. The pointed end is bent at right angles to the main body. Discovered around 1794 during tin streaming on the River Fowey near St Blazey, Cornwall, it was found at a reported depth of *c.*60ft below the ground surface. The antiquarian Philip Rashleigh, writing a few years after the discovery, suggested that the object was a Druid's hook used for gathering mistletoe, although as he acknowledged this interpretation was dependent on the assumption that 'The celebrated golden hooks . . . for pulling down and gathering mistletoe, were probably neither gold or made to cut . . .' (*Archaeologia* vol. 12, 1796, 414-15; see also the curious note in the *Gentleman's Magazine* 1830, 227). Also near St Blazey, tin streaming at Benallack, Middleway in 1796 resulted in the discovery of a Middle Bronze Age rapier together with a (probable) palstave some 40ft below the ground. Penhallurick (1986; 1997) also notes further rapiers, spearheads, palstaves, socketed axeheads and cauldrons of Middle to Late Bronze Age date.

Penhallurick rightly rejected the idea that any of these objects could have reached their resting place by accident, but otherwise offered little in the way of speculation as to why they were put there. Despite a disliking for the term 'ritual', he nonetheless felt its use appropriate for the finds from streamworks, proposing that 'Miners, like fishermen, from Cornwall or elsewhere, were very superstitious within recent times. It is very likely that tinners of an earlier age, having extracted good ore from their workings, felt it necessary to give some trifle back, be it to Mother Earth, God, or the underground sprites or "knockers" of Cornish folk-lore' (Penhallurick 1997, 28). Similarly, Sharpe (1992, 35) suggested that 'perhaps a proportion of the tin mined was being "returned to its source" as a propitiatory act'.

Less direct evidence for the exploitation of south-western tin during the Bronze Age has also come under consideration recently, a key stimulus being the realisation that Dartmoor, long recognised as rich in prehistoric settlement evidence, was home to a highly organised and bounded landscape from at least the Middle Bronze Age onwards. The extensive reave systems – land boundaries subdividing substantial areas of Dartmoor during the Middle and Late Bronze Age (see Fleming 1988) – suggest an intensity of occupation and farming at considerable odds with modern perceptions of the moor. Dartmoor is also home to more recent activity, both agricultural and industrial, and it is the latter, in particular the more recent exploitation of its tin, that underlies much recent speculation about the nature and significance of tin exploitation in the Bronze Age. The surface remains of pre-industrial streamworking are not always easy to date, and their proximity to earlier settlement traces has often been noted. One of the earliest examples occurred in Richard Polwhele's *History of Devonshire*, published in 1797, in which he noted that 'In the parishes of Manaton, Kingsteignton, and Teigngrace, are many old Tin-works of this kind, which the inhabitants attribute to that period, when wolves and winged serpents were no strangers to the hills or the valleys . . . and indeed all the valleys from Heathfield to Dartmoor, bear the traces of shoding and streaming; which, I doubt not, was either British or Phenician' (quoted in Newman 1998, 4).

A little later, and on slightly more solid ground, more archaeologically useful accounts of the surviving traces of ancient activity on Dartmoor included Ormerod's (1864) descriptive account of hut-circle settlements which concluded with the following:

Although these hut-circles extend over so large an area of country, many enquiries have not enabled me to discover the slightest local tradition either as to their date, or the persons who erected them, or the purposes for which they were built. One point, however, in connexion with them must strike the eye of the geologist, namely that there are traces of 'tin streaming', or of 'the workings of old men', or both, near to every group of huts. Where the traces of searching for tin are extensive, the huts are many; where it is otherwise, the huts are few. The huts, too, are rarely absent from traces of 'tin streaming'. (Ormerod 1864, 307-8)

Subsequently, the idea that the early settlement evidence on Dartmoor was primarily due to the presence of tin fell in and out of favour (see Price 1985). It has been argued on occasions that a primary motivation for constructing and maintaining the reave systems on Dartmoor was to control exploitation of the moor's metal resources, although this is an explanation that overlooks the agricultural potential of Dartmoor during the Bronze Age and perhaps relies too much on assumptions about the precise nature and relative significance of metal extraction at the time. Thus Price (1985, 136) has argued that 'the mounting evidence of social and territorial organisation seems to me to indicate an enormous investment of time and labour that could well have been more profitably employed elsewhere if agriculture were its sole cause. By linking the system of land management and allotment with a need to support those engaged in tin working, this objection is removed.' However, as Andrew Fleming (1988, 109) has pointed out, similarly extensive and complex field systems elsewhere have no connection with the extraction of metal. Exploitation of local tin deposits seems plausible, and may well have been a source of wealth and prestige to those able to exert some control over it. That the entire system of land boundaries on Dartmoor was geared towards supporting those engaged in that exploitation seems less likely, and is a suggestion that rather belittles the relative importance of agricultural produce during prehistory.

More direct evidence for tin exploitation comes in the form of actual pieces of ore or smelted tin from Bronze Age sites. These are, however, remarkably few in number, even in the south-west, and although they too represent strong circumstantial evidence, they do not represent unequivocal proof of the use of local ore sources. During the mid-1950s, an Early to Middle Bronze Age settlement site at Trevisker, St Eval, Cornwall (ApSimon and Greenfield 1972) was partially excavated in advance of the building of a school, permission for which had been granted just a few years after the site itself was designated as a Scheduled Ancient Monument. Two cassiterite (tin ore) pebbles were found within the fill of a small post-hole within a circular house, while elsewhere on the site a feature designated Structure B, comprising two parallel lines of large stones up to 18ft long and 9ft apart, was interpreted by the excavators as 'low dry-stone wall bases for what may have been a timber-framed building with a ridged, thatched roof'. Whether or not one agrees with that interpretation, the artefactual material within it included a large deposit of cassiterite pebbles regarded as 'a valuable clue to the intensive exploitation of gravel deposits on which "stream-tin" production depended' (ApSimon and Greenfield 1972, 355).

Around the same time that Trevisker was being excavated, Aileen Fox was overseeing the investigation of a broadly contemporary site on Dean Moor, located in the upper Avon valley of southern Dartmoor. The threat this time was the South Devon Water Board's plan to construct a dam and large reservoir, flooding the site and its surroundings. A cassiterite pebble was found within the floor deposits of one house, while a small fragment of tin slag was found in the hearth of another (Fox 1957). As at Trevisker, there was no evidence for the smelting of tin, or any other form of metalworking, occurring on site. In 1972, china clay extraction on the St Austell granite in Cornwall was preceded by the excavation of a number of barrows and associated features (Miles 1975). One, designated Caerloggas I, was a small enclosure defined by a roughly circular bank up to 1.3m high and surrounding an area up to 12m in diameter and containing a remnant tor. The enclosure, clearly multi-phase in use and construction, lay at the western end of a line of three monuments, the other two being barrows. The interior of the enclosure was scattered with artefacts including two joining fragments of an Early Bronze Age bronze dagger and, separately, seven small pieces of tin slag. The break in the dagger and also breaks in the slag probably occurred before the objects were buried (Miles 1975, 38). Finally, one Late Bronze Age hoard from western Cornwall is known to have contained a piece of tin: 'I may here mention that in a bank of stone contiguous to, and perhaps a portion of, one of these cliff castles – that at Kenidjack – a workman recently found and brought to me two remarkably fine bronze socketed celts. With them was a broken paalstab, a piece of bronze cast off from the mould, a quantity of well-smelted copper, and some roughly-smelted tin' (Borlase 1881, 181).

Occasional finds of tin have occurred further afield, but no other reliable occurrences are known from the area of exploitable tin sources in the south-west. Again, the poverty of firm evidence offers a stark contrast to statements such as that of Price (1985, 130), who felt that 'Because tin was such a highly prized and relatively rare raw material it seems doubtful whether the skilled metalworkers of the period would have overlooked the existence of a potential source of supply from an area where they were evidently present in large numbers'.

Mining in context

Despite the wealth of information now available, the copper mines and tin sources themselves remain curiously isolated from general discussion about the Bronze Age. We know broadly when they were used and we know more or less how the ore was extracted, but how this fitted into the 'bigger picture' remains an area of considerable uncertainty. Timberlake (2001) has attributed this in part to a 'conceptual gulf separating the positions of the field investigators/interpreters of the archaeological landscape and the archaeological scientists. Few outside the world of archaeo-metallurgy have entered the debate and examined the implications of all this data, much of which concerns the distribution and very nature of the mining sites themselves'. He rightly criticised the fact that the proven existence of metal extraction sites has had little impact on academic discussion of the circulation of metal during the Bronze Age, let alone the social context and organisation of mining, though that is now beginning to change as more information on the mines becomes available and accessible.

Ironically, Timberlake (2001) contrasted this situation with the study of Neolithic stone extraction sites: 'Investigations into flint mining and stone axe quarry sites prior to 1985 helped revolutionise perceptions of contemporary technology, trade, and to some extent social organisation within the British Neolithic . . . Neolithic flint mining and stone axe quarrying has been much better studied with respect to both its place and space within the contemporary landscape.' I say ironically, because in recent years our perception of flint mines and stone quarries has altered considerably, these changes being rooted in the realisation that there were real problems with the existing data and the ways in which it was being interpreted. However, they were also stimulated by new fieldwork which took a fresh look at these sites, their products, and the broader cultural context of both. The best known example is probably Mark Edmonds and Richard Bradley's investigations of the quarries at Great Langdale in the Lake District (Bradley and Edmonds 1993), while renewed attention has been paid to flint mines (Barber et al. 1999). The ideas that have emerged over the last 15 years or so with respect to Neolithic stone sources have considerable implications for the way we interpret Bronze Age metal sources.

It is highly debatable whether there were genuine economic or practical needs to mine flint in the Neolithic. Likewise, the targeting of other stone sources went far beyond the simple need to obtain usable raw material to make tools with. As has already been noted, for flint, the mines were not the only potential sources of suitable stone. Anyone familiar with the chalk downs of southern England, for example, will be aware of the abundance of flint on the surface and in hillside or cliff-face exposures, and fieldwork in a number of locations suggests strongly that exploitation of such sources was widespread, and probably the norm. Mined flint has noteworthy practical advantages – the depth below ground of the buried seams means that the flint is relatively free from frost damage and the effects of glaciation. Fewer flaws mean greater control over the knapping process. In the Neolithic, the size of the mined nodules will have facilitated the manufacture of larger core tools including axes. However, the efforts involved in recovering flint from such depth suggests that more than just economic criteria were determining where and why mining occurred. The flint mines were not the only sources around, nor were they necessarily exploiting the best quality flint. Moreover, the amount of flint both worked and unworked left behind at the mines suggests that flint mining could be a rather wasteful activity.

The 'axe-factory' sites offer interesting parallels. Work at the aforementioned Great Langdale site has shown that there too neither the best quality nor the most easily extracted material was being targeted. As Richard Bradley (2000, 85-7) has noted, sites such as Great Langdale considerably undermine attempts to discuss prehistoric extraction in terms of efficiency, labour investment and maximising of output. Applying the economic solutions of the modern western world just will not work when trying to understand the purpose of these places. Thus at Langdale,

> some of the most suitable stone for making work tools was left unused, whilst inaccessible exposures with the same physical characteristics were employed instead. The character of the place seemed at least as important as the qualities of the material found there. Moreover, a survey of the entire distribution of the parent rock shows that . . . people chose to quarry the stone in precisely those areas that were located furthest from the lower ground. They also selected quarry sites overlooking the steepest gradients. In each case, the effect was the same, for it helped to isolate these places from the sphere of everyday activity (*ibid.*, 85-6).

Together, the evidence from 'axe-factories' and flint mines, though geographically and geologically distinct, and necessarily subject to quite different methods of extraction, suggests that they have much in common. For the 'axe-factories', Bradley emphasises the importance of their location – they are often quite prominent features in the landscape, some of them visible for a considerable distance: 'They were often located in spectacular but unusually inaccessible places, where the individual quarries would be difficult to find by chance. For the most part they were located well beyond the limits of the settled landscape in areas that might be hazardous to reach . . . As often as not, work tools could have been made from other exposures if the same raw material without experiencing any of these hardships' (*ibid.*, 87-8). Many of the known flint mines appear likewise to be located away from the general distribution of contemporary sites, the inaccessibility and danger here though relating more to the depth of the flint underground and the means of accessing it.

All in all, then, a statement such as that made by Colonel Lane Fox at the outset of archaeological investigation into flint mining – that the pits at Cissbury were dug 'for the purpose of obtaining flints' (Lane Fox 1869) – is essentially true but at the same time far too simplistic. The role of such sources and their products in contemporary landscape and society was far more complex. A consideration of survey and excavated evidence suggests that exploitation of Neolithic stone sources was likely to have been episodic or intermittent, perhaps on a seasonal basis. The sheer scale of the surviving remains at places like Grimes Graves (and,

29 *Part of the area of Neolithic quarrying at Great Langdale in the Lake District. Pike o' Stickle, the triangular peak visible just left of the centre of the photograph, may have been a favoured raw material source for axe production because of its distinctiveness as a topographical feature and its relative inaccessibility as much as for the suitability of the rock itself. 'The precarious and inaccessible location of these quarries may have helped to shape the meanings attached to the axes themselves . . .' (Edmonds 1995, 79).*
© Crown copyright. NMR

indeed, Great Langdale) can give a misleading impression of large-scale working. In fact, the remains visible today represent the accumulated outcome of centuries of small-scale exploitation.

At a time when the population probably comprised small kin-based communities for whom local and ancestral authority was all important, visits to these places may have been incorporated into the seasonal round of subsistence and social activities, as people criss-crossed the landscape, moving between familiar places along well-established paths. Moreover, there are likely to have been restrictions on who could visit and work the sources, with ethnographic evidence suggesting that both procurement and the working of raw material were seen as highly skilled, specialist tasks – specialist in the sense that participation was often limited along lines of age and gender. Furthermore, the performance of these tasks could be highly ritualised, while those participating 'could use their skills to either enhance their social position or to maintain a degree of separateness from the community' (Topping in press).

The relevance of this lengthy diversion into the Neolithic might not be immediately apparent, but there are clear points of comparison to be drawn with Bronze Age copper mining in particular. As with flint, for example, the occurrence of copper mining was inevitably constrained by the availability of suitable and accessible raw material – indeed for metal the availability of source material was far more restricted. Thus Timberlake (2001, 181) has noted a broad correspondence between the location of definite and possible prehistoric copper mines with the main areas of copper mineralisation and the known spread of mining in more recent centuries. However, there are some obvious gaps. Areas where medieval and later copper mining is known, but Bronze Age mining is not, include (in addition to those already discussed) south-west Scotland, north-west Yorkshire, Shropshire and other areas on the Welsh-English border, the Quantocks and Exmoor. Moreover, some places with an extensive history of copper exploitation in recent times – Cumbria, Snowdonia, Devon and Cornwall – similarly lack good evidence for prehistoric extraction beyond a scatter of hammer stones. Timberlake (*ibid.*) summed up the situation by contrasting the relatively abundant Bronze Age evidence from mid-Wales, 'a region that returned only 7,000 tons of recorded copper concentrates throughout the whole of the nineteenth and early twentieth centuries, and Cornwall, a county that has produces many millions of tons of copper ores during historic times – yet has provided us with barely any evidence for early mining and prospection'. He considered a number of possible reasons for the Cornish situation in particular – destruction by later mining, inundation or erosion of coastal working, and so on – before concluding that 'such technological or utilitarian explanations are insufficient in themselves to explain this apparent anomaly' (*ibid.*, 182).

With regard to the south-west, explanations offered for the paucity of evidence for copper extraction are increasingly tending to stress cultural factors. Timberlake for instance suggested that tin and gold were the important metals in the south-west, with the copper being paid little attention, while Herring (1997) stressed the agricultural richness of the region as a source of wealth that might have rendered prospection and mining for metals of lesser importance. Lead isotope analyses of British prehistoric bronzes (see below) has offered little firm support for extensive exploitation of south-western copper sources, although Budd *et al.* (2000) suggested that it is possible, on the basis of lead isotope data, to assign a small group of very early copper objects (two halberds from Cumbria, a flat axe from Sussex and a halberd and dagger from the Castell Coch group) to the south-west, perhaps to the St Austell-Bodmin area.

The area around Plynlimon is equally problematical, though here, in addition to the known and possible sites, there are 'a number of richer and equally accessible copper veins that were apparently ignored' (Timberlake 2001, 182), prompting the suggestion that we need to consider more than just geological and mineralogical factors when trying to understand why some places were exploited and others were not. For these mid-Wales mines, Timberlake (*ibid.*, 185-6) also considered the distribution of broadly contemporary features, primarily of a funerary nature – cairns, cists and other forms of burial – plus standing stones and burnt mounds. It would, however, be intriguing to see the full extent of earlier, Neolithic activity in the vicinity of these mines too. Given the proximity of places such as Plynlimon and the sources of rivers such as the Severn and the Wye, the suspicion must be that such funerary and ceremonial activity was at least in part connected with the physical and mythical qualities of the landscape – this was not virgin territory prior to the Bronze Age, unvisited and unexploited. The importance of particular mines may have been in part due to their presence at prominent places within a landscape already rich in meaning and symbolism for people who had frequented it for generations. As well as influencing decisions about which sites to exploit, such associations may also have enhanced the value of any raw material – copper – to emerge from the ground at these places.

Other sites – Great Orme, Parys Mountain, Alderley Edge – are not unlike the landscape setting of Neolithic and Early Bronze Age stone sources, and it seems reasonable to suggest here too that not only did the qualities of the place influence the choice of where to mine, but also added symbolic value to the metal extracted from them. The ethnographic literature features numerous examples of landscapes imbued with symbolic, or mythological, significance and prominent features such as mountains, hills, promontories and so on are often considered particularly sacred (Price 1994; Reeves 1994; Tilley 1994; Humphrey 1995) with important spiritual, mythical or magical associations.

Both Neolithic stone sources and Bronze Age copper mines are characterised by strong evidence for intermittent, probably seasonal exploitation and a lack of any permanent structures which might indicate the presence of settlement. On the basis of the evidence from Copa Hill, Cwmystwyth, Timberlake (2003) has suggested exploitation of the copper was a secondary occupation of pastoralists, though such an interpretation appears to treat copper as a resource of primarily economic value, and also overlooks the obvious comparisons with Neolithic mining and quarrying. Ethnographic evidence offers a varied picture, but again until relatively recently it is unusual to see ore being regarded solely or largely in economic terms. Periodic or seasonal visits to obtain raw material tend to take on an event-like quality, associated with ceremonies and restrictions on participation. That the people who worked Copa Hill did so in the course of seasonal movement influenced by a predominantly pastoral lifestyle is possible, perhaps even likely, but their perception of the material they mined and of the place they mined it is unlikely to have been so straightforward.

It is worth considering also the likely environmental impact of mining. Fire-setting and smelting are likely to have made considerable demands on local resources in terms of fuel, something highlighted by recent experiments and also excavations, which have uncovered substantial quantities of wood and charcoal in amongst the mineworkings and spoil. However, the effect on local woodland appears to have been fairly small in scale. At Mount Gabriel in south-west Ireland, for example, it 'appears that mining had little impact on woodland cover' (Mighall and Lageard 1999, 55). Likewise at Copa Hill, Cwmystwyth, 'the impact of any significant reduction in woodland has not been recorded within the pollen record captured by the hilltop peat' (Mighall, in Timberlake 2003, 66), although it may be possible to link some smaller-scale declines with mining. Nonetheless, the evidence suggested that 'significant woodland persisted in the Ystwyth Valley well after the cessation of Bronze Age mining. The permanent loss of woodland occurred later on during the Bronze Age and possibly into the Iron Age . . . Similar types of vegetation changes are also characteristic of other parts of upland Wales, suggesting that mining may have had no more than a small-scale effect on an otherwise common trend' (*ibid.*). That this should be so is hardly surprising. Good evidence for careful woodland management in the British Isles precedes copper mining by nearly two millennia, a notable example being the evidence for coppicing within the ditch of the Early Neolithic causewayed enclosure at Etton, Cambridgeshire (Pryor 1998). Nonetheless, it underlines the long-term planning and complex arrangements likely to have been associated with ore exploitation, suggesting that rather than being a secondary undertaking, mining and smelting were, during the Early Bronze Age at least and probably beyond, likely to have been firmly embedded within a seasonal cycle of socially and economically significant activities.

4
THE WORK OF TIME: PEOPLE, PROCESSES AND PLACES

> The [spirit medium] would cut a sheep while it was still alive and let its blood drip or sprinkle it in the mine in the name of Ntogota, the ruler of everything. She would spit saliva on it there. So many things took place there . . . They would even become possessed. They also initiated people from there. All came when they were slaughtering, even women/wives. It was an offering to the ore. The importance of why they had to slaughter a white sheep was because, if they did not, the ore would die. The ore wouldn't come out (Childs 2000, 205).

So far, little has been said about the people responsible for prospecting, mining, smelting and the numerous other activities that must have occurred in and around mines and, of course, further afield. Although a case has been made for regarding mines as special places, whose significance resided only partly in their value as a source of raw material, equally little has been said about the social context in which they were exploited and understood. There is of course a real problem here. Artefactual material and structural remains not directly connected to the extraction processes are rare indeed at excavated mines, a situation mirrored at the various Neolithic stone sources described in the previous chapter. There too, cultural debris beyond tools of extraction and the waste from primary working is pitifully small in quantity when contrasted with the situation at contemporary non-mining sites.

Who mined?

It seems safe to assume that mining, whether deep underground within the shafts and galleries at Great Orme or among the shallower fired and hammered workings there and elsewhere, was an activity as skilled as it was laborious, and was undeniably dangerous. A far less safe assumption is that such labour was solely the preserve of adult males. While a certain amount of upper body strength would have been advantageous for many parts of the mining process, size presents more of a

30 This image of Nick Jowett squeezing through a confined space underlines the difficulties and discomfort likely to have been endured when working underground, and raises questions about the ideal size of miners. Additionally, however intermittent mining was, it was clearly a skilled activity and an experience unlikely to be forgotten.
© Great Orme Mines Ltd

problem. Anyone who has experienced at first hand the Neolithic galleries at Grimes Graves, Norfolk or the Bronze Age underground workings at Great Orme will be well aware of the cramped and claustrophobic conditions in which some of the extraction occurred (**30**). This need not in itself rule out the likelihood of men-only extraction in prehistory — it may be that the restricted nature of the galleries offers evidence for techniques of mining that involved the removal of as little extraneous rock as possible. Arguably of course, the dark and dangerous conditions will have enhanced considerably the sensory experiences of the miners, contributing an additional element to an already highly ritualised task. However, there are good historical, ethnographic and archaeological reasons for considering the underground presence of women, adolescents and children in prehistory.

For the British Isles alone, the use of female and child labour in mines is well documented historically, being relatively common until the mid-nineteenth century. Only in 1842 was the employment of children under the age of ten in underground workings outlawed by Act of Parliament. Of course, the economic and social imperatives of post-Industrial Revolution Britain can in no way compare with the situation in prehistory, but it at least allows us to reject suggestions that women and children were physically unsuited to such work. Turning to the archaeological evidence, at Great Orme the recent experiences of archaeological excavation have underlined the difficulties of squeezing adult males into some of the workings, a number of those of Bronze Age date being remarkably narrow: 'Either miners were selected for their small stature, or children were used, like Victorian chimney sweeps' (Roberts 2002, 30). Absolute proof would clearly require accident victims whose bodies had been left *in situ*, something that archaeologists have yet to encounter in a prehistoric copper mine in Britain and, indeed, is remarkably rare elsewhere. Nonetheless it is worth recalling that the only skeleton so far recovered from a prehistoric mine in the British Isles for which a mining accident might offer a plausible explanation was found at the foot of a Neolithic flint mine shaft at Cissbury, West Sussex, and was identified by its excavator as an adult female (John Pull, in Russell 2001, 181-3).

A search through the ethnographic record also suggests that female and child labour underground, while far from common, is by no means unheard of. However, they were more likely to be involved in associated above-ground activity. Eugenia Herbert (1984, 44-5), in a study of the uses and meanings of copper in sub-Saharan Africa, noted that in general, 'the division of labor in many mining areas seems to have been a logical one: women and children did the surface gathering as well as the washing and sorting of ores, while men worked underground'. Inevitably, there are noteworthy exceptions, as indicated by the discoveries of skeletons of women and younger girls from some Zimbabwean mines. These and other mines also frequently featured workings that seem too narrow to have accommodated adult miners. In one extreme case, a shaft some 70ft deep and around 18in in diameter, one commentator (quoted in Herbert 1984, 44-5) naturally found it hard to 'imagine a relay of pre-pubescent girls being lowered by their ankles to dig it'. Instead, an alternative suggestion was offered – that this was a ventilation shaft whose connected mine working had not been recognised. The plausibility of either scenario is, naturally, a matter of opinion.

However, other accounts generally dating from the late nineteenth and early twentieth centuries provide further occasional records for the involvement of women and children underground. Goucher and Herbert (1996, 49) noted that at Banjeli 'Ore was mined especially by women and children and possibly by slaves as well. Miners usually, they dug it out of surface pits but sometimes also out of underground shafts.' They quoted one eyewitness from 1914: 'It was pitiful to see some of them, with babes at their breasts . . . digging out the ore with a curious horse-shaped tool. Besides being a hard occupation, it is also a dangerous one. Only a day or so before our visit, one of the miners had been killed owing to a shaft falling in' (*ibid.*).

Nonetheless, on the whole the ethnographic evidence broadly suggests that adult males were more likely to undertake the underground mining, with rules and taboos governing participation in a manner similar to those for metalworking (see below), these rules generally constructed along lines of age and gender. Often, for women it was not merely their participation in mining and associated tasks that was forbidden. For example, referring to the Kivu of Zaire, Buleli (1993, 469) noted that

> Sexual abstinence was widespread . . . for all metallurgical activities including prospecting, extraction of ores, their reduction and forging. For the Benye-Mikebwe, this sexual ban was rigorous and lasted throughout the prospecting period. In addition, the prospectors would sacrifice a chicken before departing on a search, to increase the chance of success. For the Mamba-kasenga and Banyabisha, on the other hand, where supplies of ore were abundant, prospectors had no such inhibitions. The discovery of a deposit gave rise to great celebrations, in the course of which goats were strangled and prospectors drank banana beer.

However, there were clearly occasions, dictated either by economic, practical or cultural necessity (or any combination thereof) when other members of the mining group could become involved, and there is no reason as yet to assume anything different for Bronze Age Britain.

Processing

Although good evidence from the British Isles remains sparse, it is assumed that much of the work necessary for preparing the mined ore for the first smelt occurred fairly close to the mines themselves. These primary stages – termed beneficiation, or ore concentration – involve fairly straightforward if laborious processes of crushing and sorting in order to separate out as much as possible of the copper minerals from the ore-bearing rock. The initial stage involved pounding and crushing the extracted rock with stone hammers – probably hand-held and little modified – and flat stones used as anvils. Some of this work may have taken place within the mineworkings themselves in order to avoid moving around more rock than strictly necessary. The extracted rock will, of course, have been considerably broken up by the mining process itself, particularly if fire-setting had been used. After crushing, the mineralized fragments – the copper ore – would have been picked out by eye and further fragmented if necessary to remove any remaining rock matrix. The presence at some mines of grinding tools such as stone mortars and pestles (Great Orme) and saddle querns (Cwmystwyth) suggests that they may have been employed in the final stages of ore concentration. The efficiency of this lengthy, multi-stage crushing and sorting process is underlined by the general absence of copper minerals from the spoil heaps at the mines.

The next phase, smelting, is even more problematic, again due to a lack of surviving evidence. The ore will have been reduced to metal, probably in stages, within furnaces at temperatures of at least 1,100°C, but traces of such processes have so far proved elusive. Consequently, among other gaps in our knowledge is the form in which extracted metal actually left the mines (**31**). Explanations for the apparent invisibility of this stage in the process revolve around the simplicity of the technology and the as-yet-limited extent of archaeological fieldwork around the mines. The relatively straightforward smelting processes presumed to have been used probably produced little slag and required nothing in the way of permanent structures, making it very difficult to identify such activity archaeologically. That the potential to discover smelting sites exists has been demonstrated at Ross Island, in the south-west of Ireland, where what has been described as a 'work camp' associated with Beaker pottery, pits associated with metallurgical processes, and a few fragments of slag have been found close to Early Bronze Age copper mines (O' Brien 1996).

Just as the ethnographic data, with exceptions, favours a predominance of male miners, so women and children generally appear to have been responsible for the production of ore concentrate from mined rock (Herbert 1984, 44-5) though not, of course, for the actual smelting (see below). Indeed, the role of women and children in the surface collection and preparation of ore has been compared by some to their equally frequent role as gatherers and preparers of agricultural produce. Herbert (1993, 27-8) also suggested that surface collection, sorting and crushing generally involved a lesser degree of ritualization than did mining itself, and 'the greater the degree of ritualization, the more likely it is that women will be excluded or relegated to minor roles'. Paradoxically, of course, not only was their work crucial to the whole operation, women and children also made some of the most time-consuming and labour intensive contributions to the whole ore preparation process – the crushing, grinding and sorting of the mined ore, the production of charcoal, and the transportation of both ore and fuel to the furnaces (Herbert 1993, 123), all highly skilled activities crucial to a successful outcome.

From ore to object

As with most other aspects of prehistoric metalworking, there is much about the actual production of finished objects that remains in the realms of speculation. There are, of course, basic and undeniable scientific facts – the melting point of copper, for instance – but how such important milestones on the way to making copper or bronze objects were reached is not always easy to recognise. Moreover, when dealing with pre-literate, pre-scientific societies it is also important to look beyond our quite narrow modern perceptions of what constitutes a technological process in order to understand the broader context and significance of metalworking.

To begin with the physical evidence, there are some surviving remnants of the casting and finishing processes – crucible sherds, mould pieces, odd bits of metal removed from cast objects, the odd anvil. Experiments have been undertaken to

31 (Above) *An unusual palstave-type chisel plus an ingot fragment from the Malmains Farm hoard (see **9**). The former reminds us that the hoard record is likely to be unrepresentative of the range of objects in circulation during the Bronze Age – hoards of this date in the south-east are dominated by palstaves, in Kent almost to the exclusion of other types of object. The latter underlines how little we know about the means by which metal circulated during the Bronze Age, despite decades of debate. Ingot (or 'cake') fragments are a common feature of the so-called 'founder's hoards' of the Late Bronze Age and often comprise pure, unalloyed copper. Tin, however, simply does not occur in any great quantity. Clearly unalloyed metal was circulating, perhaps in some quantity, yet at the same time recycling of old objects was a frequent occurrence. As the Langdon Bay collection plus individual items from 'hoards' and single finds show us, some cast metal objects were themselves travelling considerable distances before deposition or recycling, yet the mechanisms, political and economic, that facilitated this movement remain poorly understood. Moreover, if we step back from the Late Bronze Age, the picture becomes less than clear. In the Middle Bronze Age, for instance, the Malmains Farm ingot fragment is almost unique for the British Isles. But how common were such pieces in the Middle Bronze Age? Incidentally, the ingot fragment from Malmains Farm is, at 186g, three times the weight of the dirk/dagger from the same hoard (see **52**). Chisel approx. 17cm in length; ingot approx. 4cm in width.* © Dover Museum

32 (Right) *Excavations at Ewanrigg, Maryport, Cumbria in the 1980s encountered an Early Bronze Age cremation cemetery comprising 26 burials, in addition to two inhumations, one of the latter being accompanied by a Beaker and probably representing the first burial in the sequence. The cremations were arranged in a rough circle around a natural knoll. The pit pictured here contained a Collared Urn, laid on its side, with an 'accessory cup' beneath it and the 'connecting rod' beside it. The cremated human remains may belong to a male, but little else could be gleaned from them. The sand and gravel around the lip of the pit was reddened, possibly 'due to chemical change brought about either by the ash or by the insertion of hot ashes' (Bewley et al. 1992, 328). The base of the pit contained a series of stakeholes around its perimeter, and one wonders if they had held a structure associated with the burning noted at the mouth. The 'conecting rod', 17cm long, may have been a tuyere (i.e. a bellows nozzle) although an alternative scenario sees it as a tube connecting the bellows to the nozzle. Better fired than the pottery from the cemetery, 'Because of the uniformity of the firing it seems likely that it was deliberately fired for a considerable period under oxidising conditions' (Longworth, in Bewley et al. 1992, 345). The possibility that it could have seen service in pottery firing, metalworking and cremation not only underlines the broadly comparable technology but the cultural factors at play in all three. The pottery could have been better fired if the makers so wished.* © Bob Bewley

THE WORK OF TIME: PEOPLE, PROCESSES AND PLACES

try and replicate the likely techniques used. Surviving artefacts have been closely studied for clues about the methods used to make them. However, much is missing. We have no *in situ* furnace structures, no complete moulds with all associated fixtures and fittings present and correct, no collections of metalworkers' tools — indeed, no definite locations at which metalworking occurred. We may point to some sites as places where some objects may have been cast, but the excavated evidence is always ambiguous, capable of other interpretations. The number of bronze objects surviving from the Bronze Age far exceeds the amount of evidence for their manufacture, the imbalance underlined by the fact that to date only one definite example of a tuyere or bellows nozzle has been found from the entire British Isles (**32**), yet it is difficult to imagine any of those thousands of bronzes being made without the use of at least one every time.

Moulds of stone, clay and bronze (**33-4**) are known from the Bronze Age. Like the objects they were used to cast, information about provenance and context is minimal, with many being recovered by accident. The Early Bronze Age is represented solely by stone moulds. Later periods are represented by all three materials, though most known examples of clay and bronze belong to the Late Bronze Age. It seems more than likely that most castings were undertaken using moulds of clay,

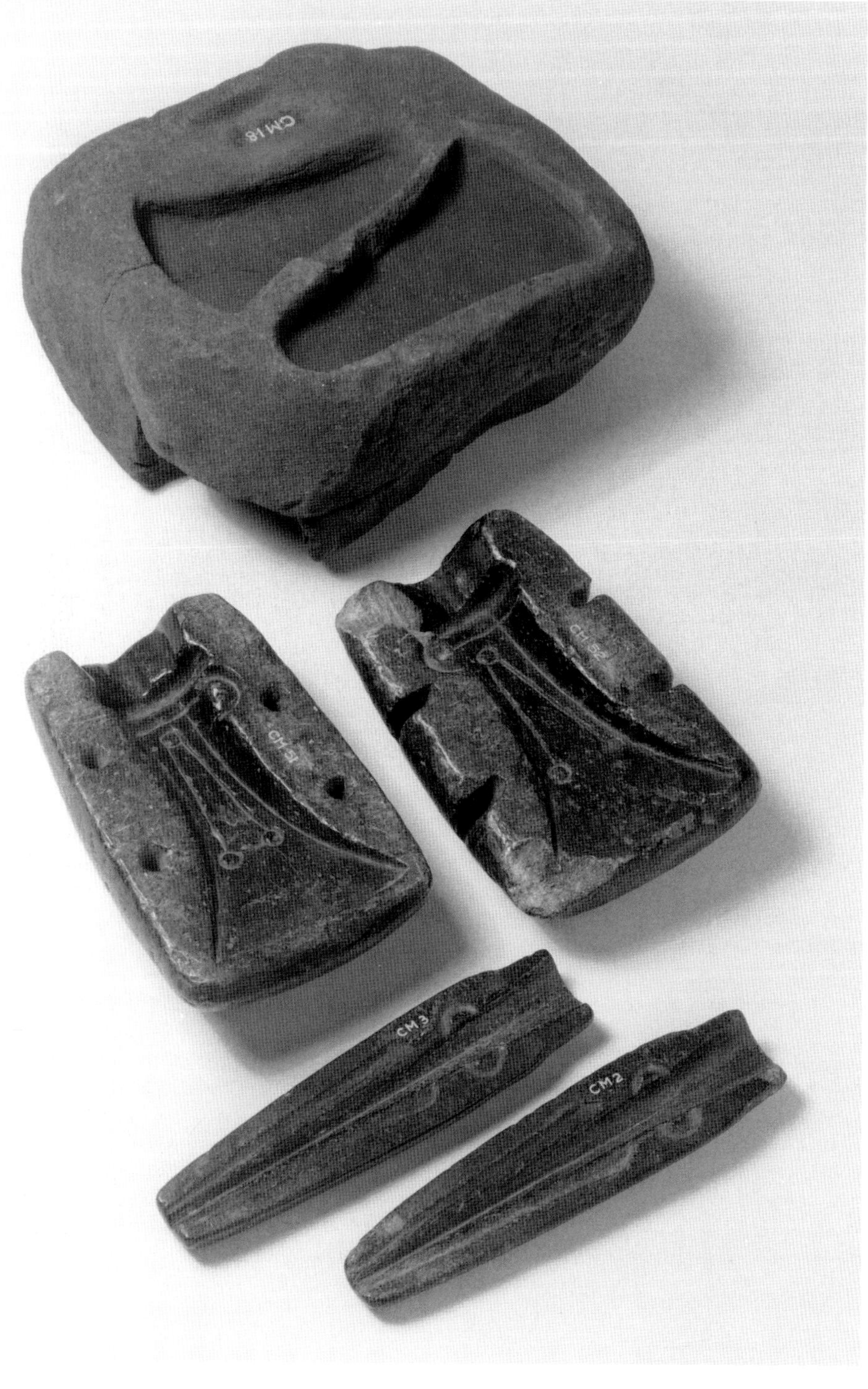

CM18
CM3
CM2

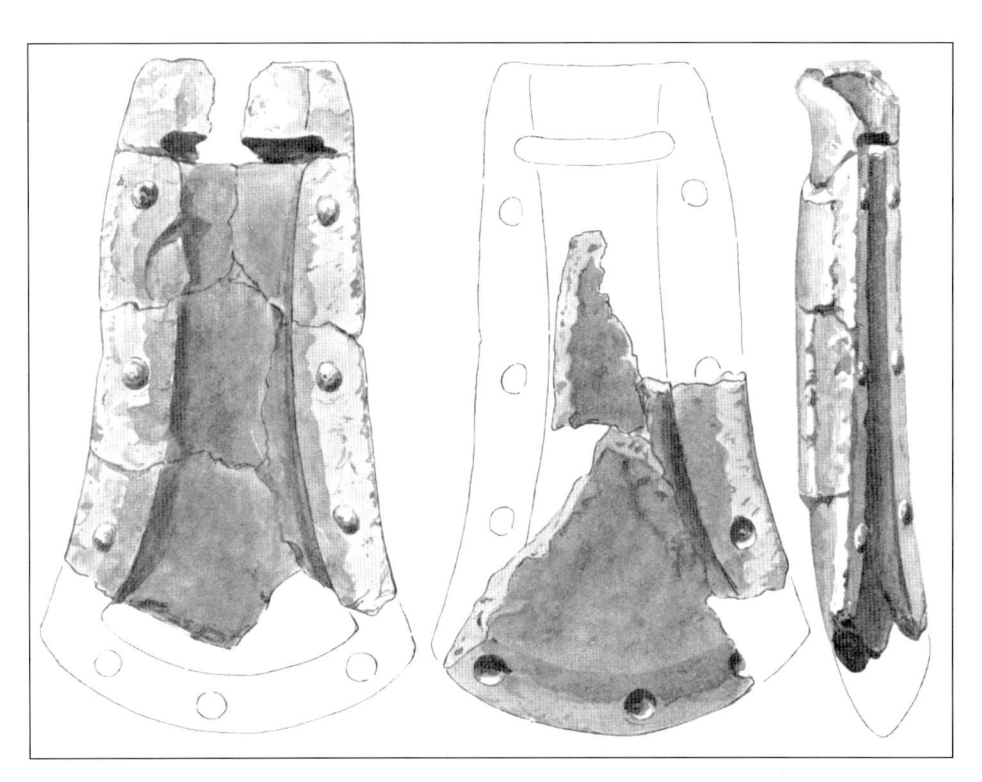

33 (Left) *Three examples of moulds for the casting of bronzes, all from Scotland. From the top, (a) open stone mould for the casting of flat axeheads, found at Culbin Sands, Moray, in the nineteenth century; (b) two-piece, or bivalve, stone mould for socketed axeheads, found at Rossken, Ross-shire; and (c) another bivalve stone mould, this time for the casting of side-looped spearheads, from Campbeltown, Argyll.*
© National Museums of Scotland

34 (Above) *The remains of a clay mould for casting a socketed axehead, found at Jarlshof, Shetland (Curle 1932-3, 113 fig. 32). See also* **38** *and* **39**. *More than 200 mould fragments for swords, axeheads, gouges and sunflower pins plus pieces of slag, crucibles and other debris were recovered from the site, primarily during the 1930s. Areas of burning and, in one house, a sand-filled pit are among features suggested by the excavator to have been involved in metalworking. The apparent remoteness of this sizeable assemblage did not fit comfortably with prevailing ideas about the relative cultural sophistication of different parts of the British Isles. Curle (1932-3, 125) suggested the presence of 'a travelling smith, coming from the south, with his raw material and his craftsmanship acquired in the more advanced regions of the mainland'. Later, Coles (1959-60, 48) conjured the image of an Irish smith 'who had retreated to the last outpost of the Bronze Age world at a time when Iron Age tools were being traded and produced in mainland Britain'* though how early they were in regular use in the British Isles is unclear. The earliest datable assemblage of clay mould fragments – a collection of over 150 pieces – was found among Middle Bronze Age midden debris dumped over the infill of a Neolithic flint mine shaft at Grimes Graves, Norfolk. These fragments represent perhaps no more than three separate moulds, each used once for the casting of basal-looped spearheads and probably dating no earlier than *c*.1300 BC (Needham 1991).

Throughout the Bronze Age, there was a gradual trend towards more complex casting technology, permitting the creation of a greater range of metal objects. The earliest castings occurred in simple one-piece stone moulds, a single block of suitable stone usually shaped in order to ease handling and with at least one levelled surface into which was cut a matrix of the desired shape and size. Though frequently referred to as 'open' moulds, the matrix was almost certainly covered with stone or wood in order to prevent oxidisation of the metal. The range of object types of Early Bronze Age date represented by surviving stone moulds is not large – assorted axehead types, the odd knife, some awls and bracelets – but is broadly representative of the range of types known from the same period. Stone moulds could, unlike those of clay, be reused many times, while some also feature matrices for the casting of more than one object. A four-sided block of carboniferous grit found in 1961 'more or less in mid-stream in the Walleybourne Brook, a small tributary of the Cound Brook which flows into the River Severn at Cound, a few miles below Shrewsbury' (Thomas 1972) featured six. The block had clearly been worked to produce a more or less rectangular longitudinal section, the matrices cut into the four long sides. The block was a maximum of 22.6cm long, and the six matrices represented five flat axeheads ranging in length from 6.5cm to 12.7cm, plus a rod or awl – a hollow measuring *c*.6.35cm long, 0.55cm wide and 0.25cm deep. Even more impressive is the mould from Foudland near Insch, Aberdeenshire which featured nine matrices, though not all appeared to have been used (Cowie 2000).

More complex castings required more complex moulds. From the later phases of the Early Bronze Age, most castings took place in two-piece moulds. Some more complicated items required even more complex arrangements. Stated simply, two opposing and matching mould pieces would be created, these being held firmly in place for casting operations by various means, including short dowels, organic binding material, or a tightly fitting outer wrap of coarse clay. Stone two-piece moulds could again take the form of rectangular blocks with matrices cut into more than one face. A good example here is the block from Bodwrdin, Anglesey (Britton 1963; Manby 1966) which featured a matrix on each of its four sides. Presumably each side was accompanied by a matching pair.

The Bodwrdin block was carved from sandstone, the long faces ground and polished to a smooth, level surface and the two ends also ground, albeit to a much lesser extent. Two of the matrices were for the casting of end-looped, socketed spearheads of a type belonging within the 'Arreton' phase of metalworking, towards the end of the Early Bronze Age (Needham 1979). A third side represents what was described by Britton as a shallow groove – perhaps it was intended for the casting of a long thin bar of metal, perhaps intended to be worked into an armlet or bracelet. The fourth side is the most puzzling. Manby (1966) noted that 'the implement from this matrice would appear to have been a socketed chisel with two opposed loops and a broad crescentic edge . . . However, a double looped socketed chisel . . . would be an implement entirely unknown at present in any archaeological context...'. Moreover, a socketed chisel of any description is otherwise unknown until the Late Bronze Age, several centuries later than the spearheads represented by the first two matrices.

Explaining this is difficult, though this is not the sole instance of a mould matrix being unmatched by a known object – the Late Bronze Age assemblage of mould debris from Dainton, Devon (Needham 1980) is another such example. There is, of course, no guarantee that all four matrices were carved at the same time, and curation of an object over several centuries is an increasingly recognised phenomenon of the Bronze Age. More importantly, the Bodwrdin mould reminds us that the depositional practices of the Bronze Age were far from random, and have not left us with a representative sample of the bronze objects made and used. Moreover, it highlights the problem that while the technology clearly existed for the casting of socketed – hollow – objects by the middle of the second millennium BC, the actual casting of socketed objects – axeheads, spearheads, chisels and so on – did not become commonplace until the end of the second millennium BC. That more sophisticated castings were possible did not mean that more sophisticated objects rapidly became the tools or weapons of choice. The role of cultural factors in determining the preferred form of those tools and weapons clearly needs to be borne in mind.

Clay moulds, as already suggested, appear likely to have been the norm throughout the Late Bronze Age and probably during the Middle Bronze Age for most castings. Unlike their stone counterparts, they could be used only once, and the need to break them open to retrieve the freshly cast object means that at best they are only likely to survive as fragments. Their friable nature doesn't bode well for their long term survival in the ground, and the best-known and best preserved examples are those which had been buried in pits, probably not too long after use.

Manufacturing clay moulds can appear a fairly straightforward process when described in outline, though in reality it involves a sequence of steps that can be spread over several weeks, particularly for larger items such as swords. Again, most were two-piece moulds with additional features added to facilitate the pouring in of the molten metal and the suspension, where necessary, of a 'core' to allow the casting of hollow or socketed items. Generally, moulds comprised at least two layers of clay, the inner bearing the matrix being of finer quality than the outer. The two halves of the mould would be formed from clay probably derived from local sources, and perhaps held within a wooden support or frame of some kind. There is evidence that the clay moulds for some longer items such as swords may have featured narrow wooden rods inserted lengthways through the mould for additional support, though the manner and timing of their use is not entirely certain.

After applying a coating of, say, charcoal or ashes to prevent it adhering to the clay, a pattern or template of the desired object would be pressed into each of the two halves of the mould, thus creating the opposing matrices. These patterns may have been made of a variety of materials. There is good evidence for the use of wood – a wooden sword found on Orkney has been considered a likely candidate. Its length, at 711mm, is longer than most swords from Scotland, though shrinkage of the mould through drying and firing before use would reduce the probable length of any casting to a more typical length of perhaps 640mm (Ó Faoláin and Northover 2000). Further support for the use of wood includes the presence of grain impressions inside a clay matrix fragment found at Jarlshof, Shetland. Another possibility is lead. Objects of lead from the British Bronze Age are rare but not unknown – the metal is more often encountered as an addition to tin bronze from the Middle Bronze Age onwards, probably as a means of facilitating casting. Items such as the lead palstave found recently near Maidstone (**35-6**) may well have seen service as patterns for the creation of clay moulds.

They may also have been associated with the use of bronze moulds. Complete and fragmentary bronze two-piece moulds are known from a number of primarily Late Bronze Age contexts, mainly hoards, and there has been some debate about their suitability for the repeated casting of bronze objects, despite the considerable investment in time, labour and materials involved in their manufacture. An alternative possibility is that they were used for the casting of lead patterns (e.g. Tylecote 1986, 92). Supporting evidence for this hypothesis includes the presence of traces of lead in several bronze moulds, including those from Roseberry Topping and from the Isle of Harty, Kent. An example from New Street, Cambridge contained 'half of a badly fitting lead socketed axe' (*ibid*.), though whether or not the lead axe fragment was actually found inside the mould is unclear.

Of course, making the mould is only a small part of the casting process. It is not proposed to detail all the likely and essential steps here, but some key points are worth emphasizing. As already noted, there is little evidence surviving for furnace structures although some fragments of fired clay may indeed derive from them. The furnace itself need comprise little more than a simple clay structure to contain a charcoal-fuelled fire. Bellows would presumably be used to force air onto the furnace via holes in its walls in order to raise the temperature within the furnace. The bellows themselves were probably made entirely from organic materials, and consequently unlikely to survive in the archaeological record, though the nozzle, or tuyere, and perhaps a connecting rod to attach the bellows to the nozzle, were probably made of clay. However, as already noted, they too are rather scarce.

Copper itself has a high melting point of around 1,086°C, but experimental work suggests that it may need to be heated as high as 1,300°C in order for it to

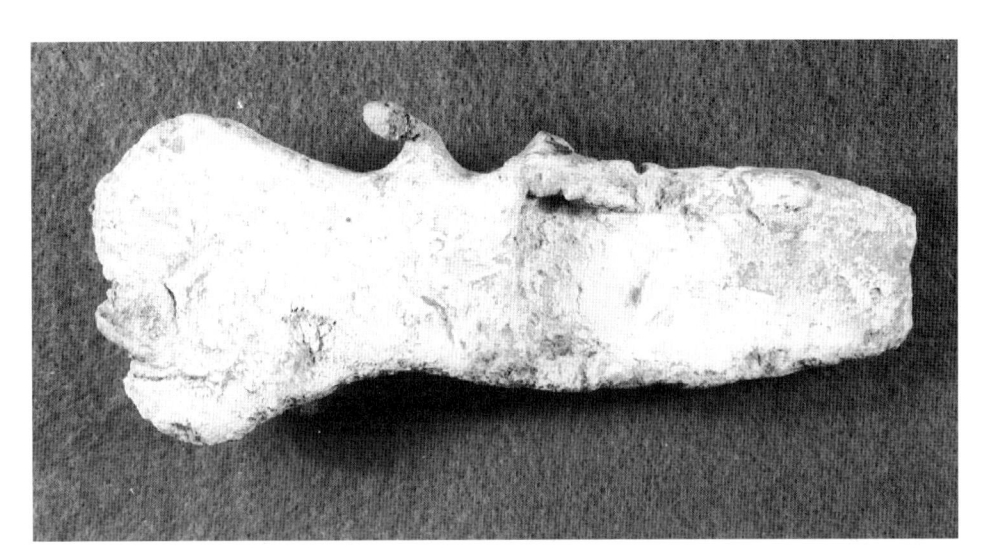

35-6 *Front and back views of a lead palstave found near Maidstone, Kent, and one of the many objects to have come to attention in recent years through the Portable Antiquities Scheme (see appendix)*

stay molten long enough to retrieve it from the furnace and pour before it starts to cool and solidify. The addition of around 10 per cent tin can lower the required temperature by around 100°C as well as improving the flow of the metal and the quality of the final casting, while adding lead to the mix can also facilitate casting by increasing the fluidity of the metal. Of course, recovering a crucible complete with molten metal from an enclosed furnace is no straightforward operation.

Neil Burridge (www.bronze-age-craft.com), who has undertaken many replica castings, suggests the use of a wooden paddle in order to lift the crucible from the fire, and then 'green' wood sticks in order to pick the crucible up for pouring. The small size and relatively open nature of many Bronze Age crucibles suggests that the act of pouring needed to be undertaken rapidly in order to counteract the rapid heat loss caused by removal from the furnace. Burridge has suggested that there may be as little as 12 seconds available to retrieve the crucible and pour the metal into the waiting mould. A key part of this process is, of course, knowing when the metal has reached the desired temperature and is ready to be removed from the furnace and poured. Many have suggested that colour may have been used as the main indicator – Burridge notes that a bright yellow colour in the heart of the furnace would indicate that a sufficient temperature had been reached to melt the metal. He also argues that this would best be done in the dark, suggesting that perhaps much if not all metalworking was undertaken at night.

The limited time available for pouring would clearly have the potential for causing problems with the casting of longer or larger items, notably swords and rapiers. Experimental work has borne this out, highlighting the difficulties of creating weapons of the same length, for example, even when using the same mould or pattern. Tylecote (1973, 4) for example noted that 'out of 1,100 rapiers from the British Isles only two are in any sense identical' and suggested that the difficulties of pouring the molten metal into the mould played a large part in this variation in form. Of course, casting – in the sense of using a mould to create something that was almost the finished article itself – was not the be all and end all of metalworking in the Bronze Age. By the end of the period remarkably elaborate items were being worked from sheet metal (**37**), items such as shields, buckets and cauldrons, some of the former being described as 'virtuoso pieces of craftsmanship in beaten bronze' (Cowie 1988, 31). Working sheet metal was not, of course, a novelty of the later phases of the Bronze Age – Early and Middle Bronze Age gold objects were for the most part created in this way.

Where are the smiths?

Whilst their products are relatively abundant, traces of the metalworkers themselves (**colour plate 6**) are scarce. For example, tools unequivocally connected with metalworking are difficult to identify – many potential pieces of a smith's equipment such as hammers could of course perform many other tasks.

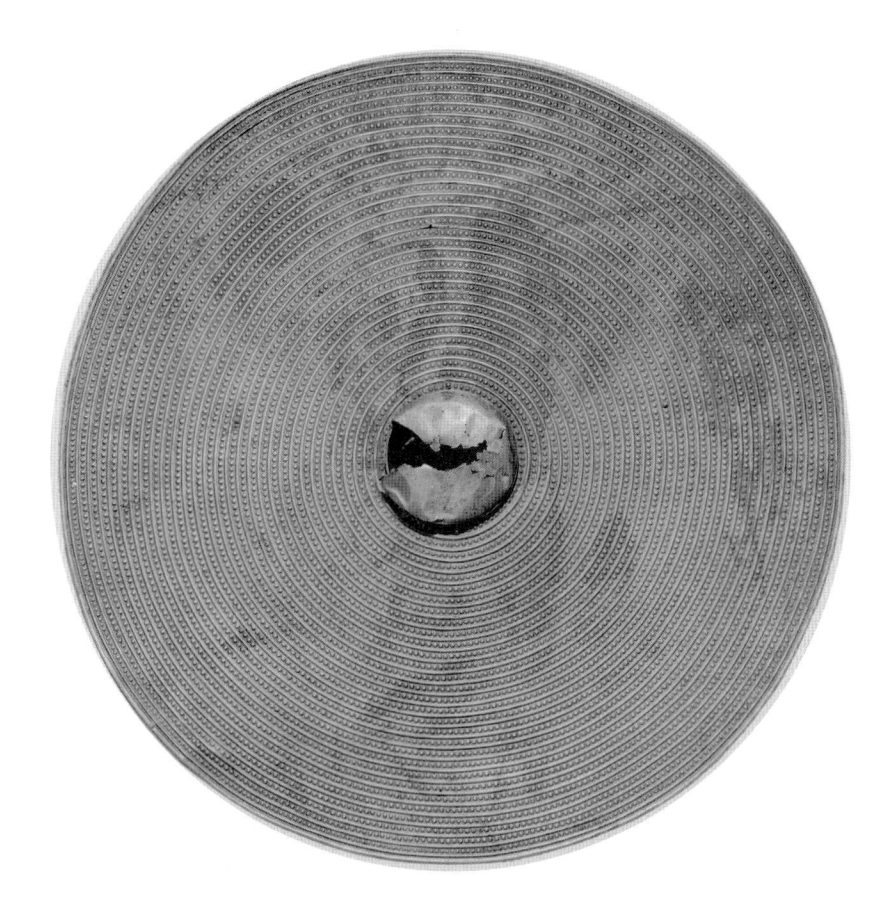

37 *The bronze shield from Yetholm, Roxburghshire, Scotland. Bronze shields 'virtuoso pieces of craftsmanship in beaten bronze' (Cowie 1988, 31) are quite remarkable objects in terms of their visual appearance and the amount of work involved in their creation, and even more remarkable when one considers the experimental work demonstrating their sheer uselessness in defending against other Bronze Age weaponry (Coles 1962). Wooden or leather shields, examples of which are known from Ireland, will have provided considerably more protection. Nonetheless, several bronze shields bear traces of damage suggesting that they may have seen action, although an alternative scenario was offered by the recent discovery of a bronze shield during excavations near South Cadbury Castle, Somerset (Coles et al. 1999). There, a shield had been placed face down within a silted up ditch, its central boss resting in the top of a stakehole. Then, a sharp object, probably a wooden stake, was driven through it with some force no less than three times before the shield was left.*

Shields also provide an excellent example of creative techniques that did not involve casting. To quote from Cowie (1988, 31-2) again, 'From an ingot, the smith would have hammered out a sheet of bronze to a thinness of about 0.35mm, a process involving periodic annealing to prevent the metal becoming brittle. After planishing — flattening the surface with a smooth-faced hammer — to remove any dents, and trimming of the sheet to size, the shield would have been ready for decoration and strengthening. This would probably have involved the use of a bed of heated pitch or possibly damp clay to provide the required yielding surface to carry out the repoussé work. Wooden or metal punches of suitable shape would be used to carry out the work of embossing the metal, and in so doing the shield would acquire additional strength. After the forming of the central boss and definition of the decoration, the work would be completed by turning in the outer edge and riveting on the folded sheet metal handle. Small tabs were added for the attachment of straps to allow the shield to be carried, worn over the shoulder or hung for display. When freshly polished, such shields would have gleamed impressively as the light was reflected off their surface contours — some of the Yetholm type shields having up to 30 ribs and 6,000 individual bosses'. © National Museums of Scotland

Definitely linked with the working of metal objects are the few bronze anvils to survive from Bronze Age Europe (Ehrenberg 1981a; Needham 1995), but most if not all represent highly specialised rather than general purpose tools. Typical here is the example found at Lichfield, Staffordshire, one of several items discovered by a metal detectorist in 1990-1. Though conforming broadly to what one might characterise as a stereotypical anvil form – a solid block with a wedge-shaped tang or spike projecting from its underside – at less than 4cm long and 5cm high, its potential uses were clearly limited. Indeed, minute gold particles found embedded in the surface suggest that it was uses 'at least in its later phases, for goldworking' (Needham 1995, 130). Likely products suggested by Needham included penannular bar bracelets.

Although anvils and hammers of bronze belong mostly to the later stages of the Bronze Age, the period when sheet bronze working was at its peak in terms of both quality and quantity, the diminutive nature of most known anvils suggests that they played no part in the production of such pieces. Instead, Ehrenberg (1981a, 140 suggested that 'they were used only for fine and decorative work, where a precision tool was needed to shape comparatively intricate pieces'. The larger pieces, and indeed most general metalworking tasks involving hammering, probably involved anvils or cushions of stone or perhaps wood.

As already noted, the places where metalworking occurred are equally scarce. The very few possible locations include Jarlshof, Shetland (**38-9**), a site that produced both metal and metalworking debris, but here as elsewhere there are problems. Mould debris, whether of stone, bronze or clay, resembles the products of those moulds in some important respects, chief among them being the means of discovery and the manner of deposition. Like bronzes, too many have been discovered by accident, by non-archaeologists, and effectively lack a context. Those that have been recovered during excavation seem not to have been deposited in a manner that suggests mere discard or disposal. The presence of bronze mould fragments in hoards has already been mentioned, but more pertinent here are cases such as Norton Fitzwarren, Somerset (Ellis 1989) and Springfield Lyons, Essex. In both cases, quantities of clay mould debris deriving from the casting of weapons were found in the course of excavation. At Norton Fitzwarren, the context appears to have been a large posthole adjacent to an entrance into a Late Bronze Age palisaded enclosure, the 70 fragments probably representing a single mould used to cast a Ewart Park-type sword. At Springfield Lyons (Buckley and Hedges 1987) the deposits occurred in the northern ditch terminals of the western and eastern entrances into the site. In both cases it is clear that the deposited material represents material selected for deposition rather than a wholesale dumping of general metalworking debris. At neither site was there any other indication that metalworking had actually occurred in the vicinity.

Most of the few excavated mould assemblages are characterised by the sort of features noted at Norton Fitzwarren and Springfield Lyons – deposition in a pit (which may of course help preserve the delicate fragments and skew the record somewhat) of some of the debris associated with very limited episodes of casting, perhaps just one or two objects. At several other sites, such as Dainton in Devon, Fimber in Yorkshire and Grimes Graves in Norfolk, the emphasis has again been on weaponry. Equally problematic is the distribution of identifiable mould fragments or pieces, which show a tendency to turn up on the fringes of, or outside, the main area of distribution of the objects they produced. Ewart Park sword moulds from the Scottish Islands, such as the Shetlands, are a case in point, while Needham (1981) has shown how moulds for 'Stogursey' or 'South Welsh' socketed axeheads come from farther afield than the axeheads they were used to make.

But what of the metalworkers themselves? The British Isles has yet to produce a grave containing a skeleton surrounded with the tools of the trade, although some examples are known from the continent. Of course, the changing burial traditions suggest that if such a find were made, it would belong to the Early Bronze Age. Some candidates have been claimed, but perhaps the best known is also the most recent: the so-called 'Amesbury Archer' (a.k.a. the 'King of Stonehenge' and, with a nod to his possible origins, 'Swiss Toni').

Excavated at Boscombe Down, near Amesbury in Wiltshire, by Wessex Archaeology in May 2002 (Fitzpatrick 2002, and www.wessexarch.co.uk), his grave proved to contain the largest quantity of artefacts yet recovered from a single burial of Bronze Age date in the British Isles. Among the most notable items accompanying the skeleton of a 35 to 45-year-old man were two gold 'basket earrings' (the inverted commas indicating debate about the precise function of these objects), three copper tanged knives (the metal sourced to possible locations in France and Spain), a 'cushion stone' possibly used in metal-working, no less than five Beaker vessels, numerous worked flints plus an antler flint-working tool, a nodule of iron from a 'strike-a-light', 16 flint barbed and tanged arrowheads that appear to represent a collection of arrows originally scattered over the legs of the body, and two stone wristguards. The wristguards plus the arrowheads prompted the early coining of the name 'Amesbury Archer', while suggestions of a date of *c.*2400-2200 BC, broadly contemporary with the earlier sarsen phases at Stonehenge, led to the press dubbing him the 'King of Stonehenge', the monument itself lying a few miles to the west.

More recently, however, oxygen isotope analysis has suggested a possible central European origin for the gentleman concerned. This, in conjunction with the date, the Beakers and the copper and early gold objects, has seen the emergence of a new narrative linking the 'Archer' with the earliest metalworking. Indeed, it is being suggested that the man's social status may have been to a considerable degree due to his ability to obtain and work metals at a time when few in the region would have possessed such skills.

There are other possibilities, of course – the presence of copper, gold and the cushion stone no more makes him a metalworker than the Beakers make him a potter, the tools and flints make him a flint knapper, or indeed the arrows and

38 *One of the near-circular courtyard houses at the Late Bronze Age/Early Iron Age settlement at Jarlshof. A succession of these houses were excavated, mainly in the 1930s. They appear to have been constructed sequentially, each replaced in turn by a new structure to the south, but they clearly overlapped in use. The principal dating evidence was the metalworking debris, the socketed axeheads, 'Ewart Park'-type swords and socketed gouges in particular highlighting the Late Bronze Age date of the phases with which they were associated, although they do not appear until a relatively late stage in the settlement's history (excluding, of course, the later Iron Age and Norse activity).* © Euan Mackie

39 *An aerial view of the site at Jarlshof, with all phases of activity visible. The site was partially exposed by violent storms at the end of the nineteenth century, and was briefly explored at the time. The main phase of exploration of the prehistoric settlement occurred over several seasons from 1931 under the leadership of A.O. Curle. Unfortunately, the manner in which those excavations were undertaken and published makes interpretation difficult, and probably contributed to the site's relatively low profile in the archaeological literature over the years. One wonders if it might have disappeared from view altogether were it not for the metalworking debris. The nature of occupation and the processes by which the debris found by Curle accumulated can perhaps be better understood following more recent excavations at the nearby and contemporary site at Sumburgh (Downes and Lamb 2000).* © Crown copyright. RCAHMS (John Dewar Collection)

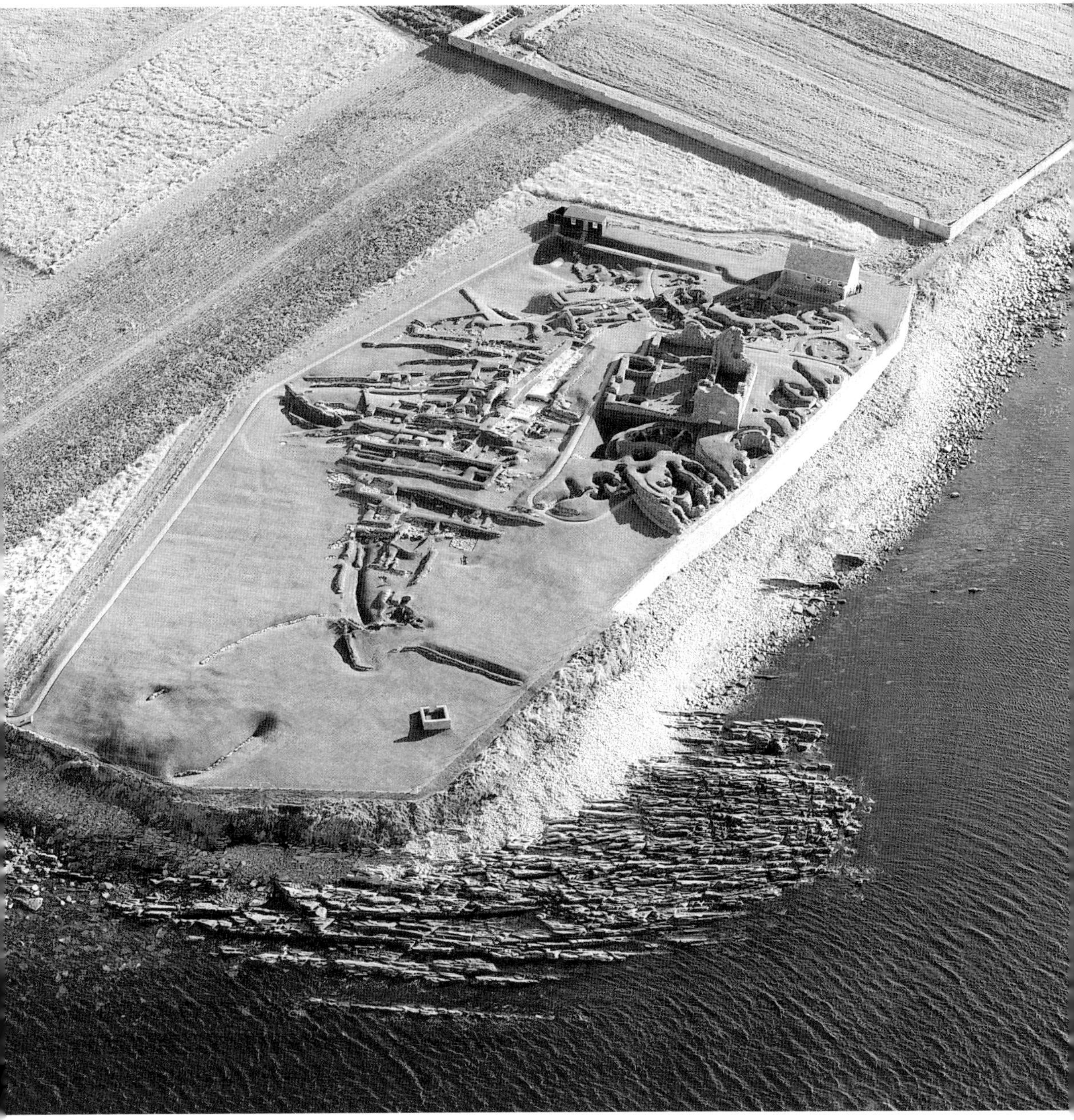

wristguards make him an archer. Clearly an important and perhaps powerful individual, the fact that he was accompanied in the grave by the accoutrements of hunting (and perhaps warfare), flint-working, metalworking, fire-making and fine pottery recalls the evidence from ethnographic case studies for the appropriation by the social elite of symbols of important crafts and activities for political and religious purposes (see p.132 for an example associated with iron-working). Perhaps his status resided not in hands-on involvement in the creation of copper and gold objects (or ceramic or stone ones) but in his ability to acquire and control their use, and a perceived association with the cultural and mythical values symbolised by these crafts and their products.

The ethnographic evidence shows metalworking to be very much a male-dominated activity. The African evidence in particular also shows it to be an activity replete with references to fertility and reproduction. Collett (1993, 502) offered the example of the Chishinga: 'The furnace . . . was regarded as the smelter's wife for the period of the work and to sleep with his human wife meant . . . adultery . . . to commit adultery whilst the wife is pregnant means . . . that the child will die, and so by analogy the furnace would not produce good iron'. There are numerous reported instances of, for example, the furnace being regarded as female, the bellows as male; terminology can be explicitly sexual, with the act of smelting (or casting) conceptualized as a procreative act. Consequently, many of the taboos relate to the non-participation of women, particularly those of child-bearing age, in the metalworking process. Of course, women had often been excluded explicitly from prehistoric metalworking on other grounds, Childe arguing that the 'casting of bronze is too difficult a process to be carried out by anyone in the intervals of growing or catching food or minding her babies. It is a specialist's job' (Childe 1936, 9).

Budd and Taylor (1995), in arguing for the need to consider more than just the technological processes when evaluating the significance of metalworking, did not just reject Childe's rather outdated assertions about women's capabilities: 'There is no a priori reason why, for example, entire family groups should not have been involved in ore gathering, or why metal casting could not have been the exclusive preserve of women (the logistics of child care can hardly have been beyond the organizational capabilities of a metal-using society' (*ibid.*, 138). However, although the ethnographic (and historical) records offer instances of female and child involvement in many stages of the metallurgical process, the direct participation of women at least in smelting or casting is indeed rare, and the reasons are predominantly cultural, as expressed through rules and taboos among other things, and can indeed reflect the commitment of mothers (and other female members of society) to other tasks including the care of children. This is not a feature exclusive to metalworking – Senior (2000, 71) noted that 'most crafts in most ethnographic cultures around the world are practised by a specific gender'.

Hurcombe (2000) has recently considered craft production from the perspective of cultural context, with specific reference to notions of time.

Among the crafts she considered from the ethnographic record was iron-working. As she noted, 'Virtually all craft processes can be divided up into common stages: collecting, preliminary processing, storage, preparation, primary product, storage, preparation and secondary product' (*ibid.*, 92). Involvement in any or all of these stages requires varying degrees of knowledge, experience and aptitude, none of which need have any gender restriction unless the particular cultural context requires it. The same applies, of course, to access to the resources essential for craft production. While any or all of these tasks may involve a considerable investment of time, iron-working in particular involved a commitment to large blocks of continuous time, particularly during the smelting phase. Hurcombe noted that overall, 'The comparison of craftwork outlined here has suggested differences in the construction of male and female associated crafts. It may have been more difficult, or simply not the best arrangement, for the biological sex responsible for children to conduct specialist craft activities which required extended blocks of continuous time' (*ibid.*, 106).

Variable and distinctive: the social status of the metalworker

The image of the itinerant smith is frequently encountered in the archaeological literature concerning the Bronze Age. Among earlier generations of prehistorians, Gordon Childe was a notable advocate on their behalf and was probably more responsible than anyone else in establishing them as a 'fact' of Bronze Age life. To Childe, this unique position accorded to the metalworker arose from the complexity of their craft and its wider implications: to grasp the fundamentals and potential of metallurgy 'demanded a power of inference and synthesis unusual in barbarians. The discoverers . . . may justly claim a place among the founders of science' (Childe 1930, 3). Consequently,

> the masters of these mysteries, the first smiths, were perhaps the first independent craftsmen. Any hunter or farmer could make a flint knife or arrow-head and grind out a stone axe-head in his spare time. His wife could stitch together robes out of skins, even spin and weave, and mould and fire clay pots. The art of the smith was so complicated that prolonged apprenticeship was required. His labour was so long and exacting that it could not be performed just in odd moments of leisure; it was essentially a full-time job. And the smith's products were so important to the community that those engaged directly in food production must provide for his primary needs in addition to their own. Among primitive peoples to-day the smith always does enjoy such a privileged position as might be expected (*ibid.*, 4-5).

Going beyond even the practical and economic importance of their wares, 'the possession of these secrets would easily gain credit for supernatural powers among barbarians to whom all stones looked much alike' (*ibid.*, 5). Subsequently, the itinerant metalworker, supported by customers eager for objects either to ease their daily toil or to allow an elite to retain their social position became firmly embedded in Bronze Age narratives. Their role, position and lifestyle became further elaborated over the years. Thus

> the life of the smiths and pedlars who manufactured and distributed these wares was doubtless hard and perilous. They were rewarded neither with great riches nor with a high rank in society [but] European metalworkers were free. They were not tied to any one patron or even to a single tribal society. They were producing for an intertribal, if not international, market . . . Their very itinerancy and far flung commercial contacts [would] fertilise native genius . . . Whoever had the perseverance to earn initiation into the appropriate mysteries of techniques . . . could escape the necessity of growing his own food and shake off the bonds of allegiance to an overlord or the more rigid fetters of tribal custom (Childe 1958, 169)

As Richard Bradley later noted in reference to the same passage, this was 'an endorsement of free enterprise . . . unexpected from a life-long Marxist' (Bradley 1990, 27). However, the mobile metalworker was for some time an important cog in the wheels of culture history. As Trigger (1980, 161-2) pointed out, an adherence to an *ex oriente lux* approach to the transmission of culture and innovation across Europe meant that *someone* had to be on the move, particularly as the complexities of metallurgy meant that many believed that it (and a number of subsequent technological advances) could have been invented only once. However, although they suited Childe's aim of presenting a European Bronze Age that was culturally and politically distinct from that of the Near East, despite a considerable dependence on the latter for innovation, the idea that wandering smiths adapted their productive output to suit local preferences is clearly an unsatisfactory explanation for the tremendous geographical and chronological variation evident in metal objects and metalworking technology across Western Europe. At times, of course, it would have required these metalworkers to adopt progressively simpler techniques as they travelled west and north. Moreover, by separating the smiths from the societies they were supplying, Childe also blurred somewhat the evidence for the various invasions and migrations, the progress of which was, of course, often charted with reference to the distribution of key metal artefact types. But beyond all this, the specialisation and separation demanded by Childe and his contemporaries is simply not required by the archaeological evidence (particularly for the British Isles), and neither does it receive much support from the ethnographic record. The productive output of Bronze Age metalworkers is unlikely, for example, to have required year-round dedicated employment any more than flint knapping, pottery making or basket weaving.

Rowlands (1971a) used the available ethnographic evidence – something Childe rarely did – to investigate the assumptions prehistorians were making about the organisation of metalworking and the status of smiths. The evidence he presented offered something of a contrast to established ideas: 'The proposition of the "detribalized" metalworker having few social ties, being able to travel to work where he pleases is the basis for the concept of the "itinerant smith" which in turn has played an essential role as an agent of diffusion . . . Significantly, however, the existence of a "free travelling", itinerant smith divorced from any social context is rarely found in ethnographic contexts' (Rowlands 1971a, 214). Instead, 'in the majority of ethnographic examples the smith is embedded in a particular social and cultural context, and, even if to some extent "itinerant", does not necessarily belong to a subgroup of distinct origin and cultural identity' (*ibid.*). Apart from questions of mobility and social ties, Rowlands also suggested that 'The status of smiths in ethnographic contexts ranges from fear, contempt and loathing to respect and awe' (*ibid.*, 216).

The shift in understanding offered by Rowlands' study seems to have been slow to filter through to the archaeological literature more generally, though by the end of the 1970s some aspects had been incorporated into general syntheses of the Bronze Age. Thus instead of the smiths being itinerant, 'at most they may have travelled around villages within a restricted locality, but would have had a base workshop in their home village, and a fixed position within their own community' (Burgess 1980, 274). For the most part, the smith was 'an otherwise ordinary farmer and member of the community' (*ibid.*, 275), though Burgess suggested that some more highly skilled metalworkers might be employed by chiefs primarily to concentrate on making more prestigious items, including weapons. Overall, Burgess (1980, 275) felt that

> the organisation of metalworking was probably complex. Looking overall at the distribution patterns, and mindful of the lack of evidence for major workshops and industrialization, a combination of operations seems likely. Village craftsmen, perhaps part-timers, would have concerned themselves with simple, functional items, especially tools and perhaps cheap trinkets, and with repairs; status craftsmen, more skilled, perhaps supplied weapons and prestige ornaments to those in authority; and itinerants, operating within the territory, would have met the demand for specialities and served those communities without their own metalworker.

Crucially, of course, much of this scenario was based around analyses of the geographical distribution of key types which, as we have seen, tended to rely on traditional explanations of deposition.

Howard (1981, 25ff), like Rowlands, observed a great deal of variability in the social positions and roles of smiths, whatever metal they worked with, but also noted that their status was 'always distinctive', a phrase that covers all manner of situations but something continually emphasized by other commentators. Muhammed (1993) for example quoted a mid-nineteenth-century source describing smiths in Darfur and other areas as 'a hereditary caste . . . dishonest and, living mostly confined to their own community, [who] did not mix with non-smith members of society. No ordinary non-smith would make marital links with them, and they were disliked by people in the region' (Muhammed 1993, 461). Radimilahy (1993) meanwhile described the situation in Madagascar and Indonesia, where 'ironworkers hold a privileged but ambiguous position . . . In Madagascar, ironworkers are considered to be close to the sovereign by virtue of the service they offer him. Even though their position is not economically advantageous, their influence is no less important. They were granted certain privileges' (Radimilahy 1993, 480-1).

In fact, links with the social elite take many forms among ethnographic accounts, and are not always so straightforward. Reid and MacLean (1995), for example, described the appropriation of symbols of iron and ironworking for political and religious purposes in the kingdom of Karagwe during the early to mid-nineteenth century. There, the symbolism represented by the smith and his craft was drawn on by the king in order to mediate between the natural and cultural worlds, and thus to maintain political and ideological control: 'At the ceremony of the New Moon, the king, hidden behind a screen and with a ritual anvil of copper and brass planted beside him would renew the fertility of the country: the success of the crops, the flow of milk, and the birth of calves' (Reid and MacLean 1995, 153).

However, in documenting the variety evident in the roles and status of metalworkers in sub-Saharan Africa, Herbert (1984; 1993) suggested that attempts to generalise are doomed to failure simply because so much variability exists:

> Feared, revered, despised . . . smiths have traditionally been viewed as a people set apart from the rest of mankind by the nature of their work and the common practice of endogamy, or at least marriage within prescribed groups . . . True, the smith occupies a clearly inferior position among [some] peoples . . . Often, too, the smiths are ethnically different or at least regarded as 'others' . . . In the agricultural or mixed-farming societies that predominate south of the desert, this inferiority is decidedly rare. On the contrary the smith plays a central and powerful role in both the natural and supernatural spheres. In fact, the distinction itself is false, since the roles are intimately connected and since such dualism is alien to African thought. The smith functions as priest, artist, shaman, magician, initiator precisely because his work demands not merely manual skills but esoteric knowledge to manipulate the dangerous forces at play in the extraction of ores and in their transformation into finished objects . . . (Herbert 1984, 23).

Consequently the frequent presence of smiths as important characters in mythology — including creation myths — is worthy of note rather than surprise (Herbert 1984, 33-4).

The manipulation of esoteric rather than purely 'scientific' knowledge is, then, arguably key to understanding the significance of the metalworker and, to a certain extent, of his products. Lahiri (1995) for example drew attention to the need to work with copper of high purity in India, especially when creating objects to be used in more overtly ritual contexts. Hosler (1994; 1995) meanwhile described the situation in pre-colonial and historic west Mexico, where the two properties of metal of greatest concern to metalworkers and the society they served were sound and colour which, according to Hosler, 'strikingly demonstrates the ways in which symbolic and ideological factors can shape technologies. Ancient metallurgy emphasised certain physical properties, sound and colour, which expressed fundamental religious beliefs, and . . . those beliefs were embedded in, and perpetuated through the technology and its products' (Hosler 1995, 113).

The ritualised aspects of metalworking and the cultural values represented are in most cases not as overt as these examples, where production is geared specifically towards sacred rather than profane ends. Generally, there is a more complex interplay between smelting or casting and the values and beliefs of the group to which the metalworker belongs. Again, this is particularly apparent in the ethnographic and historical studies of both iron and copper working in various parts of Africa (for example Herbert 1984; 1993; Childs 1991; Rowlands and Warnier 1993; Schmidt 1996; 1997). The manner in which metalworking was undertaken — the actions performed, the sequence of events, the materials used, the inclusion and exclusion of certain individuals — refers throughout to ideas about the cosmologies, or wider systems of belief shared by members of a particular social group, that helped to provide organising frameworks within which all social practices and relationships, including metalworking, could occur. At the same time, of course, adherence to particular ways of doing things also reaffirms those beliefs, including the sort of age and gender distinctions referred to earlier. In all stages of the metalworking process — mining, smelting, casting and so on — all associated activities would contribute to a successful outcome, not just those that we today might list beneath the heading 'technology'. This includes the performance of rituals; the burial of 'medicines' or other substances beneath the furnace; the observance of taboos and other restrictions, usually based on age and gender, which determined who could participate in the various stages of the process; even the timing and location of the smelting or casting operation. Adherence to such strictures, as well as contributing to a successful outcome, would help to reinforce the underlying beliefs as social norms.

Thus the apparently 'ritual' aspects of production should be seen as essential to the success of the whole procedure. Generally, for metalworking — as indeed for other crafts — no distinction is evident in the ethnographic record between technology and ritual (or 'magic'). Technology is, instead, firmly embedded within social contexts and within a broader conceptual framework that offers a means of understanding the world and structuring human behaviour, rather than comprising a series of logical, scientific procedures that exist independently of any cultural context.

Of importance in understanding the place of metalworkers and the significance of metalworking is, of course, beliefs about the nature of the raw material itself. The African ethnographic record suggests that smelters and smiths often saw themselves as participants in a natural process by which certain materials were transformed into something that could be adapted to culturally useful ends (Rowlands and Warnier 1993). The role of the smith was to facilitate this process, helping via the careful application of taboos, rituals and technological expertise to remove any likely impediments, and thus protect against perceived sources of danger both to the participants and to the outcome of the whole process. As Eliade (1978, 8) characterised it, miners and metalworkers 'collaborate in the work of Nature . . . In a word, man, with his various techniques, gradually takes the place of Time: his labours replace the work of Time.' This again serves to reiterate the point that 'technology must be understood in a cosmological context. [It] is embedded in belief systems about social relationships and the natural world' (Goucher and Herbert 1996, 55).

In skimming the surface of a vast subject, it has hopefully become clear that understanding prehistoric metalworking requires more than a grasp of the science and the technology – that the application of metalworking techniques requires a full consideration of its cultural context in order to appreciate its significance beyond the production of efficient tools and weapons, 'cheap trinkets' and the like. How much of the above reflects the reality of Bronze Age Britain is, of course, highly debatable, particularly as the course of nearly two millennia is likely to have seen some fundamental change in the status of metalworkers and their products, while the specifics of contemporary belief systems are largely beyond us. Nonetheless, the sparse archaeological evidence and the relatively abundant ethnographic literature allows a case to be made for prehistoric metalworkers being socially, if not politically, powerful individuals (probably male) whose abilities could nonetheless be appropriated for political ends. One presumes that the craft and those that carried it out were regarded with a degree of respect and perhaps awe by the general population, and the treatment of their products suggests that at least part of their value resided in the raw material and its metaphorical or mythical associations. These are issues which will be returned to in the final chapter, though. Now it is time to look at some of those products more closely.

5
WORLDLY GOODS

It is not the intention in this chapter to provide a detailed and descriptive catalogue of the full array of metal objects made during the Bronze Age in the British Isles. Time, space and readability require an alternative and more selective approach, focusing instead on particular types and key themes. Hopefully what follows, while far from comprehensive, will provide a reasonable impression of the sheer variety of copper and bronze artefacts to have survived the centuries, but is primarily intended to offer some idea of the many ways in which they could have been used and understood.

For many prehistoric artefacts, our assessment of their likely function is ultimately grounded in a visual appraisal of their form. Do they resemble anything in use today? Do they bear any similarity to anything known from the historical or ethnographic record? If no clear answer is forthcoming, then perhaps consideration of shape, size and key features might help, as may their archaeological context (if they have one, of course). Arriving at a satisfactory answer is seldom a straightforward process. A Bronze Age 'sword' looks fairly similar to swords of more recent vintage, once allowances are made for things like materials, casting technology, cultural choices and the manner of contemporary combat techniques and so on. In contrast, though, a socketed axehead is difficult to parallel with recent or modern axeheads and can perplex the uninitiated – and indeed did puzzle antiquarians – especially if incomplete when found.

The early stages in the identification and interpretation of artefacts are seldom apparent in more recent discussions, where identity and function are often taken for granted. Most basic assessments of form and function, and the consequent selection of names and labels, had taken place by the end of the nineteenth century. Little of the terminology used by John Evans (1881) for example, would be unfamiliar to the modern student of Bronze Age metalwork. Consequently, the element of guesswork and assumption involved is often overlooked, perhaps to the detriment of a fuller appreciation of the functional possibilities embodied within, say, an awl (see below), as a particular label once accepted can influence or even limit our perceptions of how a particular object, however straightforward it may seem, may have been used.

In some cases, of course, the applied terminology has proved to have little long-term significance. A good example here is the *palstave*, a name assigned to a particular and distinctive class of developed flanged axeheads widely used throughout the Middle and Late Bronze Age. The name itself derives from an Icelandic word for a bladed tool 'used to break the ice in winter, and to part the clods of earth, which, in Iceland, is dug and not ploughed' (Yates 1850, 74). The Icelandic icebreaker in fact bore little resemblance to the Bronze Age axehead, and today the latter is recognised as but one stage in the long-term development of the axehead, with scarcely a mention of clods being parted. The survival of the name palstave however serves as a reminder that even identifying these objects as possible axeheads in the first place was by no means a straightforward process for the antiquarians who first mused over them (see below).

Razors

In other cases, of course, the appropriateness of the accepted label seems more assured – dagger, for example, or bracelet. Alternatively, terms such as 'bugle-shaped object' offer clear testament to modern ignorance. However, as already implied, even the most plausible label remains just that, and it is essential not to apply too limited a definition. Here, the question of 'razors' is particularly relevant. Thin, sharp blades, occasionally highly ornamented (**colour plate 9**) are a well-known if relatively infrequent find from the Bronze Age, present at various times in hoards and in graves as well as turning up alone, either in excavations or devoid of context. Evans (1881, 217-21) did not discuss their potential uses, merely noting that a number of small tanged blades were regarded as being razors. The extent of the debate over their function was succinctly if unwittingly captured by C.M. Piggott in her discussion of the British examples: 'For many years it has been assumed that these bronze knives were used for shaving, since it was difficult to imagine what other purpose they could have served, and we can be reasonably certain that such was, in fact, their use' (C.M. Piggott 1949, 121). In fact, as has been noted more recently by David Coombs (in Pryor 2001), their interpretation as 'razors', i.e. as something whose 'primary function . . . is to remove facial hair and perhaps also cranial hair' (Kavanagh 1991, 78) is assumption, not proven fact.

To be fair, Piggott's paper was very much within a longstanding tradition of typological and chronological analysis which, in retrospect, tended to regard function and wider social significance as very much secondary concerns. Far greater emphasis was attached to arranging the known corpus into a satisfactory sequence of development, establishing a suitable pedigree via comparison with continental material, and then attempting to apply real calendar dates to the sequence. Prior to the advent of radiocarbon dating, of course, hurling oneself headlong into the typological minutiae of bronzes was essential to the construction and confirmation of chronological and cultural frameworks, the quest for continental parallels and ancestors often being the only means of attaching dates to a relative sequence of development.

However, contemporary ideas about the transmission of culture and innovation, and the tendency to view the Neolithic as being of little consequence to understanding the Bronze Age, could lead to a rather limiting and bronze-orientated view of society, as demonstrated by Piggott's suggestion that on balance, 'it can be reasonably argued that the fashion of shaving may have been introduced from the Continent via the western sea-routes at a time early in the first millennium BC . . . The custom of shaving had a much longer history in the Mediterranean countries, but in view of the evidence from the British Isles it is improbable that the habit spread as far north much before, I suggest, the eighth century BC' (C.M. Piggott 1949, 126). The possibility that sharp blades of flint, for example, might have been adequate for cutting facial (or other) hair was not considered.

The Bronze Age objects known to us today as razors would, of course, make perfectly plausible shaving tools. Indeed experimental work has demonstrated this:

> Modern experiments have shown that the blades with convex curve and the double-sided blades are better than a straight edge for shaping beards and trimming the neck and cheek. In an experiment using a copy of the Pollacorragune [Galway, Eire] razor . . . Conor MacHale, a student in the Depart of Archaeology, UCD, experimented to see how well it functioned. Using soap and water to ease the discomfort of dry-shaving, he found that quick short strokes were more effective than the longer, slower strokes used with a modern razor. He shaved cheeks, sideburns, moustache and chin hair. It was possible to remove stubble but he did not achieve as smooth a finish as with a modern razor. He found also that it was possible to remove hair from the scalp with the same blade . . . Other experiments have shown that it is easier if a few days' growth has accumulated and if the stubble is well soaked, preferably in hot water. The blade required frequent sharpening, which was done with sandpaper and leather (Kavanagh 1991, 85).

However, as fine sharp blades 'razors' may have had many other uses – both on the body (nails, hair, eyebrows, scarification, etc.) and on other materials, as personal craft-knives for instance. Going beyond mere function, there is of course the question of context and frequency of their use. Does their relative scarcity compared to, say, axeheads or swords mean that few men went cleanly shaven, or at least kept beards and moustaches trimmed? Or is that relative scarcity more to do with particular depositional practices – the appropriate means of disposal of an item so intimately connected with an individual? Or could it be argued that for most people, the functions for which these bronze blades were cast were in fact undertaken using objects of stone? If so, then were the bronze razors a more prestigious item, used by the select few? Or were they even used by the living at all? As Piggott herself noted, razors are numbered among the few classes of object to occur in funerary contexts in the Early and (mainly) Middle Bronze Age, prompting the suggestion that some, especially the more finely decorated examples, 'may have been made simply for the final ritual shaving of the corpse, and may not have been necessarily part of the owner's lifetime equipment' (Piggott 1949, 122), a suggestion re-iterated more recently by Jockenhovel (1980), who noted occasional finds of human hair with razors on the continent (*ibid.*, 246). He further suggested that the idea of ritual shaving of the corpse was supported by the presence of razors in some women's graves. John Barrett (1994, 110), referring to the inclusion of items such as razors and tweezers in Early Bronze Age graves, suggested that use either in the preparation of the corpse or by the mourners during the funerary process was a probable reason for the presence of these objects alongside the remains of the deceased.

A key site here is a barrow at Winterslow, Wiltshire 'excavated' in 1844 by the Reverend A.B. Hutchins, whose account is worth quoting at length:

> One foot and a half from the top of the barrow, towards the south, my labourers came to a strong arch-work composed of rude flints wedged together remarkably secure, without cement of any kind . . . Having carefully removed the flinty safeguard, I was highly pleased with the view of the largest sepulchral urn . . . the mouth of which was placed downwards and perfectly entire . . . With the assistance of my two men, the urn was removed, and immediately some linen, beautiful to the eye and perfect for a time, of a mahogany colour, presented itself to our view, and resembled a veil of the finest lace. I made an accurate drawing of the linen which originally contained the burnt bones, of a yellow hue; underneath there were blood-red amber-beads, of a conical form, with two holes at the base, a small pin of mixed metal, and among the bones some human hair, short, brittle, and of a bronze colour, four beautiful amber beads, and a small fluted lance-head of mixed metal. A small urn was placed beside the large one, on the same floor, surrounded by flint stones, but containing nothing besides bones (Hutchins 1845).

One can imagine the Reverend Hutchins dismay at the contents of the second urn, though his apparent disregard for the remains of a human being, in contrast to his clear delight at the relative material wealth of the first, is probably as typical of contemporary barrow diggers as it is disappointing in a man of the cloth.

The barrow itself received little attention for almost a century, the contents of the excavated grave meanwhile finding their way into Oxford's Ashmolean Museum. In 1938, Stevens and Stone published a short article attempting to identify the barrow on the ground, and providing some comment on its contents. Regarding the hair, they noted that as with some of the grave goods, it did not appear to have been burnt. Assuming it came from the deceased, 'it is not inconceivable that the hair was removed before burning and that it was placed in the urn with the unburnt amber beads and other objects later' (Stevens & Stone 1938, 177; fig. 1 in their paper features photographs of items from the burial, including the hair). A decade or so later, J.L. Stoves analysed the hair at the suggestion of Leslie Grinsell. Noting that most of the pieces were under half an inch long, he identified it as eyebrow hair. As there was clearly more than might be accounted for by one person's pair of eyebrows, he suggested that the quantity present in the grave 'precludes the deceased as the sole origin, an interesting result in view of the present day custom among certain Eastern peoples of shaving the eyebrows as a sign of mourning' (Stoves 1947). Following Stoves (1947), Barrett (1994, 123) interpreted this grave deposit as further evidence for the separation of the act of firing the corpse from the deposition of cremated remains, the latter representing the occasion for the performance of the 'final acts and obligations of the mourners'.

However, re-examination of samples of the hair by Dr Ann Priston from the Metropolitan Police, London's Forensic Science Laboratory suggested that the Winterslow hair did not come from eyebrows, but was almost certainly 'facial hair, shaved off' (Kavanagh 1991, 86). Priston had also examined the hair of Lindow Man (Priston 1986) and felt that the Winterslow hair was much finer than Lindow Man's facial hair. How many people are likely to have contributed is unclear. However, if any came from corpse, it still must have been removed prior to cremation. Otherwise one or more mourners must have shaved (or trimmed facial hair) as part of the rites of mourning or burial. The presumption must be, then, that the razor found in the grave was the one used to remove the hair. Interestingly, though, the form of this razor is highly unusual, Thurnam (1872, 451) noting that its peculiar form, and in particular the decoration – it was 'beautifully ornamented with parallel flutings down the centre' – was remarkably similar to the leaf of the ribwort. Can we then suggest that such blades might also have been used for the harvesting and preparation of particular herbs? Woodward (2000, 114) suggested something similar for other small bronze blades occasionally found in graves. Although the cultivation and use of hallucinogens and allied substances is very much a live topic for prehistory, a search through published literature and the less reliable internet has so far found no real evidence for any such properties for ribwort, though potential medicinal uses are wide ranging, from eczema to haemorrhoids.

Returning to the shaving hypothesis, Treherne (1995) has considered the wider implications of the presence and use of objects such as razors in funerary contexts. The use of things like razors, tweezers, awls and so on may have allowed mourners to dress the body in a particular way after death and prior to burial (or cremation). The image fixed in death will presumably have represented the idealised appearance of the individual in life and, indeed, as Treherne noted, 'from the mid-second millennium in much of Europe there was an explosion in metal ornaments designed to accentuate every part of the body and its movement . . .' (ibid., 110). The human body itself provides a rich medium for display and differentiation, not just in life but also in death, and not marked purely by the presence of particular objects in the grave around the remains of the deceased but also by the use of some of these objects to dress the corpse.

The fact that some razors bear clear evidence for use and resharpening suggests that such items were used by the living as well as for the dead, and if we accept the likelihood of a shaving/hair-cutting function then clearly questions need to be asked about the context and frequency of use. Kavanagh (1991, 86-7) for example suggests that shaving was unlikely to have been something undertaken daily. She also argued that rather than shave oneself, it was likely that a second person was employed to carry out the task. In an age without mirrors or other reflective surfaces apart from water, this is clearly a plausible suggestion, but need not rule out the idea of someone shaving himself or cutting their own hair. Indeed Kavanagh went further, suggesting that the people buried with the razors (in Ireland at least) may have used them in life to perform particular services for the community, primarily in the context of ritual or funerary practices.

Items such as razors can also perform an invaluable service for the archaeologist as well. While much of the various chronological schemes constructed for metalwork over the years depended primarily on axeheads, razors were of crucial importance in revising the British Bronze Age chronology during the late 1950s and early 1960s, when it was realised that the clear association of some with both Deverel-Rimbury pottery (until then considered Late Bronze Age) in graves, and Middle Bronze Age metalwork hoards, led to the backdating of the principal pottery style for the Late Bronze Age in southern Britain and all its associations, briefly opening up a gulf between the end of the Middle Bronze Age and the start of the Iron Age, a gulf occupied for a while solely by metalwork.

Display and ornamentation

The various reasons offered to account for both the functions of razors and their presence in some graves serves to underline the difficulties involved in understanding the significance of grave goods. The case of the 'Amesbury Archer' has already been noted, for example, while Stuart Piggott's (1938) *Wessex Culture* is an excellent example of a tendency to interpret grave goods in terms of material wealth and social power. As Alison Sheridan (2003, 18) recently reminded us, 'We have . . . become used to thinking of prehistoric jewellery and accessories in terms of what they tell us about status. The wealthier the grave, and the more exotic, rare and well-crafted the possessions, the more powerful the individual is said to have been. It has become almost a commonplace of archaeological thinking'.

Prehistoric reality is unlikely to have been so straightforward, and as Sheridan reminds us, the significance of grave goods is unlikely to rest in modern notions of material value. Among the examples she offers are beads and buttons of jet and amber. Clearly an element of the 'exotic' will have played a part in establishing the status of such objects among the people who used them, but these are also materials with other properties: 'Jet and amber . . . are known to have been attributed magical powers in more recent times – mainly, it is thought, because of their

40 *A pair of copper neck-rings or 'diadems' found in the parish of Lumphanan, Aberdeenshire before 1832. The larger of the two has a maximum diameter of 172mm. Circumstances of discovery are unknown, but a similar item from Yarnton, Oxfordshire found prior to 1875 was close to the head of a probable crouched inhumation. The fact that they are pure copper might place them amongst the earliest phase of metalworking in the British Isles. However, it could be that unalloyed copper was reserved for the finer, ceremonial items for a while after tin bronze was introduced.* © National Museums of Scotland

electrostatic properties. Rub them, and they develop a static charge. Jet and amber were used for amulets by the Romans and Vikings, and were widely employed in the Middle Ages and down to the recent past for healing, divination or for turning away evil spirits' (Sheridan 2003, 18).

Rather than dwelling on status, with the implications that the term carries for social hierarchies and power relations, it might be more fruitful to consider possession of particular objects, in life or in death, as indicators of identity – the social categories to which an individual might belong. As noted above for razors, and below for spearheads, identity can to a considerable extent be represented by one's appearance, including the sort of objects one possesses, whether for use or display. Age and gender are just the two most obvious criteria for determining one's social affiliations, and consequently the material culture one might be expected to use either in everyday life or on special ceremonial occasions. Indeed, it may be that a greater emphasis on the 'ornaments' might offer a broader insight into the sort of social categories recognised by the users rather than the prehistorians, shifting the emphasis away from items associated with notions of power and status. From a purely functional perspective, many bronze ornaments (**40**; **colour plate 7**) were undoubtedly intended to be worn, but whether they were everyday wear or special occasions only is often unclear. Those in graves might have been special possessions of the deceased, or alternatively provided by the mourners to emphasize or idealise some aspect of the deceased's identity. Some ornaments seem likely to have caused discomfort if worn for too long, or at all. Pins, including some quoit-headed examples (appearing not unlike metal badminton rackets), can easily be 20cm or more in length, and while they may have held clothing firmly in case are unlikely to have permitted rapid movement in the living.

Indeed, among the graves, hoards and unassociated material throughout the Bronze Age is a remarkable array of bronze material hidden beneath the term 'ornaments'. Some distinctive types have attracted particular attention, but the majority have seldom been the focus of discussion, the context (if any) of their discovery offering little clue as to the likely use they may have been put to. Thus the numerous annular and penannular bronzes contained within the hoard from Marden, Kent, may include finger-rings, bracelets, anklets, armlets, items to be sewn into clothing or linked together by some other means. They may have been a collection drawn from the everyday wear of numerous individuals or part of the ceremonial gear of just one person. They may not even have been intended for human use at all, perhaps part of the finery associated with a horse. Whatever, in every case it is worth recalling the resources likely to have been put into the processes of manufacture and acquisition.

Awls

Along with knives and daggers, awls (**41**) feature as one of the most common metal items in Early Bronze Age graves, and again underline the extent to which the provision of grave goods cannot be regarded in too simplistic a manner. The case of awls is particularly intriguing. Fleming (1971, 160-1) saw their inclusion in graves as supporting evidence for pastoralism in Early Bronze Age Wessex: 'It is impossible to devise a true test of significance in this situation, but it is tempting to recall the traditional ascription of the awl to the leather-working industry. If the people . . . were mainly pastoralists, they might be expected to display more evidence of leather-working than mixed farmers would.' Certainly leather-working represents a plausible use for such tools, but the idea that leather was more likely to be worked by pastoralists represents a rather simplistic picture of Early Bronze Age society, crafts and exchange. Furthermore, leather-working is clearly far from being the only possible function for awls. Clarke *et al.* (1985, 86) for example noted their potential use for the manufacture of gold and jet items, suggesting their use was 'perhaps restricted to the production of prestige objects'. The association of awls with craft activities is undeniable, though what their presence in graves tells us about the people with whom they were buried is less clear-cut. Evidence for or

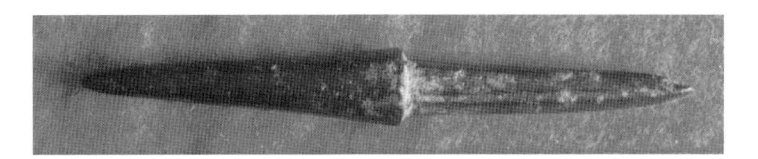

41 *An awl, one of many forms used throughout the Bronze Age. This example is from Rochester, Kent, and was reported via the Portable Antiquities Scheme*

against pastoralism is best sought in other aspects of an admittedly sparse archaeological record (for the Early Bronze Age at least), while suggestions as to whether, say, leather-working was less important than gold-working are open to debate, and depends very much on the social context of production.

Spector (1991) has shown how awls used in nineteenth-century Minnesota could be viewed as 'important material symbols of women's skills and values' (*ibid.*, 395), using ethnographic data to show how particular tools could be closely associated with the accomplishments and achievements of their owners, while at the same time the tasks for which particular awls were used may have been equally closely associated with key events in the lives of women. In this respect their significance may be viewed on a par with, say, the weaponry of a warrior. Of course, awls need not have been female-only tools in the Bronze Age. However, that their significance extended beyond simple utilitarian needs is also suggested by deposition patterns from the Middle and Late Bronze Age, with a general absence from the (often tool-dominated) hoards contrasting with their relative frequency from domestic contexts (Needham 1986). Particularly noteworthy during these later phases of the Bronze Age is the recovery of no less than 18 from Flag Fen (Coombs in Pryor 2001, 287-8, 297, and fig. 10.19), Coombs suggesting that their deposition there was linked to important stages in the lives of 'craftsmen' such as the completion of apprenticeship or training, or death.

Weaponry and warfare

> Among primitive people weapons took a far higher place than mere domestic implements, for a man's life at any moment might depend upon the qualities of his weapons, and the keenest intellects of many generations were bent on their improvement. Every little detail has a meaning, and weapons may teach us more of those who made and used them than any other article that has come down to us (Brewis 1912, 1).

The existence of conflict and combat in later prehistory has seldom been doubted – debate has mainly centred around the manner and frequency. As we have seen, troubled times were often invoked to explain the presence of bronze (and other) hoards, and few of the incursions of people from the European mainland were considered peaceful. In any case, the enormous quantities of weaponry – sword, spearheads, rapiers and daggers – had to have been used for something.

However, what we classify today as weaponry need not have been used, nor even made, with violence in mind. As Sue Bridgford (1997, 95) noted, 'A sword may simultaneously be, or have the potential to be, a beautiful object, an efficient killing tool, a symbol of power and wealth, an implied or actual threat, a sacrifice, a gift, a reward, a pledge of loyalty and/or an embodiment of the idea of complex'.

The broader social significance of material culture, rather than a narrower focus on practical function, has been a subject of keen debate in recent years. The original creators and users of the objects we study will not have viewed them solely as inert products of technology and labour with primarily utilitarian and economic value, but will have been seen to reflect and participate in social relationships. Phrases such as 'the social life of things' (Appadurai 1986) and references to 'artefacts with personalities' (Thomas 1996) neatly encapsulate the idea that objects may have identities or possess cultural values reflecting aspects of their origin, history of ownership and use. Different aspects of those identities may come to the fore in different social contexts. At the same time, the historical and ethnographic record serves to remind us that materials may be physically and culturally manipulated in many different ways, frequently ways that are totally alien to our own experiences.

A good example here comes from the work of Roy Larick (1985; 1986; 1991), who has studied the use of spears among groups of Maa-speaking pastoralists in East Africa. Among these groups, the seemingly ever-changing form of spears helps males to move through a sequence of age grades, where graduation to each new grade alters one's status and social networks. The form of an individual's spears communicates his economic, physical and social status to whomever he meets – his age and social position determine the range of spears he may possess. The males pass through age grades at regular intervals and spear styles identify then as members of a specific cohort and grade. Interestingly, it is the warriors who are responsible for innovation in spearhead form and style, bringing in new formal elements or innovations as each new generation consciously seeks to distinguish itself from the preceding one, something that can also involve the modification of jewellery, clothing and song.

Working with metal rather than stone offered the potential for a greater morphological variety among tools and weapons in particular, and for the latter would have clear implications for the manner of use and thus the nature of combat as well as display. One of the earliest possible weapons to be cast in copper was the halberd, a blade that visually can seem little different from some dagger forms. The distinguishing characteristics include a slight asymmetry or gentle curvature of the blade, and a seeming misalignment of rivet holes suggesting a handle or haft at right angles to the blade, unlike daggers. Some supporting evidence also comes from continental rock art which features occasional images of halberd-like weapons being wielded on the end of rather long poles. Such hafting arrangements would underline their unsuitability as a weapon but support ideas of a more prestige-based display role, particularly in the earliest phase of metalworking when form, material and colour would all have been new.

As Coombs (1975) noted, they would have been a somewhat clumsy weapon. Not ruling out a functional use, he saw them more as an indicator of rank or social class. Of course, they could have symbolised much more, including the ability to possess and work metal, and to harness its potential. Given the Late Neolithic background of the first metal use, one can visualise their use in processions and ceremonies associated with the major henge monuments, for example. None the less, the possibility remains that some saw more purposeful action, presumably with a rather shorter haft that those rock art images imply. Some continental examples feature damage along their inner edge which might be consistent with more violent usage (Schuhmacher 2002, 280).

Discussion of halberds is further hindered by problems of classification and the manner of their deposition. For the former, it has been noted that 'Halberds present a problem of classification which still has to be resolved at the international scale. Most British finds have an insular character, but nevertheless with close relatives in neighbouring lands' (Rohl and Needham 1998, 86). The origin and chronology of the halberd in Europe has recently been considered by Schuhmacher (2002), who approached the problem of classification thus: 'Although we can distinguish several variants, most of them resemble each other so much that an independent evolution in each region is scarcely credible' (*ibid.*, 263). Given Schuhmacher's regional scope – from Iberia to Central Europe, and from Ireland to North Africa, this is some claim, and one that is almost certainly far too simplistic. Understanding halberds is not helped by depositional behaviour either – rare in graves (unlike daggers, which they closely resemble), they are more common in hoards, but those hoards tend to contain only other halberds. Moreover, halberd hoards are hardly widespread in the British Isles, with a tendency to occur in the Highland Zone, despite the wider occurrence of halberds generally.

Schuhmacher's review of the European evidence suggests that the earliest dated occurrence of metal halberds is in Ireland and Great Britain, though this is not quite the same as saying that the halberd was invented in these islands – there is no guarantee that the earliest elsewhere were considered appropriate for deposition, while as much work remains to be done on continental chronologies as on that for Britain and Ireland. Consequently, Schuhmacher's suggestion that 'The "idea of the halberd" began to be diffused from Ireland and Great Britain. From the outset, however, it was not only an idea that was transmitted, but also the design' (Schuhmacher 2002, 282) requires further investigation.

Like halberds, the earliest metal daggers offer problems of classification too, as Needham (1999, 187) noted while discussing Early Bronze Age metalwork from the Barrow Hills, Radley area. Of six implements being considered, he argued that only one could be formally classed as a dagger, with the remainder termed 'knives' or 'knife-daggers' apart from one which might 'alternatively be attributed to the forms known as razors and razor knives' (*ibid*.). As he explained, 'These terms tend to be applied rather loosely and are not yet defined to be mutually exclusive of one another. This does, however, have the virtue of emphasising our ability to judge whether shape, size or some other attributes would have been considered most important in the classification recognised by the people using the articles' (*ibid*.). Indeed, Needham suggested that the size variation evident among the earliest, tanged, daggers 'had more to do with raw material availability than with considerations of social status, whereas at a later stage there is a sense of a legitimate and meaningful distinction between larger implements (daggers) and smaller ones (knives etc.), a distinction that could have evolved to meet both utilitarian and symbolic needs (for example gender differentiation)' (*ibid*.). Morphological overlap, as far as daggers are concerned, was not only restricted to the earliest phases of the Bronze Age. At the end of the Early Bronze Age, the first items recognisable as spearheads also bore a remarkable resemblance to contemporary dagger forms (**colour plate 8**).

The dagger (**42**) has commonly been seen as a weapon, with its primary roles comprising combat or display, perhaps both. Certainly as a form of weapon not readily identifiable among earlier lithic implements, it could be argued that the change of raw material to the more malleable copper and its alloys prompted changes in the nature of conflict. Indeed, some have gone further, viewing the more efficient weaponry of the Early Bronze Age, and by implications bronze itself, as a key step towards a society in which personal wealth and power were of greater import than before:

> The beginnings of patriarchal society started right here with the discovery of metal. For this was the very first moment when great physical power alone could guarantee a person's place in the community – and that person was almost certain to have always been male. But, most importantly, the arrival of metals meant a severe shift in the possibilities of what violence could achieve. Whereas in the Neolithic period a successful stabbing would have been a considerable achievement, with the coming of bronze weapons bodies could be ripped asunder, limbs hacked off and enemies decapitated. Casualties in these new inter-tribal squabbles were suddenly more brutalised than ever before and there were far more deaths than Neolithic tribes had previously witnessed (Cope 1998, 125).

The dagger is clearly best suited to fighting at close quarters. In contrast, throughout the Neolithic most evidence for conflict and warfare in the British Isles focuses on occurrences of arrowheads, for example at the Early Neolithic causewayed enclosures of Crickley Hill, Gloucestershire and Carn Brea, Cornwall.

WORLDLY GOODS

*42 Malmains Farm hoard (see also **9** and **31**): although the term 'dagger' may seem perfectly appropriate, the arcane practices of Bronze Age metalwork typologists would normally see this object termed a 'dirk'. The term is used to describe short, slender, double-edged weapons presumed to be best suited to stabbing. The distinction between these and the 'rapiers' is arbitrary – beyond a certain length, the weapon is better suited to thrusting rather than stabbing, but the 'certain length' at which the dividing line is drawn does not necessary represent any such functional distinction. In the Middle Bronze Age, dirks (and related objects such as daggers and rapiers) generally occur as single, unassociated finds. Occurrence in a hoard is rare. Chronology and sequential development of dirks are among the least satisfactory of established Bronze Age typologies, and are generally unencumbered by independent dating evidence. Maximum length of the Malmains Farm 'dirk' is 142mm*

The arrowhead was not, curiously enough, replicated in bronze in the British Isles, or indeed in continental Europe, the numbers known being tiny. Instead, the Early Bronze Age saw the widespread adoption (at least in graves) of the barbed and tanged arrowhead, often of flint, and in many cases representing some of the finest quality examples of the knapper's art from prehistory. Quite why this should be the case is unclear, from a technological viewpoint. A metal equivalent of contemporary lithic arrowhead types was clearly within the capabilities of the Early Bronze Age metalworker, so presumably we need to look for a cultural explanation, both for the prominent position of stone arrowheads in the Early Bronze Age, and for the few bronze examples that do exist. Intriguingly, one of the handful of bronze barbed and tanged arrowheads known from Britain, that contained within the Middle Bronze Age hoard from Penard, Wales, was sampled during the recent programme of lead isotope analysis of British bronzes (Rohl and Needham 1998). It proved to be anomalous in a number of respects (in addition, of course, to its very presence in British hoard), comprising no less than 40 per cent lead. That lead itself was 'unlikely to be from Britain, it matches well some galenas in western central Europe (Vosges, Hess, Erzgebirge). The arrowhead has evidently flown far' (*ibid.*, 100).

But to return to the blades, since the late nineteenth century it has been seen as the start of a process that led almost inevitably to the sword, the dirks and rapiers of the Middle Bronze Age essentially being viewed as extended daggers, before the advent by the Late Bronze Age of the sword, a far more effective fighting tool and one which probably represented further changes in the nature of combat. Much has also been made of the appearance, particularly during the Late Bronze Age, of more enclosed settlements, enclosure being regarded, in part at least, as a protective or defensive method. In fact, as the discussion earlier of South Lodge showed, enclosure might take many forms, and be undertaken for a variety of reasons.

The inevitability of this progression from short to long blade can easily be overstated, particularly when one considers functional requirements and other cultural factors in addition to technological capabilities, though often there is something of a chicken and egg situation. The appearance of the leaf-shaped sword in the Late Bronze Age (principally the Wilburton and Ewart Park types in the British Isles) has often been associated with the more widespread use of the horse, coming as it does around the same time that assorted paraphernalia associated with horse riding (harness and other equipment of bronze, bone and other materials) became relatively plentiful in the archaeological record. Moreover, the leaf shape, with a notable broadening of the blade nearer the point than the hilt, would render such weapons suitable for use on horseback, allowing it to be brandished in a slashing motion rather than the thrusting motion best suited to the earlier rapiers or daggers. However, analysis of edge damage suggests that some rapiers at least were likely to have been used 'in an unsuitable slashing motion, which is a more natural movement, is indicated by the tears found on the rivet holes on the handles of many such weapons' (Osgood *et al.* 2000, 23).

All three – dagger, rapier, sword – will clearly have had as much potential as items for display as they did as weapons. However, the display potential of bronze weaponry is most evident among another category of object – the shield. Numerous examples are known from the British Isles and beyond, though they occur in far lesser quantities than the weapons. Experimental work in the 1960s demonstrated clearly that bronze shields were wholly unsuited to performing a defensive role against attack by a sword, for example. Wooden or leather examples offered much greater protection. While some bronze shields might have been backed with wood or leather, the intricate detail and highly skilled and time-consuming process of manufacture only goes to underline further the probability that bronze shields were to be seen rather than wielded in anger.

To a considerable extent, terms such as dagger, dirk and rapier represent labels applied in a fairly arbitrary manner. Size rather than morphology determines the barriers between each of these three categories, but there is no clear evidence that any real break exists in the size distributions to justify this tripartite division. Of course, the longest rapiers and the shortest daggers can clearly be distinguished formally and visually from the intermediate 'dirks', but as one approaches the middle of the range, the subjectivity of this classification process becomes only too apparent. Moreover, it is important to remember that Bronze Age 'dirks' and 'rapiers' bear little relation to weapons known by these names in more recent times.

Indeed, at the lowest end of the size distribution, the limitations of the notion 'dagger = weapon' also become clear. The surviving knife-dagger (another has been lost) from the Manton Barrow (Preshute G.1, Wiltshire: Annable and Simpson 1964, 47) is barely 5cm long, which would if intended as a weapon confirm the close nature of combat in the Early Bronze Age. However, such items are equally likely, if not more so, to have been personal possessions perhaps signifying affiliation to a particular social group, perhaps based on age or gender as much as social rank. As functional items, such hilted blades would have been suitable for any number of tasks, ranging from the cutting of skins to umbilical cords. The Manton Grave contained numerous items of bronze, gold, amber, shale, stone and pottery accompanied by a crouched adult inhumation. The skeleton was identified at the time of excavation as an elderly female, although the bone report, by Beddoe (in Cunnington 1907a, 1907b) doesn't inspire confidence. The bones were re-interred after the excavation, so confirmation is not possible.

Analysis of edge-wear (and other forms of damage) on weapons from all stages of the Bronze Age demonstrates that many were used, and probably in an offensive or defensive manner. Nicks and tears on sword blades suggest metal-on-metal contact, for example. However, human remains bearing unambiguous evidence of wounds caused by daggers, rapiers or swords are absent from the archaeological record. Moreover, some such weapons bear clear evidence of other forms of use. Some, for various reasons, were never used – as weapons, that is – at all. Many of the damaged, broken or fragmentary swords available to us today were clearly already in an imperfect state when deposited, and there is good evidence that the damage or breakage may have been an integral part of the deposition process. This has on occasion been referred to as 'ritual killing' of the object, rendering it useless (in this world at least), though there are other, sometimes related possibilities (see below).

Some of the swords and spears found at Flag Fen were analysed by Sue Bridgford, who has also examined large numbers of similar weapons from elsewhere in Britain and Ireland. Bridgford has contrasted the prolonged and highly skilled process of producing swords in the Bronze Age with the treatment meted out to some at the end of their lives:

> A sword not only epitomised the threat of organised violence but also symbolised the power acquired by those prepared to use it . . . The deposition of swords, often deliberately broken, in what were clearly ritual contexts . . . speaks volumes for the importance which warfare had assumed within the culture of the period and how weapons were used to symbolise the attitudes of society towards it . . . In addition to their practical and symbolic importance swords represented a substantial investment of time and expertise on the part of the swordmaker. Their long, thin blades are difficult to make moulds for and are not easy to cast without flaws . . . which would render them useless as a practical weapon. Moreover, the amount of work involved in producing a fine finished surface and sharp even edges without access to modern power tools is far from negligible. If there were any specialist bronze workers at all during the Late Bronze Age then sword makers must be the most likely candidates. (Bridgford 1998, 206-7)

However, despite the evident pride and care, as well as labour and materials, lavished on creating an object that must have enhanced the social status of whoever was to own or use it, 'A number of swords have evidently been subjected to elaborate rituals of destruction, including burning, which are not consistent with the performance of the simple preliminaries to recycling' (*ibid.*, 216).

As we shall see, the deposition of swords in water during the Late Bronze Age is something that has been linked with the otherwise invisible funerary rites of the period. Cremation is presumed to have been the norm for the Late Bronze Age, though disposal of the dead in bodies of water has also been suggested. At Flag Fen, Bridgford suggested that 'It is . . . possible that in some at least of the weapons the organic parts were removed by burning, perhaps during some form of cremation rite. On the other hand, none of the weapons bears the incontrovertible signs of exposure to the higher range of temperatures that can occur in pyres (*c.*900°C . . .) exhibited by certain other weapons. The lower temperatures at the edge of a pyre, however, or the protection afforded by the pelvis and trunk of a body . . . could result in the burning of organic material without noticeable damage to the metal' (Bridgford, in Pryor 2001, 310). In addition to evidence for burning, 'Some items, such as certain swords, were faulty and could never have been used . . . Some of the swords . . . had broken along casting flaws . . . which indicates that their previous use life had been neither stressful or prolonged . . . Bridgford has convincingly shown that some of the cutting edges of the leaf-shaped swords showed signs of damage. This appears to have been caused by deliberate bashing against something hard, rather than by battle damage or wear during regular ceremonial use' (Pryor 2001, 427).

One of the best examples of non-use concerns a discovery made at Oxborough (**colour plate 11**; compare with **43**) in Norfolk in 1988, described succinctly by Stuart Needham as 'a stunning ceremonial dirk of Plougrescant-Ommerschans type' (Needham 1990c, 239). The finder, a Mr Allen of Stoke Ferry, really did stumble across it, actually stubbing his toe on the butt end which was projecting from the soil. The dirk was vertical, point downwards in the peaty soil. At 71cm long (*c.*28in) and weighing nearly 2.4kg, it is a fairly hefty weapon and, as the photograph shows, an impressive looking one. In addition, it can never have been used as a weapon. Despite clearly being brought to a 'finished' condition after casting, the edges were left blunt, the highly regular finish suggesting that the final form of the blade edges was the intention of whoever made it. Furthermore, the finely finished butt bears no traces whatsoever of any hilt, nor are there any rivet holes with which to attach one. This (along with other British and Continental examples of the type) was not a 'blank' intended for finishing at some later date. It is the completed article. As Needham noted, conversion to a functioning weapon 'was out of the question . . . except by melting down and recasting' (*ibid.*, 247). In other words, the Oxborough Dirk, and others like it, was probably made with the full knowledge that it never would function as a weapon. Similar points have been made about dirks and rapiers more generally: 'in view of the inordinate size and extreme length, narrowness and fragility of many blades, and very often

43 Not all weaponry, ceremonial or otherwise, is as spectacular as the Oxborough dirk. Equally, it is not always apparent what a given piece of metal actually represents, something that should present a challenge now that finds such as this may, in certain circumstances, constitute 'treasure'. The item pictured here is another reported through the Portable Antiquities Scheme, and has been identified as a fragment of a rapier blade. It was found at Lakenheath, Suffolk. © Suffolk County Council

the weakness of the hafting arrangements, it is generally agreed that many dirks and rapiers may only ever have been intended for use as prestige or ceremonial items rather than employed in actual combat' (O'Connor and Cowie 1995, 347). A similar scenario appears to have existed for some broadly contemporary (later Middle Bronze Age) spearheads, some so long that they could never have functioned satisfactorily as weapons. Needham noted in particular the basal-looped spearhead from Wandle Park, Croydon, which probably around 80cm long, excluding any wooden shaft.

Similar claims have been made for the barbed spearheads of the Late Bronze Age, some of which are among the more unpleasant items the bronze specialist is likely to handle. The possibility of a ceremonial use stems from difficulties in identifying a sensible practical function. Despite bearing a formal resemblance to other types of spearhead, there are one or two important differences, the most notable being the barb at the base of the blade. This implies a purpose different from other spearheads, but what? Fishing was a possibility that had been raised by the later nineteenth century, stemming at least in part from the boggy or riverine provenance of some finds and a passing resemblance to harpoon points. However, Sir John Evans (1881) disagreed, arguing that 'such weapons are too clumsy to have been used for the capture of fish of any ordinary size, and would have made sad havoc even of a forty pound salmon' (*ibid.*, . . .). He preferred to see them as having been intended for 'attacking large four-footed game, either by thrusting or darting . . .' (*ibid.*).

Subsequently, they have been considered ill-suited even for that role. Reasons centre around the perceived unsuitability of their shape for a weapon of penetration, particularly in view of the distance between point and barb, and their body width; the thinness of some castings; and the shortness of some of the sockets relative to total body length. These and other apparent shortcomings meant that by the 1970s attention had shifted from practical use towards ceremonial display: 'To suggest a practical use for a spearhead with broad, parallel sides; wide, blunt point; large barb; short socket and projecting pins is . . . difficult. They seem to have no particular advantages in hunting or fishing; in fact they have serious disadvantages for both of these pursuits. In view of this, one cannot overlook their possible uses as ceremonial and decorative weapons like the bronze shields of this period' (Burgess *et al.* 1972). None the less, unlike the Oxborough dirk, barbed spearheads generally feature sharpened blades and tips, and some display edge (and other) damage suggesting that they weren't just looked at. Moreover, rejection of a practical function does seem to revolve around assumptions about what a spearhead should be capable of. Whatever they might have been aimed at, whether fish, four-legged animal or human, to borrow Evans' phrase it is indeed 'sad havoc' that is likely to have ensued, and that may have been the intention.

There are, of course, a few instances of undoubted spearhead use on human targets – but only a few, and even in these cases the evidence for what actually happened is highly ambiguous. The first concerns a discovery from Dorchester-on-Thames about which little is known. In 1902, H.J. Hewett reported that 'on Queenford Farm, Dorchester . . . a skeleton was dug up with part of a bronze spear broken off in the pelvis . . . ; they also found with the skeleton a perforated stone used as a charm…'. The spearhead tip probably belongs to a basal-looped type of later Middle Bronze Age date, and is still located within the original pelvis at the Ashmolean Museum, Oxford. The spearhead presumably broke during attempts to retrieve it from the victim. However, details about the discovery are scarce – for example, it is not entirely clear if a complete skeleton was ever present.

More dramatic are the finds at Tormarton, Gloucestershire (**44-6**), the result according to Osgood *et al.* (2000, 21) of 'An act of extraordinary violence'. Pipeline laying in 1968 resulted in the discovery of the skeletal remains of at least three individuals, two featuring clear weapon-related injuries: 'Skeleton 1 had a hole in the pelvis made by a lozenge-sectioned spearhead which had been driven into the victim's side as he fell (or perhaps after he had fallen). Skeleton 11 still had a bronze spearhead embedded in the vertebrae; this would have destroyed the spinal cord, causing immediate paralysis. In addition, the tip of another spearhead was discovered in the pelvis of Skeleton 11, and the skull was also damaged. Perhaps this man had received a blow to the head before being dispatched by spear-thrusts to the body' (*ibid.*, 21-2). A fairly imprecise radiocarbon date obtained from Skeleton 11 confirmed a broad Middle to Late Bronze Age date (1400-910 BC) comparable to one obtained from the Dorchester pelvis (1260-990 BC).

Those initial Tormarton finds were published soon after discovery (Knight *et al.* 1972), though with little clue as to the burial context of the skeleton. Further information emerged from more recent work at the site by Richard Osgood. The bodies had been placed within the fill of a large and fairly steep-sided ditch, which had been partly filled with limestone slabs. In total, some five individuals proved to have been buried not far from the terminal of this ditch, which appears to run some distance across the landscape. The ditch itself appears not have been left open for long before being backfilled. Such linear ditches are increasingly common features of the later Bronze Age landscape, particularly in southern Britain, representing territorial subdivisions and possibly performing a range of functions both practical and symbolic. Osgood (n.d.) noted that

44 *The linear ditch at containing the Tormarton bodies has resolutely failed to produce a vivid cropmark outlining its course and direction. However, this aerial photograph, taken by Damian Grady of English Heritage during Richard Osgood's recent excavations gives, via the line of excavation trenches, an idea of its minimum extent and a feel for its (modern) landscape setting. The skeletons were found in the area to the left of the hedgeline.* © Crown copyright. English Heritage

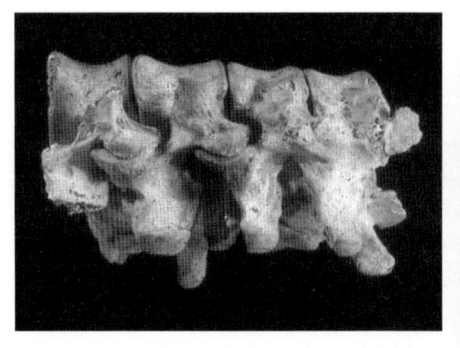

45 (Above) *The spinal column of one of the Tormarton victims, spearhead still in position*

46 (Right) *The pelvis of one of the Tormarton skeletons, a spearhead perforation clearly visible*

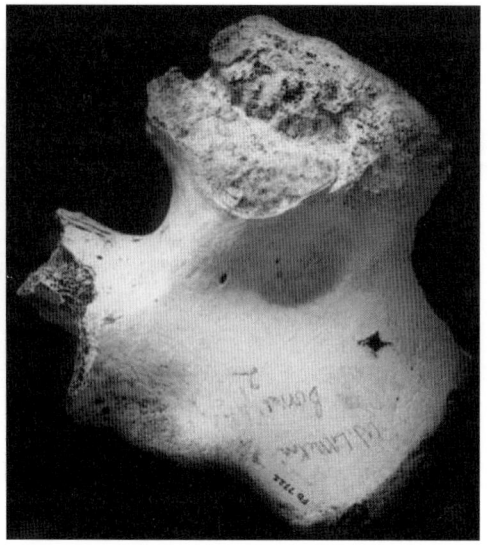

45-6 © Richard Osgood

As concluded in the report of 1972, the bodies were buried without ceremony. Dumped into a linear ditch, they were then covered with large limestone slabs which were, on excavation, surrounded by voids. These slabs perhaps represent the upcast material excavated initially to create the ditch, and used subsequently as an internal bank. One possibility is that the ditch is part of a demarcated tract of land, an element of the later Bronze Age divisions of landscape, which was attacked. If the covering material over the bodies was part of a bank inside the ditch, then this might indicate that the victims were those that dug the ditch and laid claims to the land. As the feature was slighted in covering the bodies, this would be an act one probably wouldn't have undertaken if one had invested large amounts of effort and energy in digging it.

He did note other possibilities – special deposits in or close to ditch terminals are common from the Early Neolithic onwards, and are not unknown from Late Bronze Age linear ditches. The treatment of the bodies, 'hardly smacking of the actions of grieving relatives' (*ibid.*) occurs, of course, at a time when the burial record is sparse to say the least but, spearheads aside, has a lot in common with the widely recognised Iron Age practice of apparently unceremonial dumping of the dead within pits and ditches, the meaning of which probably has little to do with modern notions of what constitutes a decent burial (see e.g. Hill 1995). Nonetheless, the evidence suggests an unpleasant end for these individuals at Tormarton: 'The bodies have been speared from behind whether on the ground or not. They may have been humiliated as part of their death as shown by the spearing of the buttocks of the oldest male. Whatever the case, it is clear that they were killed in a savage encounter . . .' (Osgood n.d.).

The axehead

The axehead, whether copper or bronze, whether flat (**47**), flanged (**48**), winged or socketed (**49**), occupies a key position in Bronze Age studies. As the sole object type to occur in considerable variety throughout the entire period, as well as being probably the most frequent find within hoards of all phases of the Bronze Age, the axehead has occupied a central role in the construction of typologies and sequences. As Barrett (in Clarke *et al.* 1985, 102) noted, 'In metalwork hoards there is considerable emphasis upon the inclusion of axes . . . Indeed the axe appears the most common element to be found in hoards of more than one object . . . almost as if it represented the core symbol about which other objects came to be arranged.' As for the Bronze Age, so for the archaeologist – many of the industrial phases used by prehistorians past and present have particular forms of axehead at their core.

47 A early flat axehead found at Malpas, Cheshire. At a little over 10cm long and 6cm wide at the blade, this is not an especially substantial item. Reported through the Portable Antiquities Scheme

48 A flanged axehead of 'Arreton' type, belonging to the latest stage of the Early Bronze Age, perhaps six or seven centuries later than the Malpas flat axehead. From Levens, Cumbria, it is c.11.3cm long, and will have been cast in a two-piece mould. Reported through the Portable Antiquities Scheme

47-8 © Board of the Trustees of the National Museum and Galleries of Merseyside

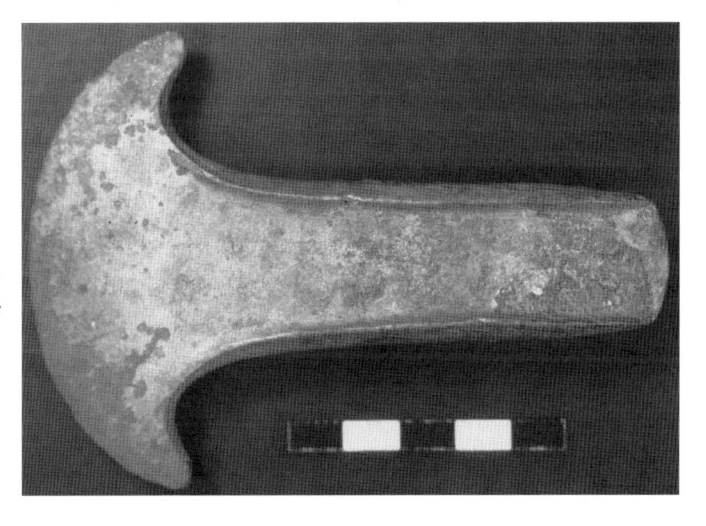

49 *Part of a Late Bronze Age hoard found by 'some woodcutters in pursuit of rabbits' in March 1843 at the Hill of Knockie, Glentanar, Scotland, but which did not come to the attention of archaeology until the 1970s. The full and remarkable story is told by Cowie (1988, 33-7), and the surviving objects published by Pearce (1971, 1977). A near contemporary account refers to 'articles including two bronze vessels . . .; seventeen spear- or axe-heads . . .; from thirty to forty bronze bracelets; six bronze rings of good workmanship . . .' (quoted in Cowie 1988), so clearly much was retained by the woodcutters. Among numerous questions to be asked about deposits such as this is the issue of the intention of those responsible for burying (or sinking) them – was deposition intended to be permanent? Jane Dickens (1996) questioned assumptions about the necessity of permanent deposition, even for 'ritual' purposes, with reference to the tjurunga of central Australia, ritually important objects which needed to be kept concealed from view. More recently, Stuart Needham (2001) has considered the issue of retrievability for Bronze Age metal deposits, suggesting that for many, recovery was clearly not impossible and, circumstances permitting, may have occurred. He notes also that regarding the more overtly votive deposits as permanent helps perpetuate the idea that clear distinctions existed between ritual and utilitarian domains.* © National Museums of Scotland

For many years, of course, there was confusion over their precise function. As has been noted, the axeheads of the British Bronze Age do not closely resemble the axes of recent times, and it was not until the later nineteenth century that experts had settled for a primary function as a woodworking tool. During the early eighteenth century, William Stukeley recognised the flat, flanged and palstave forms as differing from socketed forms only by means of their hafting arrangements, though he seems to have considered the flanged axeheads as candidates for the Druid's golden sickles: 'they were fixed occasionally on the end of their staves, to cut off the boughs of oak and mistletoe; but that, when not made use of for these purposes, they put them into their pouches, or hung them to their girdles, by the little rings or loop' (in Lort 1779). By the mid-nineteenth century, considerable debate was still underway about their possible uses. Yates (1849) argued that 'among the various uses of bronze celts, one of the most important was the application of them in destroying fortifications and entrenchments, in making roads, and earth-works, and in similar military operations'. His evidence ranged from Roman historians to Assyrian sculptures.

Unlike many other weapon or tool types, the axehead has a recognisable history measurable in millennia before the advent of metal. By the Neolithic, as Bradley (1990) has noted, the stone axe had attained both a functional and symbolic importance which were closely entwined, the contexts of use and deposition adding to perceptions of their 'special' nature. Moreover, aspects of their production seem to have enhanced their symbolic value. A key development of the Neolithic is the widespread adoption of ground and polished tools, particularly axeheads:

> This treatment of stone axes seems to improve the mechanical performance of their cutting edges and removes incipient platforms which can cause the blade to flake during use. It also allows the axehead to be held firmly in its haft. These may not be the only reasons for such complex treatment of axes, for the extent of the polished surface often goes beyond what is needed in functional terms. Less utilitarian considerations must also be mentioned here. It takes a long time to polish the entire surface of an axe, but this process gives it a distinctive appearance (*ibid.*, 44).

Indeed, this is one of many characteristics of Neolithic axehead that continues through into the Bronze Age, with the fine finishing of copper and bronze axeheads extending well beyond the areas that would have remained visible after hafting. Moreover, decorated examples feature ornamentation that also extends to areas which would have been concealed during use (**colour plate 10**). That this ornamentation existed for more than purely aesthetic reasons seems likely given resemblances between decorative traits on axeheads and pottery, for example (Jones 2001).

It seems unlikely that the earliest copper axeheads offered any real practical advantages over stone examples in terms of functional efficiency. They would have needed less frequent resharpening and would undoubtedly have lasted longer before needing replacement, but it is debatable if these were important considerations at the time. Moreover, the more restricted resource availability and the far more complex methods of production suggest very strongly that the initial adoption of metal over stone was a cultural choice rather than one dictated by purely practical needs. That axeheads may have functioned as prestige or symbolic items more than practical ones is, of course, not a novelty of the Early Bronze Age either:

> Jadeite axes and finely polished or edge polished flint axes are not utilitarian items. They are high class versions of the everyday axe but made in special materials and finely finished. They often have blunt edges and shapes which would have made them totally impractical for use in chopping wood or digging the ground. They do, therefore, represent utilitarian axes but are of such a high grade that they are practically useless except as decorative abstract items. They were not intended as practical objects but seem to embody the power of the individual who held them (Clarke *et al.* 1985, 58-9).

Of course, in detailing the likely cultural values attached to items such as axeheads and the circumstances of their creation and deposition, it is easy to overlook that they were quite handy for copping wood, among other things. As with many other types of metal object, ideas about their possible uses is limited in part by our own assumptions – they would make perfectly plausible weapons, for example – although Harding's (1976) suggestion that socketed axeheads might have seen service as agricultural implements seems less plausible: 'Axes in one form or another – preferably with straight, not convex, cutting edge – provide the necessary implement for soil cultivation' (*ibid.*, 521). A substantial part of Harding's case revolved around the assumption that the artefacts present in the archaeological record should be representative of what was in use in the Bronze Age, i.e. that deposition was random rather than deliberate, selective and purposeful. However, there is good evidence that axeheads were not used solely for cutting wood. In the late nineteenth century Pitt Rivers recorded the marks of metal blades, probably from one or more palstaves, on the sides of the ditch associated with the Middle Bronze Age settlement known as Angle Ditch (**50**: Pitt Rivers 1898), while more recently, blade marks which might also represent a palstave or perhaps a flanged axe were noted during excavation of the Early to Middle Bronze Age shaft at Wilsford, Wiltshire (Ashbee *et al.* 1989).

The uses of axeheads are coming under greater scrutiny as more wetland sites are being excavated, several of which have conditions of preservation of timbers good enough to retain traces of the tools used to shape them. Chief among these is Flag Fen (Pryor 2001), though here it is interesting to note that the blade forms

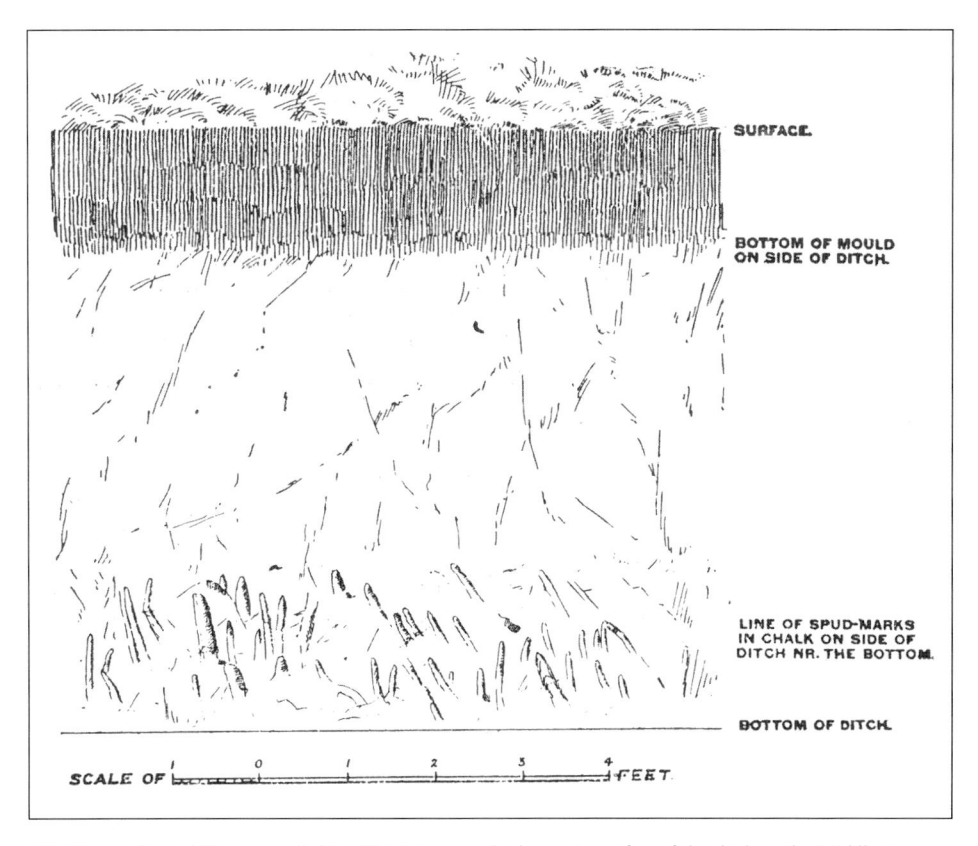

50 Traces of metal blades recorded by Pitt Rivers on the lower, inner face of the ditch at the Middle Bronze Age settlement known as Angle Ditch on his Cranborne Chase estate. That they were most clearly visible at the base seems to support suggestions that the initial backfilling was rapid, the chalk faces being less exposed to weathering

identified most closely resembled socketed axeheads, whereas the date when the timbers in question were worked (*c*.1300 BC) pre-dates the earliest known socketed axeheads in the British Isles by a couple of hundred years (**51**).

Another East Anglian site to preserve timber marks is, of course, 'Seahenge' (**52**), located at Holme-next-the-Sea, just off the Norfolk coast. An elliptical circuit up to 6.6m across comprising oak posts arranged around an upturned tree trunk, dendrochronology (tree rings) allied with Bayesian statistics has narrowed down the date of felling of the components of the monument for 2049 BC (probably between April and June) for the post circuit and 2050 BC (again between April and June) for the central tree trunk (see Pryor 2001a for an excellent account of 'Seahenge' and its investigation). The trunk and the posts proved to feature the marks of metal axes, probably the earliest so far recorded from the British Isles. Particularly noteworthy are the numbers – more than 50 different blades have been identified, a remarkable total for this early date. This

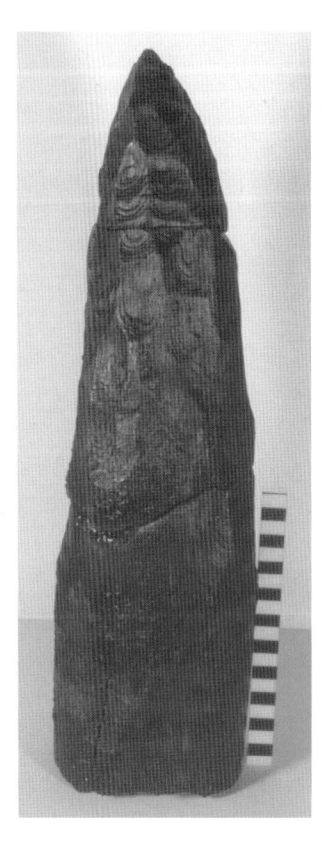

51 (Left) *Tip of a post from Flag Fen. This timber was sharpened from all sides, probably using a single socketed axehead, despite the apparently early date. The axe marks are narrower than those at 'Seahenge', and more concave or 'scooped' in profile. The excavations at Flag Fen are published in full in Pryor 2001, while an excellent and highly readable account also features in Pryor 2001a*

52 (Above) *Seahenge: timber 30 – one of the oak posts from the timber circle known as 'Seahenge' showing a particularly wide axe-mark (scale is 10cm) caused by a metal blade*

51-2 © Francis Pryor

could of course be taken as clear evidence that axes at this early stage of the Bronze Age were far more common than the hoard and stray find records suggest. It also perhaps implies the involvement of a considerable number of people in the construction of the monument, perhaps more than the local community. If, though, one assumes that metal axeheads were still comparatively rare items, then the social network associated with the monument's construction becomes even larger, particularly if we assume that each axe (or maybe a small group of axes) represented the elite members of particular communities.

And the rest . . .

As noted at the beginning of the chapter, the emphasis here has been on outlining the interpretative possibilities of a select range of object types in order to highlight both the problems and potentials of both traditional and more recent methods of analysis. In doing so, the surface has barely been scratched. There has been little mention of cauldrons, buckets, cups and bowls, with their potential for understanding the place of feasting in later Bronze Age society – their existence clearly has implications for the preparation and presentation of food, and one imagines that they were far from everyday objects. Their appearance around the same time that more traditional containers – ceramic vessels – begin to show a broadening of forms and the development of 'fine' wares is also surely of relevance.

Equally little attention has been given to tools – an extraordinary range of tools were cast in bronze, including saws, gouges, punches, hammers, chisels and so on. Considerable space could be devoted to the incredibly diverse styles of ornament, or to the many items common to the Late Bronze Age 'scrap' hoards and commonly termed 'bric-a-brac' in deference to their often fragmentary nature and to a certain vagueness about their likely function. By the later stages of the Bronze Age, bronze appears to play a part in almost every aspect of social life, from building and maintaining houses, obtaining fuel for fires, and digging ditches to constructing ceremonial monuments, killing, and feasting. This contrasts somewhat with the earlier Bronze Age, where objects are fewer, the range of types being cast is more limited, and the contexts in which they are discovered offer greater ambiguity about the possibility of practical use. While this can give the impression that, perhaps, the magic faded somewhat over the course of more than a millennium, with metal gradually taking on more of a utilitarian character, there is evidence to suggest that it remained as symbolically charged as ever, despite its more widespread availability for (one presumes) personal use.

6
THE BRONZE AGE: MYTH AND REALITY

Two decades ago, Anthony Harding suggested that 'The Bronze Age has tended to be regarded as the most turgid and indigestible of the prehistoric periods . . . by students and scholars alike' (Harding 1983, 1). Certainly, at the time, it would have been difficult to disagree. Harding had just a few years previously co-authored a major study of Bronze Age Europe with John Coles (Coles and Harding 1979) who, after many years operating within the frameworks of study for which the period was notorious, was now highly critical of the relevance of

> periodisation and typology, those Bronze Age bugbears . . . Few will doubt the care with which such multiphase episodes of the Bronze Age have been devised by Burgess, Eogan, Briard for Britain, Ireland and Atlantic France, but . . . [such] schemes are based upon metal objects, less often on pottery, and rarely if ever on settlement and economy; it is of little surprise that those archaeologists engaged in the recognition and interpretation of land organisation and use ignore the typological ordering of material that does not figure among their evidence (Coles 1982, 271).

But, as we have seen, while metalwork had become detached from mainstream studies of the Bronze Age, that was to a large part due to the manner in which metalwork had been studied and presented. However, as we have also seen there is clearly a lot more to be learned from the study of bronze than just interconnected sequential arrangements.

Over thirty years ago, Mircea Eliade suggested that much was being missed by concentrating narrowly on the scientific and technological aspects of metal (**53**): 'the purely empirical or rationalistic approach to mines, metals, and metallurgy represents a recent stage in the evolution of Western culture' (Eliade 1968, 76). He argued that the discovery of the means of manipulating metals changed the whole world of meaning :

A—Twig. B—Trench.

53 *Eliade (1978, 53), drawing on historical and ethnographic evidence, emphasised that 'a mine or an untapped vein is not easily discovered; it is for the gods and divine creatures to reveal where they lie and to teach human beings how to exploit their contents'. In his 'De Re Metallica' of 1556, from which this illustration is taken, Agricola discussed various means of finding buried veins, including dowsing, though 'this matter remains in dispute and causes much dissention among miners . . .'. Agricola himself, writing at a time when what we would regard to day as science had yet to clearly emerge from a variety of practices and beliefs, offered an opinion on the value of dowsing that is a tad more ambiguous than it may seem at first: 'Therefore a miner, since we think he ought to be a good and serious man, should not make use of an enchanted twig, because if he is prudent and skilled in the natural signs, he understands that a forked stick is of no use to him, for as I have said before, there are the natural indicators of the veins which he can see for himself without the help of twigs'* the discovery of metals and the progress of metallurgy radically modified the human mode of being in the universe. Not only did the manipulation of metals contribute to man's conquest of the material world; it also changed his world of meaning. The metals opened for him a new mythological world and religious universe . . . The symbologies, mythologies, and rituals accompanying these technological discoveries played a no less important role in shaping post-Neolithic man than did the empirical discoveries themselves (*ibid.*, 76-7).

Interestingly, Eliade contrasted the impact of metals with the earlier transition to agriculture – the adoption of domesticated plants and animals into the subsistence economy, and all that went with it, including the 'new world of meaning [that] was grasped through agricultural work' (*ibid.*) and to him represented an even more radical change in outlook and beliefs than that which accompanied metals. Over the last 15 years or so the British Neolithic itself has undergone a remarkable transformation, with the realisation that it was not enough to define the whole period (and the whole country) according to a series of material traits and a switch in the principal mode of susbsistence. Those developments will have signified far more than the population's ability to chop down more trees and grow their own food. As Thomas explained,

> The British Neolithic consisted of a set of material resources, including pottery, polished stone tools, monuments and domesticated animals. Different communities could use this technology in order to create and reproduce economic regimes, social systems and interpretations of the world. Yet while the Neolithic repertoire could be used in very different ways, it was also fundamentally transformative. Although in the present we may perceive Neolithic material culture as a set of *things*, their real significance lay in the ways in which they were used, or performed. Utilised in performance these artefacts and resources intervened in social life, transforming everyday activities. Indeed, many of the consequences of adopting Neolithic material culture will have been unintended ones (Thomas 1999, 222).

The key to understanding the significance of metal lies in part in evaluating its impact on those Neolithic 'economic regimes, social systems and interpretations of the world'.

Equally important to understanding metallurgy and its products is the need to overcome commonly-drawn distinctions between practical and ritual behaviour, distinctions that would seem to rely more heavily on preconceptions about past socio-economic behaviour than on the realities of the archaeological record. The problems of understanding the place of ritual practices and beliefs in archaeology have been discussed recently by Joanna Brück (1999), who pointed out that 'the concept of ritual is a product of post-Enlightenment rationalism and is not necessarily applicable to other cultural or historical contexts' (*ibid.*, 336). As we have seen, this is certainly the case for the studies of recent metalworking in Africa. Brück argues that viewing ritual action or activity as a distinct sphere of social practice ignores the fact that, as far as the anthropological evidence generally is concerned, 'ritual is generally considered practical and effective action by its practitioners. This is because different conceptions of instrumentality and causation inform such activities' (*ibid.*, 313). Brück reconsidered notions of ritual activity by drawing on evidence from several excavated sites of Middle Bronze Age date in southern England, focusing particularly on site structure and layout, depositional activities, and processes of site abandonment. She argued that what we might otherwise identify as distinct and separate ritual or practical actions would be better described 'as constituting a culturally specific group of *site maintenance practices* that ensured the well-being of the settlement and its inhabitants' (*ibid.*, 335).

The overall treatment of British later prehistory in recent decades underlines the problems inherent in recognising and interpreting ritual activity. The broad distinction between an earlier, Neolithic and Early Bronze Age, phase dominated by funerary and ceremonial monuments, and a later phase beginning in the Middle Bronze Age with a sharp decline in monument building and use and increased visibility of settlements and field systems has already been noted. The Neolithic and Early Bronze Age are thus characterised by the physical presence of the ancestors in the landscape, and of rituals of social practice and interaction. The monumental foci for these activities represent the most visible remains of these distant periods to survive into the modern landscape – long barrows, round barrows, causewayed enclosures, henges and so on. These funerary and ceremonial aspects of social life served to establish links between people and with places, and were given monumental and, perhaps intentionally, permanent expression in the landscape. The contemporary evidence for other activities is notoriously ambiguous and ephemeral, contrasting notably with later periods when the 'monuments' are the enclosures, fields and farms, and the ritual foci difficult to identify. Thus to an extent, what is largely a phenomenon of relative visibility has served to reinforce assumptions about the nature and practice of ritual. In fact, as Brück (1999) has made clear, it is the preconceived interpretative categories of archaeologists that have hindered a proper understanding of all such monuments by failing to consider that secular and ritual activities together represented the 'culturally-specific values, aims and rationales which shaped [prehistoric people's] practical interaction with the world' (Brück 1999, 327).

Throughout the various chapters of this book it has, I hope, become clear that the secular and symbolic aspects of metal and metalwork were likely to have been closely entwined throughout the Bronze Age. A socketed axehead was clearly an efficient wood-working tool, for example, but the manner in which many were treated at the end of their use-life (which may have been very brief indeed) suggests that at certain times and places it was the more symbolic concerns that came to prominence – bronze-working and bronze objects were heavily implicated in helping people to understand the world around them. However, as we have also seen, metal was by no means the only medium for such symbolic expression.

It was the occurrence of metal in a small proportion of early graves that first drew attention to the possibility that bronzes might represent or embody beliefs that stretched beyond their functional value. Outside of funerary contexts, the chosen places of deposition often seem connected with notions of transition and transformation – entrances, boundary or enclosing ditches, rivers and so on. At the same time the act of deposition can appear to be firmly associated with key stages in the lifecycles of both people and places, birth and death for the former and foundation and abandonment for the latter merely being among the more obvious. The involvement of metal objects in such rites would appear to derive from the fact that they too were products of a ritually-charged transformative process, one that may have held an important position in myth or cosmology and which may also have been metaphorically linked with similarly transformative activities such as pottery making, food preparation and reproduction.

For the British Middle Bronze Age in particular, Brück has discussed the 'complex symbolic discourse' implicit in the various technological and transformative processes applied to people and things. She suggests that

> the technological processes in which humans engaged (including bronze and pottery making, and the preparation and cooking of food) were conceptualised as cycles of birth, death and regeneration through the metaphor of transformation by fire, crushing and grinding. The process of biological and social growth among humans appears to have been understood and conceptualised in a similar way. Technologies such as metallurgy acted as metaphors for the production of the self. Humans, like other materials, underwent rites of passage at critical stages in their lives which required the destruction of the old social persona and the relationships this sustained, and the creation of a new self identity. At death, this was achieved through the fragmentation and burning of the body itself . . . (Brück 2001b, 157).

Thus pottery manufacture and metalworking can be viewed as a 'series of transformative cycles' which would be conceptually linked to the lifecycles of people, all capable of transformation 'from one state to another and reborn into a new life through the process of fragmentation and the medium of fire' (*ibid.*). Fragmentation of metalwork is, of course, most visible in the latter stages of the Bronze Age, a period when substantial quantities of broken and incomplete bronze and copper objects were consigned to the ground – the so-called 'founder's hoards'. However, it is important to remember that this was a phenomenon restricted not only in time, as Evans (1881) observed, but in space – they occur primarily in the south-eastern corner of the British Isles (and of course on the neighbouring continent). That fragmentation of metals occurred earlier in the Bronze Age cannot be doubted, whether the crushing and grinding of freshly mined ore or the breakage of items ready for melting and recasting. The regular deposition, as opposed to occurrence, of fragmented material began at a relatively late stage when compared to the treatment prior to deposition of other classes of material culture (e.g. pottery, quernstones, human and animal remains).

The deposition of 'founder's hoards' has in the past been attributed to many causes – the concealed stock of a dead or forgetful smith; a surplus of bronze leading to simple abandonment of excess metal; a surplus of bronze prompting discard in order to preserve the value of the remainder; a surplus caused by the coming of iron, rendering the retention of so much bronze unnecessary; and so on. However, there are problems with all of these explanations. Generally it has been assumed that the fragmentary nature of their contents stems from their status as part of the stock of a metalworker or of a metal-using community. More recently, less utilitarian theories have been advanced, inspired partly by the location and manner of deposition of some examples, but also through paying closer attention to the precise nature of the contents. It is clear, for example, that some processes of selection have been at work – some types are clearly over-represented in 'founder's hoards', some are under-represented and others are virtually absent, underlining the non-random nature of their collection. At the same time, conjoining fragments – or indeed any two fragments – from the same object is a rare occurrence indeed.

Meanwhile, Turner (1998) has looked more closely at the processes of fragmentation employed in creating these hoards. A close inspection of the broken pieces often reveals traces of hammering and damage that do not relate to the actual use of such objects but to their intentional breakage, and often that breakage of single items into smaller objects appears to have been done in a fairly systematic manner. However, Turner's analysis suggests that the methods employed were not solely concerned with making the metal easier to recycle – the results of fragmentation seem, on the whole, not to have been concerned with producing pieces of bronze that would be easier to melt down in a crucible: 'While it is possible to suggest that the degree of fragmentation is something which can be directly linked with metalworking, some more ambiguous trends can be identified which cannot be so readily explained through reference to the metalworking process' (*ibid.*, 88). Again, Turner drew an explicit link with other transformative processes, including death: 'funerary rituals are conducted through a discourse which employs metaphors derived from routine activities, in particular the metalworking process and the agricultural cycle. In this manner, the transformation of the corpse, which probably undergoes cremation, can be understood by comparing it to the processes of transformation which occur during the recycling of worn-out objects, and to the regeneration that is such a fundamental part of the agricultural year' (*ibid.*, 135).

As we have seen, it need not have been the end of a human life that was being marked. However, additional links have been drawn between metalwork deposition and funerary rites. For example, the rapid growth in the quantity of weaponry placed in water during the later Bronze Age has been contrasted with both the predominance of weaponry in earlier Bronze Age graves and the near-complete disappearance of an archaeologically visible funerary rite during the later Bronze Age (Bradley 1990, 136). Perhaps much of the weaponry discarded in this manner represented a significant shift in the nature and performance of funerary rites.

As Turner (1998) stresses, however, while metaphorical comparisons can be drawn between lifecycles of people and objects, to treat all deposits as 'displaced funerary deposits' is probably an oversimplification, although the symbolic and metaphorical properties of metal being drawn on was probably fairly consistent. At the heart of much of this activity was, of course, metalworking and the metalworker. Turner's analysis of the 'founder's hoards' of Essex and Kent suggests that the fragmentation process was not a random one, and presumably it was the smith who was responsible for the breakage of many items prior to deposition (and perhaps also for the collection and safe-keeping of the material). At other times and places the act rather than its product is less overtly referenced, it seems, although instances such as Springfield Lyons and Norton Fitzwarren show that metalworking debris itself could be used and deposited in the same manner as bronzes, while cases such as the virtually as-cast palstaves from South Dumpton Down may indicate the involvement of metalworking in such event-marking practices – those palstaves may have been specifically cast with the intention of being placed straight into the ground.

The metaphorical associations of metalworking, as we have seen, appear to reside largely in its nature as a transformative process which can be compared and contrasted with other similarly transformative acts, many of which employ comparable though not identical technology. Presumably recognition of such connections belongs to the earliest stages of metalworking practice. The association of the earliest metalworking in Britain with the users of Beaker pottery was perhaps inevitable given that the earliest copper, bronze and gold objects in graves are, when pottery is also present, invariably associated with Beakers. Indeed, it remains the case that in the British Isles, Beaker pottery is widely regarded as a funerary form, even though sherds and vessels are in fact known from a variety of contexts. However, although it is the case that in funerary contexts, it is Beakers that are most often associated with metal, a sense of proportion is required – the overwhelming majority of Beakers were not associated with metal objects, and the overwhelming majority of excavated graves do not feature metalwork.

The relatively fine finish and decoration of most Beakers sets them apart from the majority of other Late Neolithic and Early Bronze Age ceramic traditions, suggesting that the comparatively coarse nature of the latter was also a consequence of cultural choice, and something that is also pertinent given the chronological overlap between Beakers and other forms of pottery. A case in point is Late Neolithic Grooved Ware, the manufacture, use and deposition of which overlaps with Beakers. However, there is no secure association of Grooved Ware with any item of metal, although Grooved Ware can occur in abundance at sites contemporary with the earliest metal use. Neither does Grooved Ware have firm links with funerary rites.

Despite the considerable variety evident in form and decoration, and the difficulties faced in classifying and sequencing such diversity, most Beaker pots follow in general a fairly widespread tradition traceable across large areas of western Europe and beyond. However, it has also become clear that Beaker production was highly localised, with little evidence for pots moving far from their place of manufacture. Parker Pearson (1995, 98) suggested that 'the dispersed production and localised use of Beakers is seen by myself as indicative of their special context and meaning, perhaps as individualised drinking accessories'. Moreover, 'This apparently domestic mode of production raises questions about the relationship of Beakers to the individuals that they were buried with. We need to consider whether they were manufactured specifically for the funeral or whether they were directly linked to the individual, perhaps even formed out of the soil from whence that person originated' (*ibid.*, 92-3). Such ideas have been reinforced by Boast (1995), who noted a marked tendency for poorer fabrics among Beakers from graves, yet at the same time 'the surface treatment on these pots tends to be of a high standard, either burnished or smoothed. This would indicate that there is a difference between either the choice of Beakers for burial or their production, that Beakers used, or made, for burial are of a poorer quality, but are made to look good by surface treatments . . . [It] must be suggested that many pots are being made for the grave' (*ibid.*, 72-3).

The unavoidable fact that Beakers represent the first ceramic tradition to occur in association with formal burials has already been noted, but it is important here to emphasize a point already made by many about this development in mortuary practice. The treatment of human remains prior to the later Neolithic took a variety of forms, and included instances of both inhumation and cremation, with some clear regional trends visible among a wealth of data of variable quality. Recognisably complete skeletons representing the deliberate burial of reasonably intact bodies occur sporadically throughout the Mesolithic and Neolithic in a variety of contexts, but it is really only from the late Neolithic onwards that a concern with the interment of complete bodies becomes paramount. Thus Beaker pottery is not merely associated with a change in funerary rite, but arguably with the first appearance of a formal burial rite in the British archaeological record, as opposed to the performance of rites involving human remains (Barrett 1994).

The suggestion that Beakers in graves may have been made specifically to accompany the dead implies a clear link between the funerary ritual and the manufacture of a pot – the transition from life to death (or to the ancestors) being marked by the creation of clay vessel of particular form, style and a range of meanings presumably linked in some way with both the means of production and the everyday use of such vessels. Like metalworking, the creation of ceramic vessels can be characterised as a technological process, employing special knowledge, techniques and equipment in order to turn a selection of carefully chosen raw materials into a culturally useful end-product. The whole chain of processes will have been firmly embedded within social contexts – as we have seen, rather than a functional means to a utilitarian end, technology itself is firmly embedded within the broader conceptual frameworks that offer means of understanding the world and structuring human behaviour.

One particularly intriguing aspect of pottery, and one with implications for the possible metaphorical content of clay vessels and their manufacture, concerns the use of various tempering materials in prehistory. Brück (1999a), discussing the Middle Bronze Age, noted the use of broken and crushed pottery vessels ('grog') as a tempering agent in the production of new vessels: 'materials that were no longer usable in the manner originally intended entered the cycle of production at a new point. The death of a pot facilitated the creation of new vessels' (*ibid.*) and, of course, the 'death' of a pot may itself be associated with an important stage, including death, in the lifecycle of an individual. In highlighting the similar treatment afforded to both people and objects at death at a time when cremation was the overwhelmingly dominant archaeologically visible funerary rite, Brück (1999a; 2001b) focused particularly on the issues of fragmentation and regeneration, suggesting that the process of physical fragmentation, evident in the treatment and deposition of artefacts as well as in the process of cremation 'was considered an essential element of the ongoing cycle of death and the regeneration of life' (*ibid.*). Thus death could be considered as a source of life and fertility, the funerary rites representing a process of transformation from one state to another which had, as we have already seen, strong metaphorical links with other transformative processes including food preparation, pottery manufacture and metalworking. Thus the use of crushed pot as a tempering agent in new vessels further underlines the possibility that death was seen as 'the source of fertility and new life' (*ibid.*).

The use of grog as a tempering agent of course pre-dates the Middle Bronze Age. A study by Cleal (1995) of pottery fabrics in the 'Wessex' region of southern England showed its presence in the earliest Neolithic pottery traditions, but only rarely. The use of grog temper increased markedly during the later Neolithic, although it is important to remember that throughout the period and region under consideration and, no doubt, beyond, a variety of tempering agents were used, both individually and in combination. Thus although the use of grog in Grooved Ware, for instance, was notably more common than for earlier forms of pottery, the dominant inclusion in Grooved Ware was shell. For

Beakers, a majority of pots contained either grog on its own or with other material (although 41 per cent also contained flint), while grog continued to be the favoured inclusion for other Early Bronze Age forms such as Food Vessels and Collared Urns. A key point made by Cleal concerns the fact that more than purely technological criteria lay behind the selection and use of tempering agents. As she pointed out,

> crushed pot is in many ways an ideal tempering material. It is relatively easily crushed, is easy to use, has few sharp edges, provides a stable non-plastic which, on firing, has properties almost identical to the clay matrix, and does not suffer post-firing changes which would endanger or destabilise the pot . . . It was not, however, much used prior to the appearance of Grooved Ware, and although used extensively in Beakers, Collared Urns and Food Vessels, did not much feature in the ceramics of the Middle Bronze Age in large areas of Wessex . . . [O]verall, the picture is of grog as an unpopular inclusion until the appearance of Grooved Ware . . . and it is possible that there were social constraints on its use (*ibid.*).

Parker Pearson and Ramilisonina (1998, 322) briefly touched on the question of temper during their discussion of timber and stone monuments of the Neolithic and Early Bronze Age, suggesting for example that Middle Neolithic Peterborough Ware be considered as 'ancestor ware' because of a tendency towards stony inclusions in its fabric – flint, chert, sandstone and quartz – and contextual associations with the ancestral dead: 'pottery made for interactions specifically with the ancestors' (*ibid.*). These ancestral associations were contrasted with Grooved Ware pots tempered, as noted above, with shell, grog and other generally non-stony ('living') material. These observations about temper were allied to suggestions that, essentially, stone monuments were constructed for the ancestral dead while timber monuments were built by and for the living, the predominance of Grooved Ware at the latter serving to emphasize the point. Timber monuments later reworked in stone are characterised as undergoing a process of 'lithicisation' – 'the changing of a monument from wood to stone [being] a marking of the movement of the living through death to ancestorhood, as the ceremonial places which were once associated with the living became places devoid of living people where the ancestors now reside' (*ibid.*).

Grooved Ware, as we have seen, has few if any funerary or ancestral associations and, equally intriguingly, none with metalwork. Beakers on the other hand occur with both, though more so with the former than with the latter. It is also, as Cleal noted, more likely to contain grog than any other tempering agent. Thus a cycle of death and renewal is embodied within the manufacturing of many of the pots accompanying the deceased. Arguably, the vessel itself went through a process of 'lithicisation' in the act of firing – a transformation by fire from living clay to solid, durable ceramic representing the passage from the realm of the living to the realm of the dead, and presumably drawing on more than a millennium of pottery production and its associated myths and metaphors.

It would, then, be surprising if the links between the technological processes which lie behind the creation of both ceramic and metal objects were overlooked, either at a technological or a symbolic level. A number of parallels can be drawn between the two processes, even if procedures and refinements do not match precisely. However, the transformative power of fire is a key ingredient to both and offers the most potent raw material for metaphors of death and renewal. What metalwork added to the existing metaphorical melting pot of ideas is more elusive but may have concerned its potential for unlimited transformation by fire – the possibility of a repeated or endless cycle of death and renewal. Of course this is present to a certain degree in the use of grog and other materials as a temper in pottery, but with metal an entire object could be created anew through the agency of (among other process) fire, and it could happen again and again. Key questions remain to be answered, but it is noteworthy that while Beaker pottery is almost never associated with cremations, its overlapping and successor funerary vessels – the Collared Urns, Food Vessels and the like – generally accompany deposits of cremated remains into the grave.

Cremation appears to rise to prominence as the favoured funerary rite during the late third and early second millennia and clearly has both technological and, one presumes, metaphorical connections with metalworking. That the appearance and spread of metalworking was followed so closely by the rise of cremation may have been no coincidence, with the symbolism inherent in the metalworking process promoting a greater concern with the need to transform human remains by fire – instead of the process simply being represented by the firing of a pot, the dead themselves were put through the same process, but one which now drew at least as much from the metaphors of metalworking as from pottery manufacture. The links between different technological practises, including pottery manufacture, metalworking and cremation are made abundantly clear by both the associations and context of the tuyere from Ewan Rigg. Accompanying a cremation burial and fired clay vessels, consideration of the piece has centred around its possible use in metalworking, though in reality it might also have seen service at the cremation pyre or in pottery manufacture. As we have seen, the metaphorical links between metalworking and the lifecycles of people and places continue to be observable throughout the Bronze Age. Metal objects and the technology used to create them were as fundamentally transformative at both practical and symbolic levels as the material culture of the Neolithic had been.

The potential of metalwork to offer fresh insights into the lives of people in the Bronze Age should surely come as a relief to those who have previously been put off by the more traditional methods of analysis. It may, of course, be that too much is being read into the possible connections between different used of fire, or into

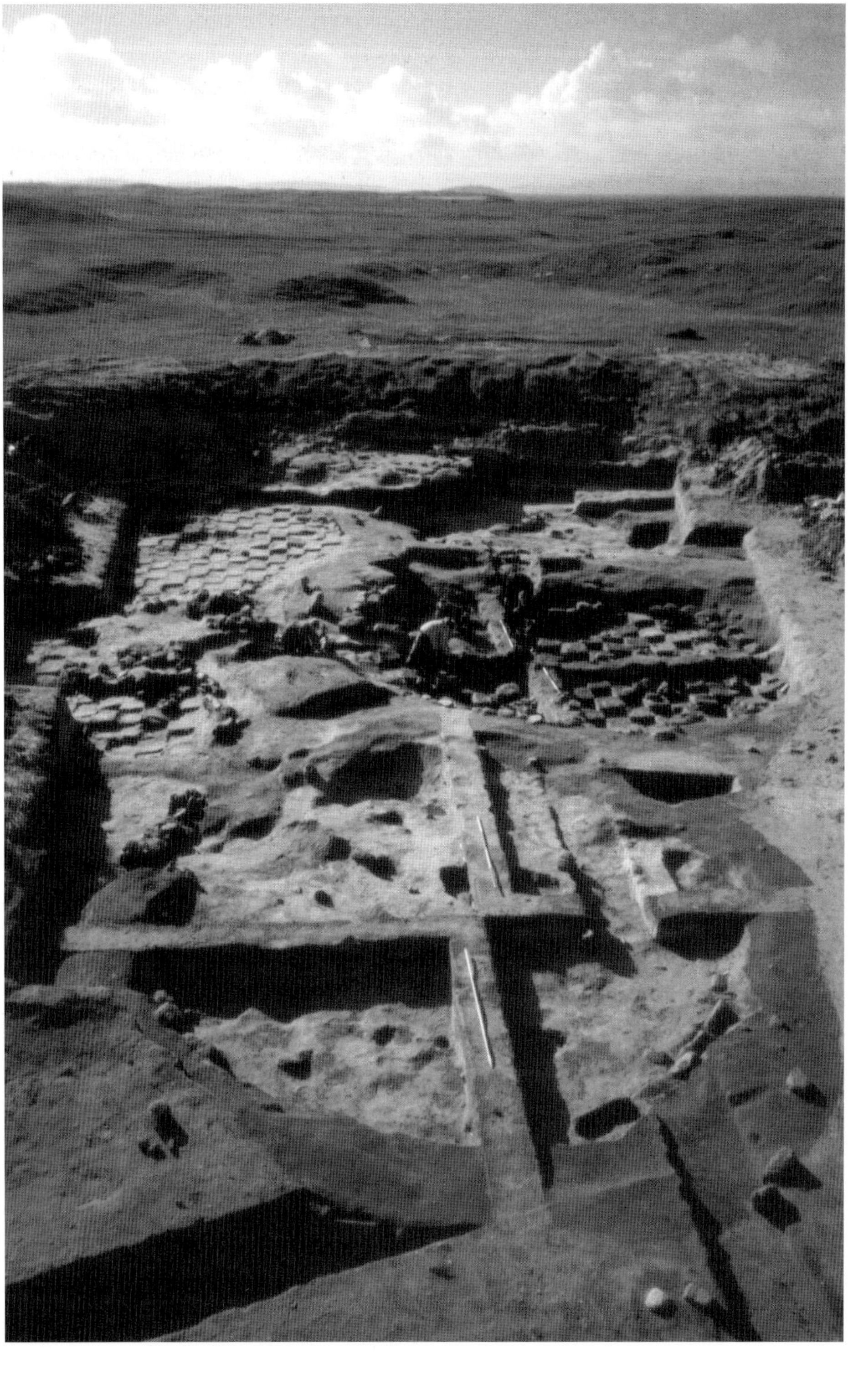

the breakage of bronzes, but it is also clear that the straightforward assumptions about metal that once dominated its study can no longer be supported even by the basic empirical and descriptive data. This has been apparent to many prehistorians for some time, but has been slow to penetrate beyond those actively involved in researching the period. In addition, new and exciting discoveries continue to occur, and here I do not just mean pretty or shiny objects with both aesthetic and cash value, but also sites like Cladh Hallan (**54**), where excavations have shown that the good folk of the British Bronze Age could indeed indulge in practices that to the modern, rational eye can seem bizarre until considered more carefully within their cultural context.

54 (Left) *The site at Cladh Hallan, South Uist, Outer Hebrides, another remote (to the modern eye) site to have produced an assemblage of metalworking debris, including mould fragments. The main feature of the site, recently excavated by the University of Sheffield under Mike Parker Pearson, was a 'terrace' of three circular houses, each of which saw several phases of use, but each of which had quite distinct histories of occupation and reuse. The central house in particular was rebuilt at least seven times over 500 years or more. Metalworking debris appears to have been particularly associated with this structure, including a scattered deposit of mould fragments from the casting of swords, spearheads and ornaments within the entrance. There was no evidence for metalworking in this area, and the moulds are presumed to have been brought from elsewhere to this spot. Other evidence suggests some metalworking may have occurred towards the rear of the settlement. However, it is some of the non-metal deposits that have attracted the most attention, including dog burials in entrances, cremated sheep burials, and human foundation deposits. In the case of these human burials, radiocarbon dating suggests that some of the bodies were centuries older than the houses whose construction they were associated with (www.shef.ac.uk/~ap/research/hebrides/hallan.html).* © Mike Parker Pearson

APPENDIX
BRONZE FINDS, PORTABLE ANTIQUITIES AND TREASURE

England and Wales

Until recently, for England and Wales at least, there was no real framework for the systematic recording of objects of archaeological or historic interest discovered by the general public rather than in the course of archaeological fieldwork (**55-6**). The Portable Antiquities Scheme was set up by the Department of Culture, Media and Sport in order to try and redress this situation. It is a voluntary scheme – with a few notable exceptions, there is no compulsion for finders to report their discoveries. Central to the scheme is a network of Finds Liaison Officers, and by the end of 2003 there should be at least one in post for all parts of England and Wales.

Ideally, any discovery of potential archaeological or historic interest should be reported to the local Finds Liaison Officer for identification and detailed recording. They can also give advice on issues such as conservation of objects. Contact details for the scheme are provided below, but advice on where to go to report an object can usually be obtained from a local museum or local authority-based archaeologists. It is hoped that the scheme will not only influence our knowledge of the history and archaeology of England and Wales, by systematically recording information about finds that has previously been collected, if at all, in a rather ad hoc manner, but will also encourage a greater awareness among finders both of the nature and significance of their discoveries, encourage and promote better recording practice by finders and others.

The Finds Liaison Officers are also involved in raising awareness of the scheme and of the importance of recording finds. This includes, of course, strengthening links between archaeologists and metal detectorists, the latter being responsible for a large percentage of the number of new finds reported every year. As has been noted throughout this book, knowing exactly where an object was found adds considerably to the potential archaeological significance of any discovery.

More information about the scheme, including a searchable database of recorded finds and a list of all Finds Liaison Officers, can be found on the internet at http://www.finds.org.uk or via more traditional methods at

Portable Antiquities Scheme
c/o Department of Coins and Medals
The British Museum
London WC1B 3DG
Tel. 020 7323 8611

For Bronze Age metalwork, an added complication for finders comes in the form of the Treasure Act of 1996, which in England, Wales and Northern Ireland replaced the less than satisfactory common law of treasure trove. Initially applying primarily to objects of precious metals (i.e. gold and silver) at least 300 years old, the Treasure (Designation) Order 2002 brought prehistoric base metals under the remit of the Act. Essentially, from 1 January 2003 any find of Bronze Age metalwork (including copper, bronze, tin, and lead) and comprising two or more objects, plus anything found in association with them, must be reported to the local coroner either within 14 days of discovery or within 14 days from the day on which it was realised that a particular find might be 'treasure'. Should a museum, whether local or national, wish to acquire the finds, they would be expected to pay the current market value. Detailed information on how the Act works, including the Code of Practice, can be found via the Portable Antiquities Scheme website, or again via local museums or local authority archaeologists. Details can also be found via metal-detecting organisations such as the National Council for Metal Detectorists (www.ncmd.co.uk).

There are some important things to remember, however. First of all, the finder should have obtained permission from the landowner to be on the land, and should inform the landowner and anyone who occupies the land of any find. Secondly, it is illegal to use a metal detector on a Scheduled Ancient Monument, or any site in the ownership or guardianship of the state. It is also illegal to remove anything from such sites without permission.

55 *A knife or, perhaps, dagger of Late Bronze Age date and 9cm in length from Malpas, Cheshire. Bearing in mind the absence of organic materials (hilt, sheath etc.), this is clearly a less visually impressive object than the functionally comparable items of earlier periods. Reported through the Portable Antiquities Scheme.*
© Board of the Trustees of the National Museums and Galleries in Merseyside

Scotland

Inevitably the situation in Scotland differs, and did so even before the Treasure Act. Under Scottish law, all objects found – of whatever date and of any material, whether single objects or collections of associated material – and for which neither the original owner nor the 'rightful heir' can be identified are the property of the Crown. Essentially this means that anything discovered that might possess some historic value should be reported. As in England and Wales, should an item be deemed 'treasure' and claimed by a museum, then a financial reward will normally follow. Again, there are important caveats with regard to keeping landowners informed and avoiding scheduled or otherwise protected sites. Should an item of potential historic interest be found, then it should be taken (or reported) to either a local museum or a local county archaeologist for advice on what to do next. Alternatively, the workings of the treasure trove system in Scotland are detailed on the internet at http://www.treasuretrove.org.uk. Further information can be obtained by e-mailing info@treasuretrove.org.uk or by contacting the following address:

> Treasure Trove Advisory Panel Secretariat
> National Museums of Scotland
> Chambers Street
> Edinburgh EH1 JF

However, in whatever part of the British Isles (or beyond) an item (or items) of Bronze Age metalwork may be discovered, the importance of getting experienced archaeological assistance, whether amateur or professional, cannot be too strongly emphasised in order to ensure that the maximum amount of contextual information is retrieved along with the objects themselves.

BIBLIOGRAPHY

Abercromby, J. 1902. 'The oldest Bronze-Age ceramic type in Britain', *Journal of the Royal Anthropological Institute* 32, 373-97.

Abercromby, J. 1912. *A Study of the Bronze Age Pottery of Great Britain and Ireland and its Associated Grave Goods.* Oxford: Clarendon Press.

Anderson, J. 1878-9. 'Notice of a remarkable find of bronze swords and other bronze articles in Edinburgh; with notes on bronze swords found in Scotland', *Proceedings of the Society of Antiquaries of Scotland* 13, 321-33.

Annable, F.K. and D.D.A. Simpson. 1964. *Guide Catalogue of the Neolithic and Bronze Age Collections in Devizes Museum.* Wiltshire Archaeological and Natural History Society, Devizes.

Anon. 1996. 'A Late Bronze Age hoard from Withersfield, Suffolk', *Journal of the Haverhill and District Archaeological Group* 6 (2), 115-22.

Appadurai, A. (ed.). 1986. *The Social Life of Things.* Cambridge University Press.

ApSimon, A. and E. Greenfield. 1972. 'The excavation of the Bronze and Iron Age settlement at Trevisker Round, St Eval, Cornwall', *Proceedings of the Prehistoric Society* 38, 302-81.

Ashbee, P., M. Bell and E. Proudfoot. 1989. *Wilsford Shaft: Excavations 1960-62.* English Heritage: London.

Barber, M., D. Field and P. Topping. 1999. *The Neolithic Flint Mines of England.* English Heritage: Swindon.

Barrett, J.C. 1980. 'The Pottery of the Later Bronze Age in Lowland England', *Proceedings of the Prehistoric Society* 46, 297-320.

Barrett, J.C. 1991. 'Towards an archaeology of ritual' in Garwood *et al.*, 1-9.

Barrett, J.C. 1994. *Fragments from Antiquity. An archaeology of social life in Britain, 2900-1200 BC.* Blackwell, Oxford.

Barrett, J.C. 1994a. 'The Bronze Age' in B. Vyner (ed.) *Building on the Past. Papers celebrating 150 years of the Royal Archaeological Institute*, 103-22. Royal Archaeological Institute, London.

Barrett, J.C. and R. Bradley (eds). 1980. *Settlement and Society in the British later Bronze Age.* British Archaeological reports, British Series 83: Oxford.

Barrett, J.C. and R. Bradley. 1980a. Preface in Barrett and Bradley (eds) 1980, 9-14.

Barrett, J.C., R. Bradley, M. Green. 1991. *Landscape, Monuments and Society. The prehistory of Cranborne Chase.* Cambridge University Press, Cambridge.

Barrett, J.C. and R. Gourlay 1999. 'An early metal assemblage from Dail na Caraidh, Inverness-shire, and its context', *Proceedings of the Society of Antiquaries of Scotland* 129, 161-87.

Beddoe, A. 1885. *The Races of Britain. A contribution to the anthropology of West Europe.* Bristol: Arrowsmith.

Benton, S. 1930-1. 'The excavation of the Sculptor's Cave, Covesea', *Proceedings of the Society of Antiquaries of Scotland* 65, 177-216.

Berridge, P. 1994. 'Cornish axe factories: fact or fiction?' in N. Ashton and A. David (eds) *Stories in Stone* (Lithic Studies Society occasional paper 4), 45-56. Lithic Studies Society: London.

Bewley, R.H., I.H. Longworth, S. Browne, J.P. Huntley and G. Varndell. 1992. 'Excavation of a Bronze Age cemetery at Ewanrigg, Maryport, Cumbria', *Proceedings of the Prehistoric Society* 58, 325-44.

Boast, R. 1995. 'Fine Pots, Pure Pots, Beaker Pots' in I. Kinnes, G. Varndell (eds) *Unbaked Urns of Rudely Shape: essays on British and Irish Pottery for Ian Longworth*, 69-80. Oxbow Books, Oxford.

Borlase, W.C. 1881. 'Typical Specimens of Cornish Barrows', *Archaeologia* 49, 181-98.

Bowden, M. and D.S. McOmish. 1987. 'The Required Barrier', *Scottish Archaeological Review* 4, 76-84.

Bowden, M. and D.S. McOmish. 1989. 'Little Boxes: more about hillforts', *Scottish Archaeological Review* 6, 12-16.

Bradley, R. 1990. *The Passage of Arms. An archaeological analysis of hoards and votive deposits.* Cambridge University Press, Cambridge.

Bradley, R. 2000. *An Archaeology of Natural Places.* Routledge: London.

Bradley, R. 2001. 'Afterword: Back to the Bronze Age' in J. Brück (ed.) 2001, 229-31.

Bradley, R. and M. Edmonds. 1993. *Interpreting the Axe Trade.* Cambridge University Press: Cambridge.

Bradley, R. and A. Ellison. 1975. *Rams Hill: A bronze age defended enclosure and its landscape.* British Archaeological Reports (British Series) 19. Oxford: British Archaeological Reports.

Brewis, W.P. 1912. 'The Evolution of the Bronze Spear and Sword in Britain', *Proceedings of the University of Durham Philosophical Society* V (I), 1-18.

Brewster, T.C.M. 1963. *The Excavation of Staple Howe.* East Riding Archaeological Research Committee: Malton.

Briard, J. 1965. *Les Depots Bretons et l'Age du Bronze Atlantique.* University of Rennes Faculty of Sciences.

Bridgford, S. 1997. 'Mightier than the pen? An edgewise look at Irish Bronze Age swords' in J. Carman (ed.) *Material Harm: archaeological studies of war and violence*, 95-115. Cruithne Press, Glasgow.

Bridgford, S. 1998. 'British Late Bronze Age Swords. The metallographic evidence' in C. Mordant, M. Pernot and V. Rychner (eds) *L'Atelier du bronzier en Europe du XX au VII siècle avant notre ère. Actes du colloque international 'Bronze '96', Neuchâtel et Dijon, 1996. Tome II: Du minerai au métal, du métal à l'object*, 205-17. Paris: CTHS.

Briggs, C.S. 1976. 'Prehistoric mining in Anglesey', *Historical Metallurgy* 10 (1), 43.

Briggs, C.S. 1988. 'Copper mining at Mount Gabriel, Co. Cork: Bronze Age bonanza or post-famine fiasco?', *Proceedings of the Prehistoric Society* 49, 317-34.

Brindley, A. 1994. *Irish Prehistory: an introduction*. National Museum of Ireland/Country House: Dublin.

British Museum. 1920. *A Guide to the Antiquities of the Bronze Age in the Department of British and Medieval Antiquities*, 2nd edition. British Museum, London.

Britton, D. 1963. 'Traditions of Metal-Working in the Later Neolithic and Early Bronze Age of Britain: Part 1', *Proceedings of the Prehistoric Society* 29, 258-325.

Brodie, N. 1994. *The Neolithic-Bronze Age transition in Britain: a critical review of some archaeological and craniological concepts*. British Archaeological Reports British Series 238: Oxford.

Brück, J. 1995. 'A place for the dead: the role of human remains in the Late Bronze Age', *Proceedings of the Prehistoric Society* 61, 245-77.

Brück, J. 1999. 'Ritual and rationality: some problems of interpretation in European archaeology', *European Journal of Archaeology* 2 (3), 313-44.

Brück, J. 1999a. 'Houses, lifecycles and deposition on Middle Bronze Age settlements in Southern England', *Proceedings of the Prehistoric Society* 65, 145-66.

Brück, J. 2000. 'Settlement, Landscape and Social Identity: the Early-Middle Bronze Age transition in Wessex, Sussex and the Thames Valley', *Oxford Journal of Archaeology* 19 (3), 277-300.

Brück, J. (ed.). 2001. *Bronze Age Landscapes: tradition and transformation*. Oxbow Books, Oxford.

Brück, J. 2001a. Preface in Brück (ed.) 2001, v-vi.

Brück, J. 2001b. 'Body metaphors and technologies of transformation in the English Middle and Late Bronze Age' in J. Brück (ed.) 2001, 149-60.

Buckley, D. and J. Hedges. 1987. *The Bronze Age and Saxon Settlements at Springfield Lyons, Essex: an interim report*. Essex County Council Occasional Paper 5, Chelmsford.

Budd, P. and D. Gale. 1994. 'Archaeological survey of an early mineworking at Wheal Coates, near St Agnes', *Cornish Archaeology* 33, 14-21.

Budd, P. and D. Gale. 1997. *Prehistoric Extractive Metallurgy in Cornwall*. Cornwall Archaeological Unit, Truro.

Budd, P. and T. Taylor. 1995. 'The faerie smith meets the bronze industry: magic versus science in the interpretation of prehistoric metal-making', *World Archaeology* 27, 133-43.

Budd, P., R. Haggerty, R.A. Ixer, B. Scaife, and R.G. Thomas. 2000. 'Copper Deposits in south-west England identified as a source of Copper Age metalwork'. http://www.archaeotrace.co.uk/stories/provenance.html

Buleli, N. 1993. 'Iron-making techniques in the Kivu region of Zaire: some differences between the South Maniema region and north Kivu' in Shaw *et al*. 1993, 468-77.

Burgess, C. 1968. 'The later Bronze Age in the British Isles and North-Western France', *Archaeological Journal* 125, 1-45.

Burgess, C. 1969. 'Chronology and terminology in the British Bronze Age', *Antiquaries Journal* 49, 22-9.

Burgess, C. 1974. 'The Bronze Age' in C. Renfrew (ed.) *British Prehistory: a new outline*, pp.165-232. Duckworth, London.

Burgess, C. 1976. 'Burials with metalwork of the Later Bronze Age in Wales and beyond' in G.C. Boon, J.M. Lewis (eds) *Welsh Antiquity*, 81-104; National Museum of Wales, Cardiff.

Burgess, C. 1980. *The Age of Stonehenge*. J.M. Dent & Sons Ltd, London.

Burgess, C. and D. Coombs (eds). 1979. *Bronze Age hoards: some finds old and new*. British Archaeological Reports (British Series) 67; Oxford: British Archaeological Reports.

Burgess, C. and D. Coombs. 1979a. Preface in Burgess and Coombs 1979, i-vii.

Burgess, C., D. Coombs and D.G. Davies. 1972. 'The Broadward Complex and barbed spearheads' in F. Lynch, C. Burgess (eds) *Prehistoric Man in Wales and the West: Essays in honour of Lily F Chitty*, 211-83. Adam Dart & Sons, Bath.

Burgess, C. and S. Gerloff. 1981. *The Dirks and Rapiers of Great Britain and Ireland*. Munich: Prähistorische Bronzefunde IV, 7.

Burstow, G.P. and G.A. Holleyman. 1957. 'Late Bronze Age Settlement on Itford Hill, Sussex', *Proceedings of the Prehistoric Society* 23, 167-212.

Butler, J.J. and I.F. Smith. 1956. 'Razors, urns and the British Middle Bronze Age', *University of London Institute of Archaeology, Annual Report* 12, 20-52.

Campbell, M. and J.M. Coles. 1962-3. 'The Torran Hoard', *Proceedings of the Society of Antiquaries of Scotland* 96, 352-4.

Champion, T. 1999. 'The Later Bronze Age' in J. Hunter and I. Ralston (eds) *The Archaeology of Britain. An Introduction from the Upper Palaeolithic to the Industrial Revolution*, 95-112. Routledge, London.

Chandler, J. 1998. *John Leland's Itinerary. Travels in Tudor England*. Sutton Publishing Ltd, Stroud.

Childe, V.G. 1930. *The Bronze Age*. Cambridge University Press, Cambridge.

Childe, V.G. 1936. *Man Makes Himself*. Watts & Co., London.

Childe, V.G. 1949. *Prehistoric Communities of the British Isles*, 3rd edition. W. & R. Chambers Ltd, London.

Childe, V.G. 1958. *The Prehistory of European Society*. Penguin, Harmondsworth.

Childs, S.T. 1991. 'Style, Technology and Iron Smelting Furnaces in Bantu-Speaking Africa', *Journal of Anthropological Archaeology* 10, 332-59.

Childs, S.T. 2000. 'Traditional Iron Working: a narrated ethnoarchaeological example' in M. Bisson, S.T. Childs, P. De Barros, A.F.C. Holl, J.O. Vogel *Ancient African Metallurgy: the sociological context*. Altamira Press, Oxford.

Clark, J.G.D. 1952 *Prehistoric Europe. The economic basis*. Methuen & Co. Ltd: London.

Clark, J.G.D. 1966. 'The Invasion Hypothesis in British Archaeology', *Antiquity* 40, 172-89.

Clarke, D.V., T.G. Cowie and A. Foxon. 1985. *Symbols of Power at the Time of Stonehenge*. Edinburgh: National Museum of Antiquities of Scotland/HMSO.

Cleal, R.M.J. 1995. 'Pottery fabrics in Wessex in the fourth to the second millennia BC' in I. Kinnes and G. Varndell (eds) *Unbaked Urns of Rudely Shape: essays on British and Irish Pottery for Ian Longworth*, 185-94. Oxbow Books, Oxford.

Cleal, R.M.J., K. Walker and R. Montague. 1995. *Stonehenge in its Landscape: twentieth century excavations*. English Heritage, London.

Clough, T.H. McK. and W.A. Cummins. 1978. *Stone Axe Studies. Archaeological, prehistorical, experimental, and ethnographic*. CBA Research Report 23; Council for British Archaeology, York.

Coles, J.M. 1959-60. 'Scottish Late Bronze Age Metalwork: typology, distribution and chronology' in *Proceedings of the Society of Antiquaries of Scotland* 93, 16-134.

Coles, J. 1982. 'The Bronze Age in Northwestern Europe: problems and advances', *Advances in World Archaeology* 1, 265-321.

Coles, J. and A. Harding. 1979. *The Bronze Age in Europe*. London: Methuen.

Coles, J.M., P. Leach, S.C. Minnitt, R. Tabor and A.S. Wilson. 1999. 'A Later Bronze Age shield from South Cadbury, Somerset, England', *Antiquity* 73, 33-49.

Collett, D.P. 1993. 'Metaphors and representations associated with precolonial iron-smelting in eastern and southern Africa' in Shaw *et al*. 1993, 499-511.

Colquhoun, I. and C. Burgess. 1988. *The Swords of Britain*. Munich: Prähistorische Bronzefunde IV, 5.

Coombs, D. 1975. 'Bronze Age weapon hoards in Britain', *Archaeologica Atlantica* 1 (1), 49-81.

Coombs, D. 1991. 'Symbolisme à l'Age du Bronze final en Europe atlantique: plaques décorées de type Watford', *Bulletin de la Société Préhistorique Francaise* 88 (2), 58-64.

Coombs, D. and J. Bradshaw. 1979. 'A Carp's Tongue hoard from Stourmouth, Kent' in Burgess and Coombs (1979), 181-96.

Coombs, D. and F.H. Thompson. 1979. 'Excavations of the hill fort of Mam Tor, Derbyshire 1965-69', *Derbyshire Archaeological Journal* 99, 7-51.

Cope, J. 1998. *The Modern Antiquarian*. Thorsons, London.

Cotton, M.A. and S.S. Frere. 1968. 'Ivinghoe Beacon, excavations 1963-1965', *Records of Bucks* 18 (3), 187-260.

Cowie, T. 1988. *Magic Metal. Early metalworkers in the north-east*. Aberdeen: Anthropological Museum, University of Aberdeen.

Cowie, T. 2000. 'An Early Bronze Age stone mould for casting flat axeheads from Glenhead Farm, Carron Bridge, near Denny', *Calatria: The Journal of the Falkirk Local History Society* 14, 97-107.

Craddock, P.T. 1995. *Early Metal Mining and Production*. Edinburgh University Press, Edinburgh.

Crawford, O.G.S. 1912. 'The Distribution of Early Bronze Age Settlements in Britain', *The Geographical Journal* 40, 184-203, 304-17.

Crawford, O.G.S. 1922. 'A prehistoric invasion of England', *Archaeological Journal* 2, 27-35.

Crew, P. 1990. 'Firesetting experiments at Rhiw Goch, 1989' in Crew and Crew 1990, 57.

Crew, P. and S. Crew (eds). 1990. *Early Mining in the British Isles. Proceedings of the Early Mining Workshop at Plas Tan y Bwlch, Snowdonia National Park Study Centre, 17-19 November 1989*. Plas Tan y Bwlch Occasional Paper No. 1.

Cunliffe, B. 1974. 'The Iron Age' in C. Renfrew (ed.) *British Prehistory: a new outline*, 233-62. Duckworth, London.

Cunnington, M. 1907a. 'Notes on the Opening of a Bronze Age Barrow at Manton, near Marlborough', *The Reliquary and Illustrated Archaeologist* Vol. 13, 28-46.

Cunnington, M. 1907b. 'Notes on the Opening of a Bronze Age Barrow at Manton, near Marlborough', *Wiltshire Archaeological and Natural History Magazine* 35, 1-20.

Curle, A. 1932-3. 'Account of further excavation in 1932 of the Prehistoric Township at Jarlshof, Shetland, on behalf of HM Office of Works', *Proceedings of the Society of Antiquaries of Scotland* 67, 82-136.

Darvill, T. 1987. *Prehistoric Britain*. BT Batsford Ltd, London.

Davies, O. 1935. *Roman Mines in Europe*. Clarendon Press, Oxford.

Dawkins, W.B. 1875. 'On the stone mining tools from Alderley Edge', *Transactions of the Manchester Literary and Philosophical Society* 14, 74-9.

Dawkins, W.B. 1894. 'On the relation of the Palaeolithic to the Neolithic period', *Journal of the Anthropological Institute of Great Britain and Ireland* 23, 242-57.

Dickens, J. 1996. 'A remote analogy? From central Australian tjurunga to Irish Early Bronze Age axes', *Antiquity* 70, 161-7.

Downes, J. and R. Lamb. 2000. *Prehistoric Houses at Sumburgh in Shetland. Excavations at Sumburgh Airport 1967-74*, Oxbow Books, Oxford.

Dutton, A. and P.J. Fasham. 1994. 'Prehistoric copper mining on the Great Orme, Llandudno, Gwynedd, *Proceedings of the Prehistoric Society* 60, 245-86.

Edmonds, M. 1995. *Stone Tools and Society*. Batsford, London.

Ellis, P. 1989. 'Norton Fitzwarren hillfort: a report on the excavations by Nancy and Philip Langmaid between 1968 and 1971', *Proceedings of the Somerset Archaeology and Natural History Society* 133, 1-74.

Ehrenburg, M. 1981. 'Inside Socketed Axes', *Antiquity* 55, 214-18.

Ehrenburg, M. 1981a. 'The anvils of Bronze Age Europe', *Archaeological Journal* 61, 14-28.

Eliade, M. 1968. 'The Forge and the Crucible: a postcript', *History of Religions* 8, 74-88.

Eliade, M. 1978. *The Forge and the Crucible. The origins and structures of alchemy*, 2nd edition. London: University of Chicago Press.

Eogan, G. 1966. 'Some notes on the origin and diffusion of the bronze socketed gouge', *Ulster Journal of Archaeology* 29, 97-101.

Evans, J. 1864. *The Coins of the Ancient Britons*. J.R. Smith, London.

Evans, J. 1872. *The Ancient Stone Implements, Weapons and Ornaments of Great Britain.* Longmans, London.

Evans, J. 1881. *The Ancient Bronze Implements, Weapons, and Ornaments of Great Britain and Ireland.* Longmans, Green & Co., London.

Evans, J. 1884. 'On a hoard of objects found in Wilburton Fen, near Ely', *Archaeologia* 48, 106-14.

Fitzpatrick, A.P. 2002. 'The Amesbury Archer: a well-furnished Early Bronze Age burial in Southern England', *Antiquity* 76, 629-30.

Fleming, A. 1971. 'Territorial Patterns in Bronze Age Wessex', *Proceedings of the Prehistoric Society* vol. 37, 138-66.

Fleming, A. 1988. *The Dartmoor Reaves.* Batsford: London.

Fontijn, D.R. 2001. 'Rethinking ceremonial dirks of the Plougrescant-Ommerschans type – some thoughts on the structure of metalwork exchange' in W.H. Metz, B.L. van Beek and H. Steegstra (eds) *Patina. Essays presented to Jay Jordan Butler on the occasion of his 80th birthday*, 263-280. Privately published, Groningen.

Fox, A. 1957. 'Excavations at Dean Moor 1954-6', *Transactions of the Devonshire Association* 89, 18-77.

Fox, C. 1923. *The Archaeology of the Cambridge Region.* Cambridge University Press, Cambridge.

Fox, C. 1933. *The Personality of Britain: its influence on inhabitant and invader in prehistoric and early historic times*, 2nd edition. National Museum of Wales: Cardiff.

Garner, A., J. Prag and R. Housley. 1994. 'The Alderley Edge Shovel', *Current Archaeology* 137, 172-5.

Garrod, J.R. 1952. 'A Palstave in "Bog Oak" at Wood Walton', *Transactions of the Cambridgeshire and Huntingdonshire Archaeological Society* vol. 7 part 4, 82.

Garwood, P., D. Jennings, R. Skeates, J. Toms (eds). 1991. *Sacred and Profane. Proceedings of a conference on archaeology, ritual and religion, Oxford 1989.* Oxford University Committee for Archaeology Monograph no. 32.

Gerloff, S. 1975. *The Early Bronze Age Daggers in Great Britain, and a Reconsideration of the Wessex Culture.* Munich: Prähistorische Bronzefunde VI, 2.

Gibson, A. 2002. Review of Brück (ed.) 2001, *Landscape History* 24, 130-1.

Gingell, C. 1992. *The Marlborough Downs: A Later Bronze Age Landscape and its Origins.* Wiltshire Archaeological and Natural History Society Monograph 1: Devizes.

Goucher, C.L. and E.W. Herbert. 1996. 'The Blooms of Banjeli: Technology and Gender in West African Iron Making' in Schmidt (ed.) 1996, 40-57.

Greenwell, W. and W.P. Brewis 1909. 'The Origin, Evolution, and Classification of the Bronze Spear-Head in Great Britain and Ireland', *Archaeologia* 61, 439-72.

Guilbert, G. and A. Vince. 1996. 'Petrology of some prehistoric pottery from Mam Tor', *Derbyshire Archaeological Journal* 116, 49-59.

Halliday, F.E. 1953. *John Carew of Antony. The Survey of Cornwall.* Andrew Melrose, London.

Harding, A. 1976. 'Bronze agricultural implements in Bronze Age Europe' in G. de G. Sieveking (ed.) *Problems in Economic and Social Archaeology*, 513-22.

Harding, A. 1983. 'The Bronze Age in Central and Eastern Europe: advances and prospects', *Advances in World Archaeology* 2, 1-50.

Hawkes, C.F.C. 1931. 'Hillforts', *Antiquity* 5, 60-97.

Hawkes, C.F.C. 1940. *The Prehistoric Foundations of Europe to the Mycenaean Age.* Methuen and Co. Ltd, London.

Hawkes, J. and C.F.C., 1943. *Prehistoric Britain.* Pelican, Harmondsworth.

Herbert, E.W. 1984. *Red Gold of Africa. Copper in Precolonial History and Culture.* University of Wisconsin Press, Wisconsin.

Herbert, E.W. 1993. *Iron, Gender and Power. Rituals of Transformation in African Societies.* Indiana University Press, Indianapolis and Bloomington.

Herring, P. 1997. 'The prehistoric landscape of Cornwall and West Devon: economic and social contexts for metallurgy' in Budd and Gale (eds) 1997, 19-22.

Hewett, H.J. 1902. 'Discoveries at Long Wittenham', *Berks, Bucks and Oxon Archaeological Journal* 8, 30-1.

Hill, J.D. 1995. *Ritual and Rubbish in the Iron Age of Wessex.* British Archaeological Reports (British Series) 242; Tempus Reparatum, Oxford.

Hingley, R. 1990. 'Domestic organisation and gender relations in Iron Age and Romano-British households' in R. Samson (ed.) *The Social Archaeology of Houses*, pp.125-47; Edinburgh University Press.

Hodges, H.W.M. 1957. 'Studies in the Late Bronze Age in Ireland: 3. The hoards of bronze implements', *Ulster Journal of Archaeology* 20, 51-63.

Hosler, D. 1994. *The Sounds and Colors of Power. The Sacred Metallurgical Technology of Ancient West Mexico.* MIT Press, Cambridge MA.

Hosler, D. 1995. 'Sound, Color and Meaning in the Metallurgy of Ancient West Mexico', *World Archaeology* 27, 100-15.

Howard, H. 1981. *The bronze casting industry in later prehistoric Southern England: a study based on refractory debris.* PhD thesis, University of Southampton.

Hughes, G. 2000. *The Lockington Golf Hoard. An Early Bronze Age Barrow Cemetery at Lockington, Leicestershire.* Oxford: Oxbow Books.

Humphrey, C. 1995. 'Chiefly and Shamanist Landscapes in Mongolia' in E. Hirsh and M. O'Hanlon (eds) *The Anthropology of Landscape. Perspectives on Place and Space*, 135-62. Clarendon Press: Oxford.

Hurcombe, L. 2000. 'Time, skill and craft specialisation as gender relations' in M. Donald and L. Hurcombe (eds) *Gender and Material Culture in Archaeological Perspective*, 88-109. London: Macmillam Press Ltd.

Hutchins, A.B. 1845. 'Notes on the opening of the Winterslow barrow', *Archaeological Journal* 1, 156-7.

James, D. 1988. 'Prehistoric copper mining on the Great Orme's Head, Llandudno, Gwynedd' in J. Ellis Jones (ed.) *Aspects of Ancient Mining and Metallurgy*, Acta of a British School at Athens Centenary Conference, Bangor, 1986, 115-21.

James, D. 1990. 'Prehistoric Copper Mining on the Great Orme's Head' in Crew and Crew (eds) 1990, 1-4.

Jockenhövel, A. 1980. *Die Rasiermesser in Westeuropa.* Munich: Prähistorische Bronzefunde VIII, 3.

Johnson, M. 1999. *Archaeological Theory. An Introduction*. Blackwell, Oxford.

Jones, A. 2001. 'Enduring Images? Image production and memory in Earlier Bronze Age Scotland' in J. Brück (ed.) 2001, 217-28.

Kavanagh, R.M. 1991. 'A reconsideration of razors in the Irish Earlier Bronze Age', *Journal of the Royal Society of Antiquaries of Ireland* 121, 77-104.

Kendrick, T.D. and C.F.C. Hawkes. 1932. *Archaeology in England and Wales 1914-1931*. Methuen and Co. Ltd, London.

Knight, R.W., C. Browne, L.V. Grinsell. 1972. 'Prehistoric Skeletons from Tormarton', *Transactions of the Bristol and Gloucestershire Archaeological Society* 91, 14-17.

Lahiri, N. 1995. 'Indian Metal and Metal-related Artefacts as Cultural Signifiers', *World Archaeology* 27, 116-32.

Lane Fox, A.H.L. 1869. 'Further remarks on the hillforts of Sussex: being an account of the excavations of the hillforts at Cissbury and Highdown', *Archaeologia* 42, 53-76.

Larick, R. 1985. 'Spears, Style and Time among Maa-speaking Pastoralists', *Journal of Anthropological Archaeology* 4, 206-20.

Larick, R. 1986. 'Age Grading and Ethnicity in Loikop (Samburu) Spears', *Journal of Anthropological Archaeology* 4, 269-83.

Larick, R. 1991. 'Warriors and Blacksmiths: Mediating Ethnicity in East African Spears', *Journal of Anthropological Archaeology* 10, 299-331.

Lawson, A. 1985. 'An unusual Bronze Age sword from Highclere, Hampshire', *Proceedings of the Hampshire Field Club and Archaeological Society* 41, 281-4.

Lawson, A. 2000. *Potterne 1982-5. Animal Husbandry in Later Prehistoric Wiltshire*. Wessex Archaeology: Salisbury.

Lawson, A. and D. Farwell. 1990. 'Archaeological investigations following the discovery of a hoard of palstaves near New Inn Farmhouse, Marnhull, Dorset', *Proceedings of the Dorset Natural History and Archaeological Society* 112, 131-7.

Lethbridge, T.C. 1950. 'Boredom in Archaeology', *The Archaeological Newsletter* 3 (6), 89-92.

Lewis, A. 1990. 'Underground exploration of the Great Orme copper mines' in Crew and Crew (eds) 1990, 5-10.

Londesborough, Lord. 1852. 'An account of the opening of some tumuli in the East Riding of Yorkshire', *Archaeologia* 34, 251-8.

Longworth, I. and J. Cherry (eds). 1986. *Archaeology in Britain since 1945: New Directions*. British Museum, London.

Longworth, I., A. Herne, G. Varndell, S. Needham. 1991. *Excavations at Grimes Graves, Norfolk, 1972-1976. Fascicule 3: Shaft X: Bronze Age flint, chalk and metal working*. British Museum Press: London.

Longworth, I., A. Ellison and V. Rigby. 1988. *Excavations at Grimes Graves, Norfolk, 1972-1976. Fascicule 2: The Neolithic, Bronze Age and later pottery*. British Museum Press: London

Lort, Rev. 1779. 'Observations on Celts', *Archaeologia* 5, 106-18.

Lubbock, J. 1865. *Pre-historic Times, as Illustrated by Ancient Remains, and the Manners and Customs of Modern Savages*. Williams and Norgate: London.

Mackay, A. 1908-9. 'Notice of two flanged palstaves of bronze from Craig-a-Bhodaich, Farr, Sutherland', *Proceedings of the Society of Antiquaries of Scotland* 43, 240-2.

Manby, T.G. 1966. 'The Bodwardin Mould, Anglesey', *Proceedings of the Prehistoric Society* 32, 349 and plate xxxv.

Marsden, B. 1999. *The Early Barrow Diggers*. Tempus Publishing Ltd: Stroud.

M'Culloch, W.T. 1862-4. 'Notes respecting two bronze shields recently purchased for the museum of the society; and other bronze shields', *Proceedings of the Society of Antiquaries of Scotland* 5, 165-8.

Megaw, J.V.S. and D.D.A. Simpson (eds).1979. *Introduction to British Prehistory from the arrival of Homo sapiens to the Claudian invasion*. Leicester University Press: Leicester.

Mighall, T.M. and J.G.A. Lageard. 1999. 'The Prehistoric Environment' in W. O'Brien, *Sacred Ground. Megalithic Tombs in Coastal South-West Ireland*, 41-59. Bronze Age Studies No. 4, Department of Archaeology, National University of Ireland, Galway.

Miles, H. 1975. 'Barrows on the St. Austell granite', *Cornish Archaeology* 10, 5-81.

Monro, R. 1882-3. 'Notice of the discovery of five bronze celts and a bronze ring at the 'Maidens', near Culzean Castle, Ayrshire', *Proceedings of the Society of Antiquaries of Scotland* 17, 433-8.

Montelius, O. 1908. 'The Chronology of the British Bronze Age', *Archaeologia* LXI, 97-162.

Muhammed, I. 1993. 'Iron technology in the middle Sahel/Savanna: with emphasis on central Darfur' in Shaw et al. 1993, 459-67.

Muirhead, A. 1890-1. 'Notice of bronze ornaments and a thin bifid blade of bronze from the Braes of Gight, Aberdeenshire', *Proceedings of the Society of Antiquaries of Scotland* 25, 135-8.

Needham, S. 1979. 'A pair of Early Bronze Age spearheads from Lightwater, Surrey' in Burgess and Coombs (eds), 1-39.

Needham, S. 1980. 'An assemblage of Late Bronze Age metalworking debris from Dainton, Devon', *Proceedings of the Prehistoric Society* 46, 177-216.

Needham, S.P. 1981. *The Bulford-Helsbury manufacturing tradition. The production of Stogursey socketed axes during the later Bronze Age in southern Britain*. British Museum Occasional Paper 13, London.

Needham, S.P. 1986. 'Late Bronze Age artefacts' in I.M. Stead and V. Rigby (eds). *Baldock. The excavation of a Roman and Pre-Roman Settlement*, 141-3. Britannia Monograph Series No. 7. Society for the Promotion of Roman Studies, London.

Needham, S.P. 1988. 'Selective Deposition in the British Early Bronze Age', *World Archaeology* vol. 20, 229-48.

Needham, S.P. 1990. 'The Penard-Wilburton succession: new metalwork finds from Croxton (Norfolk) and Thirsk (Yorkshire)', *Antiquaries Journal* 70, 253-70.

Needham, S.P. 1990a. *The Petters Late Bronze Age Metalwork. An analytical study of Thames Valley metalworking in its settlement context*. British Museum Occasional Paper 70, British Museum Press, London.

Needham, S.P. 1990b. 'Middle Bronze Age Ceremonial Weapons: new finds from Oxboroough, Norfolk and Essex/Kent', *Antiquaries Journal* 70, 239-52.

Needham, S. 1995. 'A Bronze Age goldworking anvil from Lichfield, Staffordshire', *Antiquaries Journal* 75, 125-32.

Needham, S.P. 1992. 'The structure of settlement and ritual in the Late Bronze Age of south-east Britain' in C. Mordant and A. Richard (eds) *L'habitat et l'occupation du sol à l'âge du bronze en Europe*, 49-69. Paris: Editions du Comité des Travaux historiques et scientifiques, Section de Préhistoire et de Protohistoire, Documents Préhistoriques 4.

Needham, S.P. 1996. 'Chronology and Periodisation in the British Bronze Age' in K. Randsborg (ed.) *Absolute Chronology. Archaeological Europe 2500-500 BC. Acta Archaeologica* 67, 121-40.

Needham, S.P. 1999. 'Radley and the development of early metalwork in Britain' in A. Barclay, C. Halpin (eds) *Excavations at Barrow Hills, Radley, Oxfordshire Volume 1: The Neolithic and Bronze Age Monument Complex*, 186-91. Oxford Archaeological Unit, Oxford.

Needham, S. 2001. 'When expediency broaches ritual intention: the flow of metal between systemic and buried domains', *Journal of the Royal Anthropological Institute* 7 (2), 275-98.

Needham, S. and J. Ambers. 1994. 'Redating Rams Hill and reconsidering Bronze Age enclosure', *Proceedings of the Prehistoric Society* 60, 225-44.

Needham, S., C. Bronk Ramsay, D. Coombs, C. Cartwright and P. Pettit. 1997. 'An Independent Chronology for British Bronze Age Metalwork: the results of the Oxford Radiocarbon Accelerator Programme', *Archaeological Journal* 154, 55-107.

Needham, S.P., A. Lawson, H.S. Green. 1985. *British Bronze Age Metalwork, A1-6: Early Bronze Age Hoards*. British Museum, London.

Newman, P. 1998. *The Dartmoor Tin Industry. A Field Guide*. Chercombe Press, Newton Abbott.

Nowakowski, J.A. 2001. 'Leaving Home in the Cornish Bronze Age: insights into planned abandonment processes' in Brück (ed.) 2001, 139-48.

O'Brien, W. 1994. *Mount Gabriel. Bronze Age Mining in Ireland*. Bronze Age Studies no. 3, National University of Ireland, Galway.

O'Brien, W. 1996. *Bronze Age Copper Mining in Great Britain and Ireland*. Princes Risborough: Shire Archaeology.

O'Connor, B. and T. Cowie. 'Middle Bronze Age dirks and rapiers from Scotland: some finds old and new', *Proceedings of the Society of Antiquaries of Scotland* 125, 345-67.

Ó'Faoláin, S. and J.P. Northover. 1998. 'The technology of Late Bronze Age sword production in Ireland', *Journal of Irish Archaeology* 9, 69-88.

O'Neil, B.H. St J. 1941. 'Hoard of Axes from Bourton-on-the-Water, Gloucestershire', *Antiquaries Journal* 21, 150-1.

Ó'Ríordáin, S.P. 1937. 'The halberd in Bronze Age Europe: a study in prehistoric origins, evolution, distribution and chronology', *Archaeologia* 86, 195-321.

Ord, J.W. 1846. *The History and Antiquities of Cleveland*. Simpkin and Marshall, London.

Ormerod, G.W. 1864. 'On the hut-circles of the eastern side of Dartmoor', *Journal of the British Archaeological Association* 20, 299-308.

Osgood, R. n.d. *The Dead of Tormarton. Bronze Age Combat Victims?* South Gloucestershire Council.

Osgood, R., S. Monks and J. Toms. 2000. *Bronze Age Warfare*. Sutton: Stroud.

Oswald, A. 1966/1967. 'Excavations for the Avon/Severn Research Committee at Barford, Warwickshire', *Birmingham Archaeological Society Transactions and Proceedings* 83, 1-64.

Oswald, A. 1997. 'A doorway on the past: practical and mystic concerns in the orientation of roundhouse doorways' in A. Gwilt, C. Haselgrove (eds) *Reconstructing Iron Age Societies*, pp.87-95. Oxbow Monograph 71, Oxbow Books, Oxford.

Parker Pearson, M. 1993. *English Heritage Book of Bronze Age Britain*. BT Batsford Ltd/English Heritage, London.

Parker Pearson, M. 1995. 'Southwestern Bronze Age pottery' in I. Kinnes, G. Varndell (eds) *Unbaked Urns of Rudely Shape: essays on British and Irish pottery for Ian Longworth*, 89-100. Oxbow Books, Oxford.

Parker Pearson, M. 1999. 'The Earlier Bronze Age' in J. Hunter, I. Ralston (eds) *The Archaeology of Britain. An Introduction from the Upper Palaeolithic to the Industrial Revolution*, 77-94. Routledge, London.

Parker Pearson, M. and Ramilisonina. 1998. 'Stonehenge for the Ancestors', *Antiquity* 72, 308-26.

Parker Pearson, M. and C. Richards. 1994. 'Architecture and order: spatial representation and archaeology' in M. Parker Pearson and C. Richards (eds) *Architecture and Order: Approaches to Social Space*, pp.38-72. Routledge, London.

Peake, H. and H.J. Fleure. 1931. *Merchant Venturers in Bronze*. Corridors of Time VII. Clarendon Press, Oxford.

Peake, H. and H.J. Fleure. 1933. *The Horse and The Sword*. Corridors of Time VII. Clarendon Press, Oxford.

Pearce, S.M. 1971. 'A Late Bronze Age hoard from Glentanar, Aberdeenshire', *Proceedings of the Society of Antiquaries of Scotland* 103, 57-64.

Pearce, S.M. 1977. 'Amber beads from the Late Bronze Age hoard from Glentanar, Aberdeenshire', *Proceedings of the Society of Antiquaries of Scotland* 108, 124-9.

Pearce, S.M. 1983. *The Bronze Age Metalwork of South Western Britain*. British Archaeological Reports (British Series) 120; BAR, Oxford.

Pendleton, C.F. 1999. *Bronze Age Metalwork in Northern East Anglia. A study of its distribution and interpretation*. BAR British Series 279, British Archaeological Reports, Oxford.

Pendleton, C.F. 2001. 'Firstly, let's get rid of ritual' in J. Brück (ed.) 2001, 170-8.

Penhallurick, R.D. 1986. *Tin in Antiquity*. London: The Institute of Metals.

Penhallurick, R.D. 1997. 'The evidence for prehistoric mining in Cornwall' in Budd and Gale (eds) 1997, 23-33.

Phillips, J. 1859. 'Thoughts on ancient metallurgy and mining among the Brigantes and in some other parts of Britain, suggested by a page of Pliny's *Natural History*', *Archaeological Journal* 16, 7-21.

Piggott, C.M. 1949. 'The Late Bronze Age Razors of the British Isles', *Proceedings of the Prehistoric Society*, 121-41.

Piggott, S. 1938. 'The Early Bronze Age in Wessex', *Proceedings of the Prehistoric Society* 4, 52-106.

Piggott, S. 1954. *The Neolithic Cultures of the British Isles*. Cambridge: Cambridge University Press.

Piggott, S. 1965. *Ancient Europe*. Edinburgh University Press: Edinburgh.

Pitt Rivers, A.H.L.F. 1898. *Excavations in Cranborne Chase, near Rushmore, on the borders of Dorset and Wilts, 1893-1896*, Vol. 4. Privately printed.

Powell, T.G.E. 1963. 'Excavations at Skelmore Heads near Ulverston, 1957 and 1959, *Transactions of the Cumberland and Westmorland Antiquarian and Archaeological Society* 80, 1-30.

Price, D.G. 1985. 'Changing perceptions of prehistoric tinning on Dartmoor', *Transactions of the Devonshire Association* 117, 129-38.

Price, N. 1994. 'Tourism and the Bighorn Medicine Wheel: how multiple use does not work for sacred land sites' in D.L. Carmichael, J. Hubert, B. Reeves and A. Schanche (eds) *Sacred Sites, Sacred Places*, 259-64. Routledge: London.

Priston, A. 1986. 'The Hair' in I.M. Stead, J.B. Bourke and D. Brothwell (eds) *Lindow Man: the Body in the Bog*, 71. British Museum, London.

Pryor, F. 1998. *Etton: Excavations at a Neolithic causewayed enclosure near Maxey, Cambridgeshire, 1982-7*. English Heritage: London.

Pryor, F. 2001. *The Flag Fen Basin. Archaeology and environment of a Fenland landscape*. English Heritage: Swindon.

Pryor, F. 2001a. *Seahenge. New Discoveries in Prehistoric Britain*. Harper Collins, London.

Quennell, M. and C.H.B. 1952. *Everyday Life in the New Stone, Bronze and Early Iron Ages*, 4th edition. BT Batsford and Co. Ltd, London.

Radimilahy, C. 1993. 'Ancient iron-working in Madagascar' in Shaw *et al*. 1993, 478-83.

RCHME. 1995. *A Causewayed Enclosure on Combe Hill, Eastbourne, East Sussex*. RCHME, Cambridge.

RCHME. 1996. *Skelmore Heads, Urswick, Cumbria*. RCHME survey report, RCHME, Cambridge.

Reeves, B. 1994. 'Ninaistákis – the Nitsitapii's sacred mountain: traditional Native religious activities and land use/tourism conflicts' in D.L. Carmichael, J. Hubert, B. Reeves and A. Schanche (eds) *Sacred Sites, Sacred Places*, 265-94. Routledge: London.

Reid, A. and R. MacLean. 1995. 'Symbolism and the social contexts of iron production in Karagwe', *World Archaeology* 27 (1), 144-61.

Richards, C.C. and J.S. Thomas. 1984. 'Ritual activity and structured deposition on later Neolithic Wessex' in R. Bradley and J. Gardiner (eds) *Neolithic Studies*, 189-218. British Archaeological Reports, British Series no. 133; BAR, Oxford.

Roberts, E. 2002. 'Great Orme: Bronze Age Mining and Smelting Site', *Current Archaeology* 181, 29-32.

Roeder, C. 1901. 'Prehistoric and Subsequent Mining at Alderley Edge, with a sketch of the archaeological features of the neighbourhood', *Transactions of the Lancashire and Cheshire Antiquarian Society* 19, 77-118.

Roeder, C. and F.S. Graves. 1905. 'Recent Archaeological Discoveries at Alderley Edge', *Transactions of the Lancashire and Cheshire Antiquarian Society* 23, 17-29.

Rohl, B. and S. Needham. 1998. *The Circulation of Metalwork in the British Bronze Age. The application of lead isotope analysis*. British Museum Occasional Paper 102; British Museum Press, London.

Rowlands, M. 1971. 'A group of incised decorated armrings and their significance for the Middle Bronze Age of southern Britain' in G. de G. Sieveking (ed.) *Prehistoric and Roman Studies*, 183-99. Trustees of the British Museum: London.

Rowlands, M. 1971a. 'The Archaeological Interpretation of Prehistoric Metalworking' *World Archaeology* 3 (2), 210-24.

Rowlands, M. 1976. *The Organisation of Middle Bronze Age Metalworking*. British Archaeological Reports (British Series) 31; BAR, Oxford.

Rowlands, M. and J.P. Warnier. 1993. 'The Magical Production of Iron in the Cameroon Grassfields' in Shaw *et al*. 1993, 512-50.

Russell, M. (ed.). 2001. *Rough Quarries, Rocks and Hills. John Pull and the Neolithic Flint Mines of Sussex*. Oxbow Books, Oxford.

Savory, H.N. 1971. *Excavations at Dinorben 1965-9*. National Museum of Wales, Cardiff.

Schmidt, P.K. and C. Burgess. 1981. *The Axes of Scotland and Northern England*. Munich: Prähistorische Bronzefunde IX, 7.

Schmidt, P.R. (ed.). 1996. *The Culture and Technology of African Iron Production*. University Press of Florida, Gainesville.

Schmidt, P.R. 1997. *Iron Technology in East Africa. Symbolism, Science and Archaeology*. James Currey, Oxford.

Schuhmacher, T.X. 2002. 'Some remarks on the origin and chronology of halberds in Europe', *Oxford Journal of Archaeology* 21, 263-88.

Scott, L. 1951. 'The colonisation of Scotland in the Second Millennium BC', *Proceedings of the Prehistoric Society* 17, 16-82.

Selkirk, A. 1971. 'The LANEBA', *Current Archaeology* 28, 113.

Senior, L.M. 2000. 'Gender and Craft Innovation: proposal of a model' in M. Donald, and L. Hurcombe (eds) *Gender and Material Culture in Archaeological Perspective*, 71-87. London: Macmillan Press Ltd.

Sharpe, A. 1992. 'Footprints of former miners in the far west', *Cornish Archaeology* 31, 35-40.

Shaw, T., P. Sinclair, B. Andah and A. Okpoko (eds). 1993. *The Archaeology of Africa. Food, Metals and Towns*. London, Routledge.

Shell, C. 1979. 'The early exploitation of tin deposits in south-west England' in M. Ryan (ed.) *The Origins of Metallurgy in Atlantic Europe*, 251-63. The Stationery Office, Dublin.

Sheridan, A. 2003. 'Supernatural Power Dressing', *British Archaeology* 70, 18-23.

Sherlock, S. 1995. 'The Archaeology of Roseberry Topping' in B. Vyner (ed.) *Moorland Monuments: studies in the archaeology of north-east Yorkshire in honour of Raymond Haynes and Don Spratt*, pp.119-29. CBA Research Report 101; Council for British Archaeology: York.

Smith, I.F. 1961. 'An Essay Towards the reformation of the British Bronze Age', *Helinium* 1, 97-118.

Smith, M. 1959. 'Some Somerset hoards and their place in the Bronze Age of Southern Britain', *Proceedings of the Prehistoric Society* 25, 144-87.

Sørensen, M.L.S. 1997. 'Reading Dress: the construction of social categories and identities in Bronze Age Europe' in *Journal of European Archaeology* 5, 93-114.

Spector, J.D. 1991. 'What This Awl Means: Toward a Feminist Archaeology' in J.M. Gero and M.W. Conkey (eds) *Engendering Archaeology: Women and Prehistory*, 388-406. Blackwell, Oxford.

Spindler, K. 1994. *The Man in the Ice*. Weidenfeld and Nicholson, London.

Stanley, W.O. 1850. 'Note on discoveries at Great Orme', *Archaeological Journal* 7, 68-9.

Stead, I.M. 1968. 'An Iron Age hill-fort at Grimsthorpe, Yorkshire, England', *Proceedings of the Prehistoric Society* 34, 148-90.

Stevens, F. and J.F.S. Stone. 1938. 'The Barrows of Winterslow', *Wiltshire Archaeological Magazine* 48, 174-82.

Stevenson, R.B.K. 1947-8. 'Notes on some prehistoric objects', *Proceedings of the Society of Antiquaries of Scotland* 82, 292-5.

Stewart, C. 1881-2. 'Notice of a hoard of bronze weapons and other articles found at Modadh-Mor, Killin', *Proceedings of the Society of Antiquaries of Scotland* 16, 27-31.

Stocker, D. and P. Everson. 2003. 'The Straight and Narrow Way: Fenland Causeways and the Conversion of the Landscape in the Witham Valley, Lincolnshire' in M. Carver (ed.) *The Cross Goes North: Processes of Conversion in Northern Europe, AD 300-1300*, 271-288. York Medieval Press, York.

Stoves, J.L. 1947. 'Report on hair from the barrow at Winterslow', *Wiltshire Archaeological Magazine* 52, 126-7.

Strachan, J.M. 1884. 'Notice of a find of bronze weapons at Ford, Loch Awe', *Proceedings of the Society of Antiquaries of Scotland* 18, 207-9.

Taylor, R.J. 1993. *Hoards of the Bronze Age in Southern Britain. Analysis and Interpretation*. BAR British Series 228, Tempus Reparatum, Oxford.

Thomas, J. 1996. *Time, Culture and Identity. An interpretive archaeology*. Routledge, London.

Thomas, J. 1999. *Understanding the Neolithic*, a revised second edition of *Rethinking the Neolithic*. Routledge, London.

Thomas, N. 1972. 'An Early Bronze Age stone axe-mould from the Walleybourne below Longden Common, Shropshire' in F. Lynch, C. Burgess (eds) *Prehistoric Man in Wales and the West*, 161-6. Adams Dart and Son, Bath.

Thurnam, J. 1872. 'On ancient British barrows, especially those of Wiltshire and the adjoining counties (Part II. Round Barrows)', *Archaeologia* 43, 285-552.

Tilley, C. 1994. *A Phenomenology of Landscape: Places, Paths and Monuments*. Berg: Oxford.

Timberlake, S. 1990. 'Firesetting and primitive mining experiment, Cwmystwyth, 1989' in Crew and Crew (eds) 1990, 53-4.

Timberlake, S. 1992. 'Prehistoric Copper Mining in Britain', *Cornish Archaeology* 31, 15-34.

Timberlake, S. 2001. 'Mining and prospection for metals in Early Bronze Age Britain – making claims within the archaeological landscape' in J. Brück (ed.) 2001, 179-82.

Timberlake, S. 2003. *Excavations on Copa Hill, Cwmystwyth (1986-1999). An Early Bronze Age copper mine within the uplands of Central Wales*. British Archaeological Reports, British Series 348. Archaeopress Oxford.

Treherne, P. 1995. 'The Warrior's Beauty: the masculine body and self-identity in Bronze-Age Europe', *Journal of European Archaeology* 3 (1), 105-44.

Trigger, B. 1980. *Gordon Childe. Revolutions in Archaeology*. London: Thames and Hudson.

Trigger, B. 1989. *A History of Archaeological Thought*. Cambridge University Press, Cambridge.

Turner, C.E.L. 1998. *A Re-Interpretation of the Late Bronze Age Metalwork Hoards of Essex and Kent*. Unpublished PhD thesis, University of Glasgow.

Turton, R.B. 1913. 'Roseberry Topping', *Yorkshire Archaeological Journal* 22, 40-8

Tylecote, R.F. 1973. 'Casting copper and bronze into stone moulds', *Bulletin of the Historical Metallurgy Group* 7, 1-5.

Tylecote, R.F. 1986. *The Prehistory of Metallurgy in the British Isles*. The Institute of Metals: London.

Varley, W.J. and J.W. Jackson. 1940. *Prehistoric Cheshire*. Chester: Cheshire Rural Community Council.

Warren, S.H. 1919. 'A stone axe factory at Graig Lwyd, Penmaenmawr', *Journal of the Royal Anthropological Institute* 49, 342-65.

Whimster, R. 1980. *Burial Practices in Iron Age Britain*. British Archaeological Reports (British Series) 90; BAR, Oxford.

Woodward, A. 2000. *British Barrows. A matter of life and death*. Stroud: Tempus Publishing Ltd.

Wright, W.B. 1939. *Tools and the Man*. G. Bell and Sons Ltd, London.

Yates, J. 1849. 'Use of Bronze Celts in Military Operations', *Archaeological Journal* 6, 363-92.

Yates, J. 1850. 'Note on the word "palstave"', *Archaeological Journal* 7, 74.

Yates, J. 1858. 'On the mining operations of the Romans in Britain', *Proceedings of the Somersetshire Archaeology and Natural History Society* 8, 1-34.

INDEX

Numbers in **bold** refer to illustrations

Acton Park, 42, 87
Agricola, **53**
Alderley Edge, Cheshire, 79, 86-7, 91-4, 106, **27**
amber, 140, 141, 149, **4**
Amesbury Archer, 9, 87, 125, 128, 140
Angle Ditch, Dorset, 158, **50**
anklets, 142
anvils, 38, 113, 124
armrings, 38, 59, 63, 142, **18**, **colour plates 3 & 7**
Arreton, 87, 118, **48**
Arreton Down, Isle of Wight, 56
arrowhead, 125, 146-7
awl, 66, 69, 118, 142-3, **16**, **41**, **colour plate 2**
axehead, 38, 39, 77, 118, 137, 140, 155-60
axehead, flanged, 14, 40, 54, 55, 60, 65, 155, **2**, **48**, **colour plate 10**
axehead, flat, 40, 55, 63, 98, 155, **6**, **9**, **10**, **33**, **47**, **colour plate 10**
axehead, jadeite, 14, 158
axehead, socketed, 56, 60, 63, 66, 120, 125, 135, 155, 167, **14**, **17**, **33**, **34**, **49**, **colour plate 2**
axehead, stone, 60, 97, 157-8
axehead, winged, 155, **3**, **colour plate 2**

Banffshire, **colour plate 10**
Barford, Warwickshire, 66, 71
barrows, long, 13, 166, **14**
barrows, round, 12, 17, 22, 70-74, 166, **1**
Barrow, Suffolk, 59
beads, 140, **6**
Beakers, 22, 23, 28, 30, 33, 42, 80, 112, 125, 169ff, **4**, **colour plate 3**
Beith, Argyllshire, 59
Benellack, Cornwall, 99
Ben Nevis, 63
Black Patch, East Sussex, 76
Blackpatch, West Susses, 75
Bodwrdin, Anglesey, 118-19
Boscombe Down, Wiltshire, 125
Bourton on the Water, Gloucestershire, 49, 56
bowl, 160
bracelets, 60, 66, 68, 118, 124, 142, **12**, **16**, **49**
Brading Marsh, Isle of Wight, 59
Braes of Gight, Aberdeenshire, 60
'bric-a-brac', 160

Brockagh, Co. Kildare, 65
buckets, 160
burials, 12, 13, 18, 25, 70-74, 77-8, 106, 137, 140-3, 148-9, 150, 166ff, **4**, **32**, **54**
'bugle-shaped object', 15
Burridge, Neil, 122
buttons, 140

Caerloggas, Cornwall, 101
Campbeltown, Argyll, **33**
Carhan, Co. Kerry, 55
Carn Brea, Cornwall, 146-7
cassiterite, 101
casting, 113-22
cauldrons, 99, 160
causewayed enclosure, 107, 166, **2**
Cerrig-y-Drudion, 65
chisels, 63, 66, 119, **31**, **colour plate 2**
Christianity, 77-8
chronology, 25, 39, 40, 140, **42**
Cissbury, West Sussex, 80, 91, 103, 111
Cladh Hallan, Outer Hebrides, 175, **54**
clotted cream, **colour plate 1**
Collared Urn, 172, 173, **32**
Colleonard, Banff, 56, **10**
Combe Hill, East Sussex, 55, 71, **2**
Coombe Dingle, nr Bristol, 54
Copa Hill, Cwmystwyth, 85-6, 87, 95, 106-7, 112, **colour plate 5**
Cornhill-on-Tweed, **colour plate 10**
Cragg Wood, Yorkshire, 55
Craig-a-Bhodaich, Sutherland, 63
Crawford Priory, Fife, **colour plate 8**
Crickley Hill, Gloucestershire, 146
crucible, 113, **34**
Culbin Sands, Moray, **33**
cup, 160, **49**
cushion stone, 125

dagger, 38, 56, 77, 101, 143-54, **4**, **colour plates 2 & 3**
Dail na Caraidh, Inverness-shire, 63
Dainton, Devon, 119, 125
Dalduff Farm, Kilkerran, Ayrshire, 59
Dartmoor, 99-101
Dean Bottom, Wiltshire, 75
Dean Moor, Devon, 100

189

Deverel-Rimbury, 30, 33, 36, 60, 140
Dinorben, Wales, 34
dirks, 39, 143-154, **42**, **colour plate 2**
Dorchester-on-Thames, 152
dowsing, **53**
Driffield, Yorkshire, **4**
Druids, 98-9, 157

Edington Burtle, Somerset, 54
earrings, gold, 124
East Chisenbury, Wiltshire, 76
Ecton, Staffordshire, 87
eczema, 139
Eildon, Roxburghshire, **colour plate 10**
Etton, Cambridgeshire, 107
Ewanrigg, Cumbria, 173, **32**, **33**
Ewart Park, 42, 148
Ewart Park, Northumberland, 59

Fimber, Yorkshire, 125
Finglenny Hill, Aberdeenshire, 49, 55, **9**
fire-setting, 86, 90, 93-4
Flag Fen, 9, 48, 49, 68-9, 143, 149, 150, 158-9, **17**, **51**
Food Vessels, 172, 173, **colour plate 7**
Fowey (river), Cornwall, 98
fragmentation, 166ff

Glentrool, Kirkcudbrightshire, 60
gold, 56, 122, 125, 149, 169, **4**, **18**, **colour plate 3**
Gosport, Hampshire, 59
gouges, 38, 63, **34**
Graig Llwyd, 81
Great Langdale, Cumbria, 81, 102-5, **29**
Great Orme, 82, 83, 85-90, 94, 95, 106, 109-12, **20-4**, **28**, **30**
Grime's Graves, Norfolk, 76, 80, 103, 110, 118, 125
Grimthorpe, Yorkshire, 34
Grooved Ware, 170

haemorrhoids, 139
halberds, 38, 106, 144-5
hammers, 63, 124
hammers, mining, 86, 89-91, 94, 97, **25-6**
henges, 145, 166, **1**, **6**, **9**
Highclere, Hampshire, 65
Hill of Knockie, Glentanar, **49**
Hollingbourne, Kent, 60
Hollingbury Hill, East Sussex, 56, **11**
Holme-next-the-Sea, Norfolk, 159, **52**
horse equipment, 142

Isle of Harty, Kent, 120
Itford Hill, West Sussex, 75, 76
Ivinghoe Beacon, Buckinghamshire, 34

Jarlshof, Shetland, 120, 124, **34**, **38**, **39**
jet, 140, 141, **15**

Kenidjack, Cornwall, 101
Kinneff, Kincardineshire, **colour plate 7**
knife, 125

Lakenheath, Suffolk, **43**
Langdon Bay, Dover, 47, **colour plate 2**
lead isotope analysis, 87, 147, **colour plate 2**
leather-working, 142-3
Levens, Cumbria, **48**
Lichfield, Staffordshire, 124
Llyn Fawr, 42
Lockington, Derbyshire, **18**, **19**, **colour plate 3**
Long Rigg Field, Urswick, Cumbria, 65
Loft's Farm, Essex, 76
Lumphanan, Aberdeenshire, **40**

Maidens, The, Port Murray, Ayrshire, 63
Maidstone, Kent, 120, **35-6**
Magdalen Bridge, Midlothian, **colour plate 9**
Malmains Farm, Kent, **8**, **31**, **42**
Malpas, Cheshire, **47**, **55**
Mam Tor, Derbyshire, 34, **5**
Manton Barrow, Wiltshire, 148-9
Marden, Kent, 142
Margate, Kent, **colour plate 1**
Marnhull, Dorset, 56
metal-detecting, 43, 60, 124, 177-9, **7**, **8**
metal-workers, 51, 122-34
Migdale, Sutherland, **6**
mining, 79-113
mining, environmental impact, 107
mining, flint, 14, 80, 102-5
mistletoe, 98-9, 157
Monadh-mor, Killin, Perthshire, 54
Mottram St Andrew, Cheshire, 86, 94
moulds, 63, 113, 115-22, 124-5, **33-4**, **54**
Mount Gabriel, 95, 96, 107

Nantyrickets, 95
Nantyreira, 95
National Council for Metal Detectorists, 179
neck rings, **40**
New Street, Cambridge, 120
Norton Fitzwarren, Somerset, 124, 169

ornaments, 60, 141-2, **54**
'Ötzi', 14
Oxborough, Norfolk, 65, 150, 152, **colour plate 11**

palstaves, 56, 60, 63, 65, 120, 135-6, **7**, **8**, **11**, **12**, **13**, **35-6**, **colour plate 2**
Park House Quarry, Birtley, Northumberland, 63
Parys Mountain, Anglesey, 82, 85, 88, 90, 95, 106, **colour plate 4**

pasty, **colour plate 1**
Penard, 42, 147, **colour plate 2**
Penhale Moor, Cornwall, 68
Peterborough Ware, 172
Petter's Sports Field, Egham, Surrey, 54, 76
phallus, chalk, 76
Phoenicians, **colour plate 1**
pins, 69, 88, 98, **34**
plaques, 38
Plumley Tracey, Devon, 56
Plymstock, Devon, 55
Portable Antiquities Scheme, 43, 177-9, **41**, **43**, **47**, **48**, **55**
Post-Deverel-Rimbury pottery, 36
Potterne, Wiltshire, 76
pottery, 14, 32, 36, 54, 65, 71, 76, 166, **5**
post-processual archaeology, 20
Preshute G1, see Manton Barrow
processual archaeology, 19

Quantock Hills, Somerset, 56
Queensford Mill, Dorchester-On-Thames, 71

radiocarbon dating, 34, 40, 42, 95, 96, **5**, **6**, **28**
rapiers, 38, 39, 60, 65, 99, 122, 143-54, **43**, **colour plate 2**
razors, 60, 66, 69, 71, 136-40, 141, **colour plate 9**
ribwort, 139
'ring money', 68
rings, 56, 68, 69, 142
Ripple, Kent, **7**
ritual, 74-5, 99, 129-34, 163-75
Rochester, Kent, **41**
rock art, 145
Roseberry Topping, Yorkshire, 63, 120, **15**
Rosskeen, Ross-shire, **33**
Ross Island, Co. Kerry, 87, 112
Runnymede, Berkshire, 54, 76

Salcombe, Devon, 47
Sculptor's Cave, Covesea, 67-8
'Seahenge', see Holme-next-the-Sea
shields, 59, 122, 148, **37**
Shuna, Argyll, 59
sickles, 63, 157
sickles, golden, 98-9, 157
Skelmore Heads, Cumbria, 60, **14**
'slider', jet, 98
South Cadbury, Somerset, **37**
South Dumpton Down, Kent, 60, 66, 169, **12-13**
South Lodge, Wiltshire, 66-7, 75, 76, **16**

spearheads, 56, 59, 60, 63, 65, 68, 77, 118, 141, 143-54, **33**, **54**, **colour plates 2 & 8**
Springfield Lyons, Essex, 124, 169
Staple Howe, Yorkshire, 34
St Blazey, Cornwall, 98, 99
St Erth, Cornwall, 97
St Michael's Mount, Cornwall, 54, 98
'stone axe factories', 80-1, 102-5
Stonehenge, Wiltshire, 125, **1**
streaming (tin), 98
Stuntney, Cambridgeshire, 54
'Sussex loops', 56, **11**
swords, 38, 39, 59, 65, 76-8, 120, 124, 135, 137, 143-54, **34**, **45**, **colour plate 2**

Taunton, 42, 87
'Three Age System', 11, 12, 25, 27, **colour plate 1**
tinning, **9**
'tjurunga', **49**
torcs, 56, 60, **11**
Tormarton, Gloucestershire, 61, 152, **44-6**
Torran, Argyll, 51-2
Tosson, Northumberland, 60
'Treasure' (Act; Trove), 43, 53, 60, 177-9
Trevisker, Cornwall, 100
tuyere, 173, **32**
tweezers, 138
typology, 18, 39, 163

Walleybourne Brook, Shropshire, 118
Wandle Park, Croydon, 151
warfare, 143-54
'Wessex Culture', 31, 33
Wheal Coates, St Agnes, Cornwall, 97
whetstone, **15**
Whitehaugh Moss, Ayrshire, **colour plate 8**
Whittinham, Northumberland, 59
Wilburton, 42, 48-9, 148
Willerby, 88
Willerby (Wold Farm), Yorkshire, 56, 71
Wilsford Shaft, Wiltshire, 158
Winmarleigh, Lancashire, 54
Winship, Cambridgeshire, 54
Winterslow, Wiltshire, 138-9
wire, 66, **16**
Witham (river), Lincolnshire, 77-8
Withersfield, Suffolk, 59-60
Wood Waltham, Cambridgeshire, 65
Wotton, Surrey, 63
wristguard, 125

Yarnton, Oxfordshire, **40**
Yetholm, Roxburghshire, **37**